The Sensible Cook's

52 Weeks of Healthy Cooking

Meal Plans, Recipes & Grocery Lists

That You Will Love!

Kaylan C. Vialpando

The author would like to thank her lovely family for participating in and tolerating years of experimental cooking, tasting, sampling, and munching with varying degrees of success, and for making cooking the most rewarding chore in the house.

The Sensible Cook's

52 Weeks of Healthy Cooking

www.thesensiblecook.com

Contents

Introduction

Welcome! Nice choice in cookbooks you just made, by the way. Whether you're trying to lose weight, adopt healthier eating habits, or are already an expert at healthy eating & cooking, this book can simply make it easier. You'll find healthier versions of favorite recipes, which makes eating healthier simpler and enjoyable. By using the meal plans and grocery lists, it's simpler and less expensive to eat healthy while still being able to cook meals that whole family can enjoy.

These reduced fat, sugar, and calorie recipes can be used as part of your everyday eating plan, without making you feel like you're on a "diet". Technically speaking, anyone who eats food is on a "diet". It's just that some diets are better than others, and better for you. This book is not about eliminating carbohydrates, eating raw foods, or any other standpoint of "food discrimination" for the sake of being the next great diet craze. It's more about eating wisely, most of the time. All foods are okay, in the right amounts. You want chocolate cake? Have some! It's not the occasional treat that gets us into trouble, but rather the accumulation of bad dietary choices that can sometimes leave our waistlines feeling a bit… um… compromised. If you learn to eat from all of the food groups, in the appropriate amounts, you'll find yourself feeling and looking much better. Once you've gotten past the mindset of being on a "diet" and you adopt your smarter eating as part of your everyday lifestyle, you'll find it gets quite easy to live with and you're cravings for less healthier foods will actually <u>decrease</u>! Cool huh?

This book is not meant to be a weight reduction plan in itself, although it's a great tool if you happen to be watching your calories. There's a TON of information that comes and goes in the weight loss world. Ultimately, the most effective weight loss is still a matter of having the appropriate amount of calories for your specific body. Eat too little calories and your metabolism can actually slow down and cause you to gain weight. Eat too many calories and your body will store the excess as fat, and you'll gain weight. Each too much or too little of any one food group and you can run into deficiencies, kidney and heart issues, hair loss, fatigue, poor concentration and mood control, and the list goes on. Calorie requirements and nutrient needs vary per individual. You may benefit by speaking with a medical, fitness, or nutrition professional regarding your personal caloric, carbohydrate, protein, and fat needs. This can sometimes be an area where a second or even a third opinion may be in order.

Most of the recipes in this book still contain FAT. Some fats are actually good for you, and again… in moderation. One mistake that is commonly made with reduced fat and sugar recipes (or store bought products), is that people think that since a food is fat-free, sugar-free, non-whatever-free-reduced-light version the food may be, that it's a license to eat more of it! While it might be better for you than the original version, <u>calories still count</u>. Pay attention to serving sizes and go for VARIETY in your diet. There are more healthy recipes available at The Sensible Cook website at http://www.thesensiblecook.com.

Quality of calories count too! A body that tries to function on 1500 low quality calories of fat & sugar operates and feels much different (worse) than a body that is lucky enough to function on 1500 calories of vegetables, fruits, protein, complex carbohydrates, and healthy fats. If your body was an expensive race car, would you put premium fuel in it or watered down cheap gas? Don't you think that your race car would perform better with high quality fuel? Of course it would! And your body will too. Your body will start acting like a performance machine, when you start treating it like one.

Most of us need 5 or more servings of vegetables a day! Try to get in the habit of always serving a salad and/or vegetables as side dishes to your entrees. Fresh is great, but stock up your cabinets and freezers as well so you're never caught short.

For those of you watching your blood pressure, this cookbook is not based on a reduced salt diet. An option is to remove the salt from the recipes and season with other herbs of your choice. You'll need to make good choices based on your personal health needs. If you have diabetes of any other nutritionally influenced health condition, please consult your physician regarding your personal dietary needs.

I found that if you don't tell any hesitant family members that they are eating healthy, most won't even notice the changes in taste. Whether weight is an issue or not, everyone benefits from eating healthier by lowering their risk for many diseases, increasing energy levels, assisting digestion, and even improving concentration! Good habits that can have a positive effect on your life are habits to strive for.

One more thing. Exercise is critical for weight control and overall good health. This is not new news, but it should be taken seriously and should be considered a priority for overall health. The benefits that are rewarded through exercise are numerous. Those who eat healthier AND exercise have a much higher success rate for long term weight loss & maintenance. This is a merely a sensible approach to things. It's a way of life. Enjoy It!

Okay, Here's how to get the most from this book:

Use the meal plans. This ultimately saves you time, money, stress, and unwanted calories. How? By not having to make several little trips to the store, fidgeting through your kitchen cabinets wondering what to cook, or waiting for someone to take your order & make your food at a restaurant.

Use the Grocery lists. Having a list organized by section makes it easy to get in and out of the grocery store fast. The lists assume you have nothing in your kitchen. Before heading off to the store, compare your list with what you already have on hand and mark off what you already have before taking your list to the store. Add any other items you may need...you know...toilet paper, breakfast foods, healthy snacks, laundry soap, stuff like that.

Only purchase what is on your lists. This will keep you from randomly grabbing less desirable foods. Plus, if you leave the junk food at the store (because it's not on your list), you've already eliminated most of the temptation. Saying no to the cookies that are down the street at the grocery store is easier than saying no to the cookies sitting in your kitchen. Think about it.

Single? Cook anyway. Cook up those family size entrees and freeze them already portioned out so you can grab and go later. Plus leftovers make great lunches. Easy.

"Main dishes" can be found anywhere. Look in the soup, salad, breakfast, brunch, sandwich, and veggie sections. Explore your cookbook.

Write in your cookbook. Whenever I find a recipe that I don't like, I just scratch it out right then and there in the book (that way I don't forget and make it again later on). I also rate and make notes on the recipes. For example: I might write "good", or "fair", or "I didn't like it much but Sarah really did", or " try adding more mushrooms next time". Sometimes there might be ingredients that can be switched for ones that you may be more favorable to. Experiment!

Stay flexible & use common sense. Consider these suggested meal plans. You could follow them exactly, but you don't have to. You'll also need to substitute foods based on allergies, special needs, and/or personal taste.

Be brave, sorta. Don't be afraid to try new ingredients. However, if you absolutely can't stand a particular ingredient, just omit it. Most recipes do just fine missing an item here and there. So if you hate eggplant and the recipe calls for eggplant, just don't put it in! Naturally, if the recipe uses the dreaded ingredient as the main portion of things (like Eggplant Parmesan), then just scratch that recipe off of your grocery list for the week. Otherwise, explore food a bit. It's fun to learn new tastes and expand the palette.

Okay. That's the basics. Let's get planning, shopping, cooking, eating, and feeling fabulously sensible about it.

Seasonal Meal Plans

Why are they divided up in seasons? To make the most out of your shopping dollar by considering the best time of the year to purchase certain foods. Plus, cooking methods like grilling or baking often vary according to season. Naturally, it's just a suggestion. Feel free to roam about the menus all you want. The matching grocery lists are located towards the back of this book (and also on-line at www.thesensiblecook.com). Also note: The main dish ingredients are in your grocery lists, the side dishes are not (since they are just suggestions). You may want to peek ahead at the recipe & add those to your list if you'd like.

Spring Meal Plan #1
Chicken Bonne Femme ~ page 73
"Fried" Scallops ~ page 59
Marinated London Broil II ~ page 37
Ham with Fruit Sauce ~ page 109
Meatballs & Gravy ~ page 15

Spring Meal Plan #2
Chicken & Cheesy Potatoes ~ page 79
Balsamic Pork Chops ~ page 122
Kielbasa Lime Chili ~ page 83
French Dip Roast ~ page 32
Shrimp Linguine ~ page 66

Spring Meal Plan #3
Spanish Chicken & Rice ~ page 70
Corned Beef & Cabbage ~ page 33
Costa Rican Beans ~ page 109
Gorgonzola and Vegetable Pasta ~ page 128
Spicy Baked Fish ~ page 51

Spring Meal Plan #4
Chicken Cordon Bleu ~ page 76
Stuffed Flank Steak ~ page 38
Sesame Flounder ~ page 64
Bean & Veggie Burritos ~ page 141
French Onion Meatloaf ~ page 18

Spring Meal Plan #5
Garlic Shrimp Pasta ~ page 64
Southwestern Steak Salad ~ page 153
Hashbrown Casserole ~ page 166
Tortellini Spinach & Tomato Soup ~ page 146
Sour Cream Enchiladas ~ page 18

Spring Meal Plan #6
Caraway Chicken ~ page 97
Sweet & Sour Meatballs ~ page 27
Boiled Ham & Veggies ~ page 111
Four Cheese Spaghetti ~ page 140
Beef or Chicken Fajitas ~ page 40

Spring Meal Plan #7
White Bean Chicken Soup~ page 147
Chinese Pork Chops ~ page 121
Mexican Stuffed Pasta ~ page 21
Chicken Fried Steak ~ page 46
Seared Scallops ~ page 58

Spring Meal Plan #8
Tuna Casserole II ~ page 56
Black Beans & Rice ~ page 136
Pot Au Feu ~ page 92
Herb-Marinated Steak ~ page 45
Baked Beefy Bread ~ 20

Spring Meal Plan #9
Snapper Vera cruz ~ page 52
Beef Mushroom Dips ~ page 33
Fettuccine with Mushrooms ~ page 131
Spinach Burgers ~ page 91
Chicken Carne Asada Tacos ~ page 77

Spring Meal Plan #10
Hungarian Goulash ~ page 35
Smothered Chicken II ~ page 100
Italian Salad ~ page 152
Shrimp & Scallop Teriyaki ~ page 56
Stuffed Taco Burgers ~ page 16

Spring Meal Plan #11

Pasta with Spinach & Sausage ~ page 117
Oriental Orange Chicken ~ page 98
Shredded Beef for Tacos ~ page 31
Pork, Pear, & Cranberry Salad ~ page 151
Honey Glazed Salmon & Asparagus ~ page 55

Spring Meal Plan #12

Cheesy Spaghetti ~ page 88
Southwestern Stir-Fry ~ page 122
Mediterranean Chicken Salad ~ page 153
Beef & Cabbage Wraps ~ page 16
Pasta with Broccoli & Tomatoes ~ page 134

Spring Meal Plan #13

Maple Pecan Pork Chops ~ page 112
Braised Cornish Game Hens ~ page 94
Chicken & Mushroom Pasta ~ page 93
Pot Roast & Gravy ~ page 37
Moo Shu Joes ~ 23

Summer Meal Plan #14

Spaghetti with Vegetables ~ page 129
Beef & Spicy Rice ~ page 15
Scallops & Spinach ~ page 54
Latin Chicken ~ page 76
Grilled Steak Salad ~ page 34

Summer Meal Plan #15

Thai Rice ~ page 71
Ravioli in Garlic Oil ~ page 128
Cream Cheese & Horseradish Burgers ~ page 24
Shrimp Tacos ~ page 49
Tuscan Chicken ~ page 77

Summer Meal Plan #16

Chicken Chili ~ page 84
BBQ Ground Beef Sandwiches ~ page 19
Grilled Marinated Pork ~ 127
Summer Vegetable Stew ~ page 135
Smoked Salmon Pizza ~ page 50

Summer Meal Plan #17

Rosemary Turkey Burgers ~ page 106
Pasta with Jalapeno Spinach Pesto ~ page 142
Greek Shrimp & Beans ~ page 57
BBQ Fajitas ~ page 80
Southwestern Pork Chops ~ page 116

Summer Meal Plan #18

Mexi Mac ~ page 19
Kielbasa & Roasted Vegetables ~ page 90
Shrimp Pasta Primavera ~ page 50
Smothered Chicken ~ page 84
Grilled Polenta & Steak ~ 38

Summer Meal Plan #19

Italian Pork Chops ~ page 126
Steak & Lime Pasta ~ 36
Tuna & Spinach Salad ~ page 155
Turkey Pecan Enchiladas ~ 86
Chicken & Vegetable Stir-Fry ~ page 89

Summer Meal Plan #20

Pierogies & Cabbage ~ page 130
Creamy Mushroom Steaks ~ 41
Cream Cheese Chipotle Burgers ~ page 26
Scallops Bonne Femme ~ page 51
Pepperoni & Cheese Sandwiches ~ page 156

Summer Meal Plan #21

Enchilada Bake ~ page 136
Pasta with No-Cook Sauce ~ page 129
Turkey Chili ~ page 69
Thai Pot Rice ~ page 105 or 68
Salmon with Lime Butter ~ page 61

Summer Meal Plan #22

Tomato & Cheese Spaghetti ~ page 134
Crab Enchiladas ~ page 59
Grilled Ham ~ page 117
Chicken & Corn Quesadillas ~ page 101
Sesame Beef ~ 45

Fall Meal Plan #29
Japanese Noodles ~ page 82
Cilantro Lime Chicken Salad Wraps ~ page 157
Steak Tampiquena ~ page 48
Honey Garlic Pork Chops ~ page 126
Tomato Baguette Pizza ~ page 137

Fall Meal Plan #30
Stuffed Sole ~ page 67
Potato & Ham Skillet ~ page 123
Chicken in Wine Sauce ~ page 72
Mexican Stewed Beef ~ page 42
Hamburger Noodle Soup ~ page 148

Fall Meal Plan #31
Chinese BBQ Chicken Legs ~ page 80
Tossed Shrimp Salad ~ page 154
Moroccan Stew ~ page 133
Chicken with Rosemary & Onion Sauce ~ page 82
Super Joes ~ page 23 or page 104

Fall Meal Plan #32
Polenta & Chili Bake ~ page 131
Crab Stir-Fry ~ page 54
Chicken & Artichoke Pasta ~ page 81
Balsamic Glazed Pork Chops ~ page 122
Beef, Broccoli, & Rice Skillet ~ page 20

Fall Meal Plan #33
Tortellini Soup ~ page 147
Shrimp Newburg ~ 49
Turkey Cutlets ~ page 103
Stuffed Chicken Breasts ~ page 104
Honeyed Ham Steak ~ page 108

Fall Meal Plan #34
Hawaiian Ham ~ page 120
Pesto Pork & Pasta ~ page 107
Beef Stew ~ page 43
Chicken Casserole Ole ~ page 95
Maryland Fish Fillets ~ page 65

Fall Meal Plan #35

Pasta with Ham & Tomatoes ~ page 119
Foil Fish Bake ~ page 65
Steaks with Mushroom Sauce ~ page 43
Chicken & Brie Salad ~ page 150
Pesto Ravioli & Artichokes ~ 138

Fall Meal Plan #36

BBQ Chicken Pizza ~ page 99
Linguine with Tuna Sauce ~ page 62
Beef & Snow Pea Stir-Fry ~ page 44
Chunky Tomato Soup ~ page 145
Gorgonzola Burgers ~ page 25

Fall Meal Plan #37

Baked Ziti with Sausage ~ page 121
Chicken & Dumplings ~ page 75
Vegetable Beef Tacos ~ page 22
Cod Chowder ~ page 146
Pot Roast with Veggies ~ page 41

Fall Meal Plan #38

Oriental Chicken ~ page 102
Cuban Pork Sandwiches ~ 118
Creamy Chicken & Broccoli Pasta ~ 91
Vermont Ham & Cabbage ~ page 116
Hamburger Cornbread Bake ~ page 25

Winter Meal Plan #39

Chili Verde ~ page 120
Tilapia & Tomatoes ~ page 63
Puffed Up Pizza ~ page 21
Roast Turkey with Rosemary Gravy ~ page 79
Crispix Chicken ~page 73

Winter Meal Plan #40

Oriental Chicken with Stir Fry Vegetables ~ page 87
Texas Stuffed Potatoes ~ page 70
Baked Pork Chops ~ page 115
Shepherd's Pie ~ page 32
Seafood Pasta ~ page 60

Winter Meal Plan #41

Chicken & Vegetable Medley ~ page 100
Stir Fried Scallops & Vegetables ~ page 66
Beef with Potatoes & Greens ~ page 39
Ranch Chops & Rice ~ page 114
Cheesy Vegetable Soup ~ page 143

Winter Meal Plan #42

Pork Chops with Mushroom Gravy ~ page 119
Tuna Spaghetti ~ page 55
Deluxe Chicken Breasts ~ page 78
Pepper Steak ~ page 34
New Orleans Red Beans ~ page 138

Winter Meal Plan #43

Ham Stuffed Potatoes ~ page 113
Pork & Broccoli Rotini ~ page 123
Chicken & Broccoli with Mushroom Sauce ~ page 103
Mom's Spaghetti ~ page 31
Grilled Salmon & Spinach ~ page 53

Winter Meal Plan #44

Chicken & Sesame Noodles ~ page 74
Slow Cooked Pork Roast ~ page 124
Southwest Salad ~page 152
Deviled Beef Rolls ~ page 48
Hearty Chili ~ page 27

Winter Meal Plan #45

Pecan Chicken ~ page 83
Creamy Bean Burritos ~ page 132
Fish & Potato Casserole ~ page 57
Now & Again Turkey Tetrazzini ~ page 88
Chipotle Pork Sandwiches ~ page 113

Winter Meal Plan #46

Creamy Chicken & Bacon Pasta ~ page 85
Now & Again Chicken Stuffing Casserole ~ page 87
Meat Loaf Wellington ~ page 17
Cauliflower Soup ~ page 144
Mexi-Pork Skillet ~ page 110

Winter Meal Plan #47

Now & Again Enchiladas ~ page 29
Lemon Rice & Chicken ~ page 69
Pistachio Fish Fillets ~ page 52
Penne Puttanesca ~ page 137
Marinated London Broil ~ page 36

Winter Meal Plan #48

Vegetable Chili ~ page 130
Pork Medallions in Mustard Sauce ~ page 111
Pizza Potatoes ~ page 71
Cranberry Ham ~ page 125
Chicken Chipotle Tacos ~ page 85

Winter Meal Plan #49

Quick Mexi-Chicken & Rice ~ page 97
Minestrone Stew ~ page 149
Scallop Lo Mein ~ page 58
Pork & Potato Supper ~ page 112
Olive Stuffed Chicken ~ 96

Winter Meal Plan #50

Feta Turkey Patties ~ page 93
Pork Chops & Apple Stuffing ~ page 124
Cuban Picadillo ~ page 19
Dijon Salmon ~ page 61
Cumin Chicken ~ page 72

Winter Meal Plan #51

Ravioli & Brown Butter ~ page 135
Mexican Lasagna ~ page 28
Crockpot Chicken ~ page 74
Swiss Steak Strips ~ page 35
Lentil & Spinach Soup ~ page 143

Winter Meal Plan #52

Corn & Potato Chowder ~ page 148
Mini-Meatloaf Burgers ~ page 17
Glazed Chicken Breasts ~ page 89
Linguine with Gorgonzola Sauce ~ page 140
Seafood & Yellow Rice ~ page 63

Beef

Meatballs & Gravy
Side dish suggestion: Vegetable of your choice

12 oz wide egg noodles
1 lb. ground lean ground turkey or beef
6 Tbsp plain dry bread crumbs
1½ tsp dried parsley
½ tsp dried minced garlic
¼ cup skim milk
1 cup coarsely chopped onion
1 jar (2.5 oz) sliced mushrooms, drained
1 can (15 oz) beef gravy
¼ cup fat-free sour cream

Cook noodles according to package directions. Meanwhile, in a large bowl, combine meat, bread crumbs, parsley flakes, minced garlic and skim milk. Mix well using clean hands. Form into 24 meatballs. Place meatballs in a large skillet sprayed with cooking spray. Brown on all sides. Remove meatballs from skillet and cover to keep warm. In the same skillet, sauté onion 3-5 minutes or until tender. Stir in mushrooms and beef gravy. Return meatballs to skillet. Reduce heat. Cover and simmer 5 minutes or until meatballs are cooked through. Remove from heat & stir in sour cream.

6 servings, each serving has 397 calories, 11 g fat, 50g carbohydrate, 25 g protein, 3g fiber

Beef & Spicy Rice
You control the "spiciness" of this dish by choosing your salsa and chili powder according to how hot you like it. Side dish suggestion: baked tortilla chips

1 lb lean ground beef or turkey
1 (8 oz) can tomato sauce
1 cup white rice
1 (16 oz) jar Salsa
2 cups water
1 Tbsp chili powder
1 tsp garlic powder

Brown meat and drain. Add remaining ingredients and bring to a boil. Reduce heat, cover, and simmer for 20 minutes or until rice is tender.

4 servings, each serving has 340 calories, 7g fat, 32g carbohydrate, 34g protein, 2g fiber

Stuffed Taco Burgers

Cook these in a pan or on a grill. Don't use an indoor grill (George Foreman type), because it will squish the cheese out of your stuffed burgers. Side dish suggestion: baked nacho chips

1 ½ lbs lean ground beef
¼ cup fat free mayonnaise
1 pkg. taco seasoning mix
½ cup shredded reduced fat cheddar cheese
¼ cup salsa
1 tomato, sliced
6 lettuce leaves
6 hamburger buns

Mix together the ground beef, 3 Tbsp of mayo, and taco mix. Shape into 12 thin patties.

Combine cheese & 2 Tbsp of the salsa. Spoon onto the center of 6 of the meat patties. Top with remaining patties and seal the edges. You should now have 6 "stuffed" patties.

Grill or pan cook until browned on both sides and cooked through.

Meanwhile, combine 2 Tbsp salsa with remaining 1 Tbsp mayo. Serve this salsa mixture on the cooked burgers along with a slice of tomato and lettuce.

6 servings, each serving has 315 calories, 10g fat, 29g carbohydrate, 28g protein, 2g fiber

Beef & Cabbage Wraps

No side dish needed

8 (8 inch) flour tortillas
1 lb. lean ground beef
½ cup onion, chopped
2 cups packaged shredded cabbage with carrots (coleslaw mix)
1 cup frozen whole kernel corn, thawed
¼ cup bottled barbecue or hoisin sauce
1 teaspoon sesame oil

In a large skillet cook ground beef and onion until meat is brown and onion is tender. Drain off fat. Stir coleslaw mix and corn into meat mixture in skillet. Cover and cook about 4 minutes or until vegetables are tender, stirring occasionally. Stir in barbecue sauce or hoisin sauce and the sesame oil. Cook and stir until heated.

Heat tortillas in microwave to soften (about 30 seconds). Spoon about ½ cup of the filling into each tortilla. Serve with extra barbecue or hoisin sauce.

4 servings, each serving has 446 calories, 12g fat, 51g carbohydrate, 32g protein, 6g fiber

Meat Loaf Wellington

Side dish suggestion: steamed vegetables of choice

2 egg whites, lightly beaten
1 cup meatless spaghetti sauce, divided
1/4 cup dry bread crumbs
½ tsp salt
¼ tsp pepper
1 ½ lbs lean ground beef
1 cup shredded part-skim mozzarella cheese
1 Tbsp minced fresh parsley
1 tube (8 oz) refrigerated, reduced-fat crescent rolls
Aluminum foil

Preheat oven to 350°. Meanwhile, in a large bowl, combine the egg, ⅓ cup spaghetti sauce, bread crumbs, salt, pepper, and beef. Mix well. On a piece of foil, pat beef mixture into a 12-in x 8-in rectangle. Sprinkle 1 cup cheese and parsley to within 1 inch of edges. Roll up jelly-roll style, starting with a long side and peeling foil away while rolling. Seal seam and ends. Place seam side down in a 13x9 inch baking dish that has been sprayed with cooking spray.
.
Bake, uncovered, for 1 hour; drain. Unroll crescent dough; seal seams and perforations. Drape dough over meat loaf to cover the top, sides and ends as much as you can. Seal ends. Bake 15-20 minutes longer or until a meat thermometer reads 160° and crust is golden brown. Let stand for 5 minutes.

Using two large spatulas, carefully transfer meat loaf to a serving platter. Serve with remaining heated spaghetti sauce.

8 servings, each serving has 318 calories, 16g fat, 19g carbohydrate, 24g protein, 0g fiber

Mini Meat Loaf Burgers

Side dish suggestion: Rice and veggies of your choice

1 lb. lean ground beef
¾ cup reduced fat cheddar cheese, divided
½ cup ketchup, divided
½ teaspoon garlic powder

Preheat oven to 400°. Mix together meat, ½ cup of cheese, ¼ cup of ketchup, and garlic powder. Shape into 12 balls. Flatten balls to make mini burgers. Place the burgers on a broiling pan that's been sprayed with cooking spray. Bake in the center of the oven for 15 minutes or until cooked through, turning once during cooking.

Spread remaining ketchup on top of each patty and sprinkle with remaining cheese. Bake 5 minutes more or until cheese melts.

4 servings, each serving has 260 calories, 9 g fat, 8 g carbohydrate, 35 g protein, 0 g fiber

French Onion Meatloaf

Side dish suggestion: Mashed potatoes, gravy, and corn

1 lb lean ground beef
½ pkg. French onion soup mix
¼ cup bread crumbs
⅓ cup skim milk
Ketchup (optional)

Preheat oven to 400°. In a medium bowl, combine all ingredients, mixing well. Pat mixture into a meatloaf pan, preferably one that drains (A draining meatloaf pan is a pan with holes in the bottom, set into a loaf-size pan). Top with ketchup if desired. Bake for 45 -60 minutes, or until no longer pink in the middle.

6 servings, each serving has 163 calories, 5 g fat, 6 g carbohydrate, 21 g protein, 0 g fiber

Sour Cream Enchiladas

Side dish suggestion: green salad

1½ cups water
1½ tsp chicken bouillon granules
⅓ cup flour
1 cup skim milk
1 lb. Lean ground beef
1½ tsp cumin
½ tsp chili powder
¼ tsp salt
1 (7oz) can diced green chilies
½ cup chopped green onion
1 cup nonfat sour cream
8 tortillas (8")
4 oz. Shredded reduced fat cheddar cheese

Drink water! Your body needs water to burn fat & build muscle. Even just being 1% dehydrated can slow your results.

Preheat oven to 350°. To make the sauce, combine water and chicken bouillon in saucepan and bring to a simmer. In a small bowl combine flour with milk and stir until there are no lumps. Slowly add milk mixture to simmering bouillon and stir until thickened. Remove from heat and set aside.

Meanwhile, brown the hamburger; Rinse, drain, and return to pan. Add half of the sauce to the pan along with seasonings, chilies, onion, and sour cream. Spray a 9X13 pan with cooking spray. Spread each tortilla with ½ cup of meat sauce and a Tbsp of cheese. Roll and place seam side down in the pan. Repeat with remaining tortillas. Pour any remaining sauce or meat mixture over the filled tortillas, covering all with sauce. Bake for 20 minutes. Sprinkle with remaining cheese and bake for 10 more minutes.

8 servings, each serving has 311 calories, 9g fat, 36g carbohydrate, 21g protein, 2g fiber

BBQ Ground Beef Sandwiches

Side dish suggestion: corn on the cob

1 lb. lean ground beef
½ cup BBQ sauce
¼ cup ketchup
4 hamburger buns

Brown meat in skillet. Drain fat. Add BBQ sauce and ketchup. Mix well and heat through. Serve on buns.

4 servings, each serving has 365 calories, 13g fat, 35g carbohydrate, 23g protein, 0g fiber

Mexi Mac

Start to finish time: 15 minutes! Side dish suggestion: green salad

1 box (14 oz) Deluxe macaroni & cheese dinner
1 lb. lean ground beef
1 green pepper, chopped
10 oz frozen corn, thawed
1 cup salsa

Prepare macaroni and cheese dinner according to package directions. Meanwhile, cook hamburger and green pepper until cooked through. Drain any fat. Stir in corn and salsa. Heat for 1-2 minutes. Stir in prepared macaroni & cheese dinner.

6 servings, each serving has 364 calories, 10g fat, 43g carbohydrate, 25g protein, 3g fiber

Cuban Picadillo

The raisins make this dish sound odd, but it makes sense when you taste it. Side dish suggestion: warm tortillas

1 lb. lean ground beef
1 small green pepper, diced
1 small onion, diced
1 (8 oz) can tomato sauce
½ cup sliced pimiento stuffed green olives
¼ cup raisins
1 Tbsp apple cider vinegar
3 cups hot cooked rice

Cook rice according to package directions. Meanwhile, cook ground beef, green pepper, and onion in a large nonstick skillet until meat is no longer pink; drain. Stir in the tomato sauce, olives, raisins, and vinegar. Simmer 5 minutes or until heated through. Serve over rice.

4 servings, each serving has 486 calories, 20 g fat, 49 g carbohydrate, 25 g protein, 2 g fiber

Baked Beefy Bread

Side dish suggestion: Great with a large green salad!

1 lb lean hamburger
½ cup chopped onion
1½ tsp Salt
2 Tbsp parsley
¼ cup Parmesan cheese
½ cup Reduced Fat Swiss cheese
2 egg whites (save one of the yolks)
¼ tsp Tabasco or hot sauce
¼ cup fat free mayonnaise
1½ cups Reduced fat baking mix (like Bisquick)
½ cup skim milk

Preheat oven to 400°. Cook hamburger and onion in a skillet until brown. Drain & rinse off fat from hamburger. Return meat to pan & mix in Parmesan, Swiss cheese, egg whites, hot pepper sauce, salt and parsley.

In a separate bowl mix mayonnaise, baking mix, and milk. Spray an 8x8 pan with cooking spray & spread with ½ of the dough mixture. Top with meat mixture. Cover with remaining dough & brush with reserved egg yolk to glaze. Bake for 25-30 minutes.

6 servings, each serving has 309 calories, 12g fat, 24g carbohydrate, 24g protein, 1g fiber

Beef, Broccoli & Rice Skillet

You can use instant brown rice, although you may have to adjust the water and cooking times as directed on the package. No side dish needed

1½ lbs lean ground beef
2 cups water
¼ cup fat free zesty Italian dressing
¼ tsp salt
½ tsp dried oregano
3- 4 cups chopped broccoli
2 cups instant white Rice
¾ cup reduced fat shredded cheddar cheese

Brown beef in a large skillet. Drain any fat and return beef to pan. Add water, dressing, salt, and oregano. Bring to a boil. Stir in broccoli and Rice. Cover, reduce heat and simmer 5 minutes or until rice is tender. Sprinkle with more salt, if desired, to taste. Sprinkle with ½ cup cheese. Cover. Remove from heat and let stand for one minute. Sprinkle with remaining cheese.

5 servings, each serving has 434 calories, 11g fat, 37g carbohydrate, 45g protein, 2g fiber

Puffed-Up Pizza

Side dish suggestion: green salad

1 lb. lean ground beef
1 (15 oz) can tomato sauce
1 cup diced onion
1 cup diced green pepper
½ cup water
1 ½-oz. Pkg. Dry spaghetti-sauce mix
1 cup skim milk
2 tsp Olive Oil
4 egg whites or ½ cup liquid egg substitute
1 cup flour
4 oz Part-skim mozzarella cheese, shredded
¼ cup Parmesan cheese, grated

Preheat oven to 400°. In a skillet, brown the ground beef, rinse with hot water & drain. Return meat to pan. Stir in the tomato sauce, onion, pepper, water, and spaghetti sauce mix. Reduce heat and simmer covered for 10 minutes. Meanwhile, in a small bowl, beat milk, oil, and eggs. Add flour and beat 2 minutes longer. Spread meat mixture in a 9-by-13 inch pan that has been sprayed with cooking spray. Sprinkle with mozzarella. Top with flour mixture. Sprinkle with Parmesan. Bake for 30 minutes or until puffed and golden. Let stand for 10 minutes before serving.

6 servings, each serving has 355 calories, 13g fat, 31g carbohydrate, 28g protein, 2g fiber

Mexican Stuffed Pasta

If you have a hard time finding Extra-jumbo shells, you can use manicotti shells. Side dish suggestion: green salad

12 extra-jumbo pasta shells, cooked and drained (about 8 oz)
1 lb lean ground beef
1 cup medium salsa
½ cup water
1 (8oz) can tomato sauce
1 (4oz) can chopped green chilies, drained
1 cup shredded reduced-fat cheddar cheese

Preheat oven to 350°. Cook pasta cooking according to package directions. *Do not over-cook.* Meanwhile, brown the ground beef in a skillet, rinse with hot water and drain well. Combine salsa, water, and tomato sauce in a small bowl. In another bowl, stir ½ cup of this mixture, the ground beef, chilies and ½ cup of cheese. Mix well. Pour ½ cup of sauce mixture on the bottom of an 8 X 12 inch baking dish that has been sprayed with cooking spray. Stuff cooked shells with ground beef mixture. Arrange shells in the baking dish. Pour remaining sauce over the shells. Sprinkle remaining cheese on top and bake, uncovered for 20 minutes.

5 servings, each serving has 388 calories, 9g fat, 42g carbohydrate, 36g protein, 4g fiber

Vegetable Beef Tacos

Start to finish time: 25 minutes
These are a great way to get in some extra vegetables in a fun, non-traditional way. No side dish needed

1 lb. lean ground beef
1 medium onion, chopped
4 oz finely chopped fresh mushrooms
1 large zucchini, shredded
1 large carrot, shredded
2 garlic cloves, minced
2 tsp chili powder
¼ tsp salt
¼ tsp hot pepper sauce
3 Roma tomatoes, chopped
⅓ cup chopped fresh cilantro
8 tortillas (10 inch), warmed
Shredded lettuce
1 cup shredded reduced fat sharp cheddar cheese

In a large nonstick skillet over medium heat, cook beef and onion until meat is no longer pink; drain. Remove and keep warm. In the same skillet, cook and stir the mushrooms, zucchini, carrot, garlic, chili powder, salt and pepper sauce until vegetables are tender. Stir in the tomatoes, cilantro and beef mixture and heat through. Serve in warm tortillas and sprinkle with cheese and lettuce to make tacos.

8 servings, each serving has 350 calories, 10 g fat, 41 g carbohydrate, 25 g protein, 4 g fiber

BBQ Salisbury Steak

Side dish suggestion: sautéed zucchini

1 ½ lb. lean ground beef
1 (6 oz) pkg. stuffing mix for chicken
1 small onion, diced
8 oz mushrooms, chopped
½ cup BBQ sauce

Mix beef, stuffing mix, onions, and 1¼ cups water together. Form into 6 patties. Grill, pan-fry, broil, or bake the patties until they are completely cooked through.

While patties are cooking, sauté mushrooms in a pan that has been sprayed with cooking spray until mushrooms are lightly browned. Stir in BBQ sauce and ½ cup water. Stir in additional BBQ sauce, if desired. Heat until boiling. Reduce heat and simmer gently until ready to serve. Serve the BBQ mushroom sauce over the patties.

6 servings, each serving has 295 calories, 6g fat, 31g carbohydrate, 27g protein, 1g fiber

Try not to eat right before going to bed.

Moo Shu Joes

This is what happens when Sloppy Joes and Chinese food collide. It's a yummy and unique fusion of taste. Side dish suggestion: Sautéed pea pods

2 tsp cornstarch
½ cup cold water
¼ cup barbeque sauce
¼ cup hoisin sauce
2 Tbsp soy sauce
2 tsp fresh grated ginger
¼ tsp garlic powder
¼ tsp salt
1 small onion, diced
1 red pepper, diced
1 lb lean ground beef
3 cups coleslaw mix
8 small flour tortillas

In a small bowl, combine the cornstarch, water, barbecue sauce, hoisin sauce, soy sauce, ginger, garlic powder and salt until blended. Set aside.

Spray a large skillet or Dutch oven with cooking spray. Sauté the onion and red pepper until slightly tender. Remove from the skillet and set aside. Cook ground beef in a skillet until meat is no longer pink. Drain meat of any fat, if necessary, and return meat to skillet. Add cornstarch mixture to the skillet with the hamburger. Bring to a boil; cook and stir for 1-2 minutes or until thickened. Stir in coleslaw mix, onions and red peppers. Remove from heat and blend well to combine. Spoon meat mixture into warmed tortillas, and eat like a burrito.

4 servings, each serving has 466 calories, 13g fat, 45g carbohydrate, 35g protein, 3g fiber

Super Joes *(beef version)*

The smaller you dice the veggies, the less likely kids will notice them. Side dish suggestion: salad and/or baked French fries

1 lb. lean ground beef
½ onion, finely diced
1 red bell pepper, finely diced
1 large carrot, finely diced
1 can (15 oz) tomato sauce
2 Tbsp Worcestershire sauce
2 Tbsp ketchup
1 Tbsp brown sugar
Salt to taste
8 hamburger buns

Brown the meat until cooked through. Drain off any fat or liquid, and add the diced vegetables to the skillet. Sauté for 2 more minutes. Stir in remaining ingredients, except buns. Bring to a boil. Reduce heat, cover, and simmer for 15 minutes or until the vegetables are tender. Serve in the buns.

8 servings, each serving has 242 calories, 6g fat, 27g carbohydrate, 19g protein, 4g fiber

Stuffed Taco Burgers II

Don't press down on these while cooking, or you'll lose the yummy stuffing. Side dish suggestion: Tater Tots

1 lb lean ground beef
1 pkg. taco seasoning mix
4 Tbsp chive & onion cream cheese
1 oz slice cheddar cheese, divided into 4 pieces
4 hamburger buns
1 avocado, sliced
1 tomato, sliced
½ cup salsa

Mix beef with taco seasoning. Shape into 8 thin patties. Spread 1 tablespoon of cream cheese on a patty. Top with a piece of cheddar cheese. Place another patty on top and pinch edges to seal. Repeat with other patties until you have 4 stuffed patties.

Grill or pan fry over medium heat approximately 7-9 minutes per side or until done. Serve on buns, and top with avocado, tomato, and salsa.

4 servings, each serving has 368 calories, 20g fat, 18carbohydrate, 29g protein, 4g fiber

Cream Cheese & Horseradish Burgers

Side dish suggestion: Baked chips

2 lbs. lean ground beef
2 Tbsp A-1 type steak sauce
¾ tsp seasoned salt
3 oz reduced fat cream cheese
1 tsp mustard
1-2 Tbsp prepared horseradish
8 hamburger buns
Optional accompaniments: lettuce, tomato

Combine beef, steak sauce, and salt in a bowl. Mix well and form into 16 patties.

In a small bowl, combine cream cheese, mustard, and horseradish, to taste. Spoon 1 tablespoon of this mixture into the center of a patty. Place another patty on top and seal the edges so the cream cheese mixture is secure in the inside of the burger. Repeat with remaining patties to make 8 stuffed burgers.

Grill over medium heat for 10 minutes on each side or until meat is no longer pink. Do not press down when cooking or you will squish out the filling. Serve on buns and with accompaniments if desired.

8 servings, each serving has 368 calories, 10g fat, 39g carbohydrate, 29g protein, 1g fiber

Gorgonzola Burgers

Side dish suggestion: Tomato Stacks (see index)

1 ¼ lb. lean ground beef
4 oz crumbled gorgonzola cheese, divided
⅓ cup dried oil packed tomatoes, diced and divided
¼ tsp dried thyme
1 tsp garlic powder
½ tsp salt
½ tsp pepper
4 large, plain hamburger buns, toasted
Thin red onion slices
Tomato slices

In a large bowl, combine ground beef with ¾ cup of the gorgonzola cheese, half of the sundried tomatoes, thyme, garlic powder, salt, and pepper. Shape into 4 patties.

Grill or pan-fry until cooked through.

Place burgers on the buns and top with remaining sun-dried tomatoes, gorgonzola, red onion, and fresh tomato slices.

4 servings, each serving has 463 calories, 26g fat, 21g carbohydrate, 38g protein, 3g fiber

Hamburger Cornbread Bake

Side dish suggestion: green salad

It takes about 20 minutes or so for the body to register that it is full. Slow down.

1 lb lean ground beef
⅓ cup chopped onion
2 tsp chili powder
1 tsp Worcestershire sauce
1 cup canned diced tomatoes
1 (15 oz) can kidney beans, rinsed and drained
1 cup prepared corn bread batter (made from a little package of Jiffy mix or other)

Brown meat and chopped onion. Drain in colander & rinse with hot water. Return beef & onion to pan. Add the seasonings and tomatoes. Cover and cook on low for 15 minutes.

Add the kidney beans and heat through. Spray a 1½ quart casserole dish with cooking spray & pour in the meat mixture. Prepare corn bread batter according to package directions. Cover the meat mixture with spoonfuls of corn bread batter. Bake at 425° for 20 minutes.

4 servings, each serving has 394 calories, 11 g fat, 32 g carbohydrate, 38g protein, 6g fiber

Cream Cheese Chipotle Burgers

I'm not a hamburger fan, but my husband loves them. This flavor combination has made everyone happy. Thanks to the filling, my husband gets burgers more often & I love them now too! Side dish suggestion: baked tortilla chips

4 oz reduced fat cream cheese
¾ tsp garlic salt, divided
4 chipolte chili peppers in adobe sauce, minced
1 lb. lean ground beef
½ tsp chipolte chili powder
4 hamburger buns
4 lettuce leaves
1 tomato, sliced

Combine cream cheese with half of the chili peppers and 1/4 tsp garlic salt in a small bowl and set aside.

In another bowl, combine ground beef with remaining peppers, ½ tsp garlic salt, and chipotle chili powder. Form into 8 patties.

To "stuff" the burgers, place 1 patty on a plate. Spread 1 Tbsp of cream cheese mixture to within1/2 inch of the edges. Top with another patty, and press the edges down to seal in the cream cheese. Repeat with remaining patties to make 4 stuffed burgers.

Grill or pay fry burgers 5-10 minutes per side or until cooked through (don't press on the burgers while cooking).

Place in buns, with lettuce and tomato. Enjoy!

4 servings, each serving has 396 calories, 19g fat, 24g carbohydrate, 29g protein, 1g fiber

Lose weight slowly. 1-2 pounds per week is perfect! The body can not burn off more than 2 pounds of fat per week (slightly more if you are male). Faster "weight loss" is most likely a combination of dehydration or muscle breakdown. Muscle loss slows your metabolism & causes return weight gain (and then some).

Sweet & Sour Meatballs

This recipe is also good made with ground turkey. Side dish suggestion: Serve over rice

1½ lb. lean ground beef
⅔ cup low fat cracker crumbs
½ cup minced onion
1 egg
1 tsp salt
¼ tsp ground ginger
¼ cup skim milk
2 Tbsp cornstarch
½ cup brown sugar (lightly packed)
1 small can pineapple tidbits (or chunks)
½ cup vinegar
1 Tbsp soy sauce

Preheat oven to 400°. Mix together beef, cracker crumbs, onion, egg, salt, ginger, and milk. Shape mixture into 1 inch meatballs. Place on a broiling pan in the center of the oven. Broil for 10 minutes, turn over, and broil 10 more minutes or until cooked through.

About 5-10 minutes before the meatballs are done, begin making sauce. Whisk together to cornstarch, brown sugar, vinegar, soy sauce, and pineapple juice from the can. Pour into a saucepan and heat to boiling, stirring constantly. When it starts to thicken, turn down heat to low and stir in the pineapple. Remove from heat.

Put cooked meatballs into a serving bowl and pour the sweet & sour sauce over the meatballs.

5 servings, each serving has 422 calories, 19 g fat, 28g carbohydrate, 32g protein, 1g fiber

Hearty Chili

Serving Idea: To make **Cincinnati Chili***, serve over spaghetti noodles. Top with shredded Fat free Cheddar cheese, and Fat free sour cream.*

1 lb. lean hamburger
1 lb. round steak, trimmed of all fat & sliced into thin bite-sized pieces
1 (16oz) can tomato sauce
2cups chopped onion
1 tsp salt
1 (28 oz) can diced tomatoes, un-drained
2 (16oz each) cans dark red kidney beans, drained
3 cloves garlic, chopped
4 tsp Chili powder
1 tsp Dried basil
½ tsp Pepper

Cook hamburger and steak, onion and garlic, until meat is brown. Drain off all fat. Return meat to pan. Add remaining ingredients & bring to boiling. Reduce heat. Cover and simmer for at least 20 minutes.

8 servings, each serving (chili only) has 364 calories, 9 g fat, 32g carbohydrate, 41 g protein, 8g fiber

Mexican Lasagna

Side dish suggestion: None needed. However, the optional toppings are nice.

1 lb. Lean ground beef
1 medium onion, chopped
4 garlic cloves, minced
2 cups salsa
1 can (16 oz) fat free refried beans
1 can (15 oz) black beans, rinsed and drained
1 can (10 oz) enchilada sauce
1 can (4 oz) chopped green chilies
1 envelope taco seasoning
¼ tsp pepper
6 flour tortillas (10 inches)
1 ¾ cups shredded reduced-fat Mexican blend cheese

Optional toppings:
sliced black olives
chopped tomatoes
shredded lettuce
fat free sour cream

Preheat oven to 375°. In a large skillet, cook the beef, onion and garlic until meat is no longer pink; drain. Set aside. Meanwhile, in a large bowl, combine the salsa, beans, enchilada sauce, chilies, taco seasoning and pepper. Add the ground beef mixture, and stir well to blend.

Spread 1 cup sauce in a 13-in. x 9-in. baking dish that has been sprayed with cooking spray. Layer with two tortillas (tear the tortillas to fit the pan better, if needed), a third of the meat mixture and 1/3 of the cheese. Repeat layers, two more times.

Cover and bake for 30 minutes. Uncover and bake 10-15 minutes longer or until cheese is melted. Let stand for 10 minutes before serving. Garnish with the olives, shredded lettuce, tomatoes and sour cream if desired.

8 servings, each serving has 355 calories, 10 g fat, 33 g carbohydrate, 28 g protein, 5 g fiber

Make sure that you eat enough calories. Too little calories can actually slow down your metabolism, making weight loss difficult. Generally speaking, most adult females should not drop below 1200 calories per day. Most adult males should not drop below 1500 calories per day.

Now & Again Enchiladas

This recipe makes two dinners. Serve one tonight and freeze the other one for future use. Adjust the "heat" by choosing mild, medium, or hot salsa and/or by adding extra chili powder. Side dish suggestion: refried beans and yellow rice

Sauce:
1 onion, diced
1 can (16 oz) tomato sauce
1 cup salsa
1 Tbsp chili powder
1 tsp oregano
½ tsp garlic powder
½ tsp thyme

1 lb. lean ground beef
1 lb. ground Turkey
1 onion, diced
1 ½ cups fat free cottage cheese
1 ½ cups fat free sour cream
1 can (7 oz) diced green chilies
½ teaspoon ground cumin
½ teaspoon ground coriander
12 (10 inch) tortillas
1 cup shredded reduced fat cheddar cheese

Disposable 9X13 inch baking dish (if needed)
Aluminum foil

For the sauce, start by sautéing the onion in a saucepan that has been coated with cooking spray, until the onion is tender. Stir in the remaining sauce ingredients and bring to a boil. Reduce heat and simmer for 15 to 20 minutes. Meanwhile, cook the beef, turkey, and onion in a large skillet until meat is no longer pink. Drain any fat and return meat to pan. Stir in the cottage cheese, sour cream, chilies, cumin and coriander. Remove from heat.

Preheat oven to 350°. Using a ½ cup measuring cup, scoop a heaping measuring cup of the meat mixture and place in each tortilla. Roll up and place seam side down in two 13 x 9" baking dishes that have been sprayed with cooking spray. Each dish should have six enchiladas in it. Pour sauce evenly over the top of all the enchiladas. Bake uncovered for 30 minutes or until heated through. Sprinkle with 1/2 cup cheese and bake an additional 5 minutes or until cheese is melted.

For remaining enchiladas, sprinkle with 1/2 cup cheese, cover and freeze for up to three months. When ready to use, thaw in refrigerator overnight. Bake, covered in a 350° oven for 45 minutes or until heated through.

Makes 2 dinners. Each dinner has 6 servings, each serving has 418 calories, 11 g fat, 49 g carbohydrate, 30 g protein, 3 g fiber

Cheesy Spaghetti & Smoky Meatballs

You can use regular mozzarella, if you don't want the smoky flavor. You can find smoked mozzarella in the specialty cheese section of your store. Certain brands of smoked mozzarella have a tough rind that peels away easily. No side dish needed.

Meatballs
1 lb lean ground beef
1 small onion, diced
½ cup chopped parsley
½ cup shredded Parmesan cheese
⅓ cup seasoned dried bread crumbs
1 egg
2 Tbsp ketchup
3 garlic cloves, minced
¼ tsp crushed red pepper flakes
1 tsp salt
½ tsp pepper
2 oz smoked (or use regular) mozzarella cheese, cut into 16 little cubes

Sauce
1 tsp olive oil
1 small onion, diced
2 garlic cloves, minced
⅛ tsp crushed red pepper flakes
1 (15 oz) can crushed or diced tomatoes
½ tsp salt
½ tsp pepper
¼ cup chopped parsley
½ cup shredded Romano cheese

12 oz spaghetti

For the meatballs, preheat the oven to 415°. In a large bowl, thoroughly combine all of the meatball ingredients except the mozzarella. Shape the meat mixture into 16 equal sized balls. Push a cube of cheese into the center of each meatball and re-form the meatball so that the mozzarella in completely covered with meat. Bake the meatballs for 15 minutes, or until cooked through.

For the sauce, sauté the onion in the oil until browned. Stir in the garlic and red pepper flakes and cook about 1 minute. Add the tomatoes, salt, and black pepper. Simmer, uncovered, over medium-low heat while the meatballs are cooking. Meanwhile, cook the pasta according to package directions.

When ready to serve, stir the remaining parsley and Romano cheese into the sauce. Pour sauce over hot drained noodles and stir to mix. Top with meatballs.

4 servings, each serving has 517 calories, 18g fat, 45g carbohydrate, 43g protein, 4g fiber

Mom's Spaghetti

This is my best attempt at recreating my mom's spaghetti. She never wrote her recipes down, so I had to go purely off memory and taste. It's pretty simple and kids like it. Hopefully I did it justice.
Side dish suggestion: garlic bread

1 lb. Lean ground beef
1 (28 oz) can diced tomatoes, un-drained
3 (8 oz) cans tomato sauce
1 (6 oz) can tomato paste
1 (2.25 oz) can sliced black olives, drained
8 oz mushrooms, chopped
2 tsp oregano
1 tsp basil
1 tsp onion powder
1 ½ tsp dried minced onion
1 tsp garlic powder
1 tsp garlic salt
½ tsp pepper
16 oz spaghetti

Brown ground beef; drain any fat and return to pan. Stir in remaining ingredients, except spaghetti. Bring to a boil. Reduce heat and simmer uncovered for 30 minutes, stirring occasionally. Meanwhile, cook pasta according to package directions (omitting any salt). Serve sauce over pasta.

6 servings, each serving has 382 calories, 8 g fat, 50g carbohydrate, 30 g protein, 8g fiber

Shredded Beef for Tacos   Slow Cooker

Serve with fresh tortillas, lettuce, tomatoes, cheese, guacamole, and maybe some fat free sour cream.

2-3 lb. Round roast, cut into large chunks
1 large onion, chopped
2 serrano chilies, chopped
3 garlic cloves, minced
1 tsp salt
1 cup water

Spray skillet with cooking spray. Brown meat and onions, re-spraying pan if needed. Transfer to slow cooker. Add chilies, garlic, salt, and water. Cover. Cook on high for 6-8 hours.

Remove meat to a plate. Pull meat apart with two forks until shredded. Return to crock pot. Make tacos!

8 servings, each 3 oz serving (meat only) has 147 calories, 4g fat, 2g carbohydrate, 25g protein, 0g fiber

Shepherd's Pie

Side dish suggestion: green salad

8 oz lean ground beef
1 tsp olive oil
1 large onion, chopped
⅓ cup chopped sweet red pepper
¼ tsp Garlic powder
1 cup shredded zucchini
½ cup shredded reduced-fat cheddar cheese
¼ tsp Salt
1 tsp Basil
¼ tsp Pepper
2 cups water
½ cup skim milk
2 cups instant mashed potato flakes
1 egg, beaten or ¼ cup liquid egg substitute
1 Tbsp Parmesan cheese

Preheat oven to 450°. Meanwhile, brown ground beef; rinse in hot water & drain. Heat oil in a large no-stick skillet over medium heat. Sauté onion, red pepper, and garlic for 3 minutes. Add cooked ground beef, zucchini, half of the shredded cheese, salt, basil, and pepper, and set aside.

Spray a 9-inch pie pan with cooking spray. Bring water and milk to a boil in a saucepan. Stir in potato flakes, then beat in egg and remaining half of cheese. Remove from heat. Spread about half of the potato mixture in the bottom of the pan. Spoon meat over potatoes. Spoon remaining potatoes on top. Sprinkle with Parmesan cheese. Bake for 15 minutes. Let stand for 5 minutes before cutting.

6 servings, each serving has 212 calories, 8 g fat, 22 g carbohydrate, 14 g protein, 2g fiber

> *Try drinking a glass of water about 20 minutes before eating. This can help you feel fuller & keep you from overeating.*

French Dip Roast *SLOW COOKER*

This meat is great as a sandwich, and using the juices to dip in. It's also good as a meat entrée, without making it into a sandwich at all. Side dish suggestion: steamed carrots

1 beef rump roast
½ cup soy sauce
1 tsp beef bouillon granules
1 bay leaf
1 tsp dried thyme
4 peppercorns
1 tsp garlic powder
Hoagie rolls (optional)

Trim fat from edges of roast. Combine all ingredients in a slow cooker (except rolls). Cover and cook on high for 6 hours or on low for 8-10 hours. Slice and serve as is, or make into a sandwich.

4-12 servings, depending on the size of the roast. Each 4 oz serving without bread has 184 calories, 5 g fat, 0g carbohydrate, 33 g protein, 0g fiber

Corned Beef &Cabbage

No side dish needed

1 (3-4lb) corned beef brisket
4 medium potatoes, peeled & quartered
4 medium carrots, peeled & quartered
8 small onions
3 medium parsnips, peeled & cut into chunks
2 medium rutabagas, peeled & cut into chunks
1 small cabbage, cored & cut into wedges
Salt
pepper

Place meat into a Dutch oven (or large pot); add juices and spices from package. Add enough water to cover the meat. Bring to a boil. Reduce heat and simmer, covered, for 2 hours.

Add all vegetables, except cabbage. Cover and return to boiling. Reduce heat and simmer 15 minutes. Add cabbage to pan. Cover and cook 15-20 minutes more or until vegetables are tender. Season with salt and pepper to taste.

8 servings, each serving has 411 calories, 10g fat, 46g carbohydrate, 35 g protein, 8g fiber

Beef Mushroom Dips   SLOW COOKER

This recipe is easy to adapt to make 4-12 sandwiches. Side dish suggestion: Baked French fries

Beef Round Roast- any size (each 1 ½ lbs. will serve 4)
Large Portobello mushrooms (1 for each person)
1-2 packets dry mushroom onion soup mix
Hoagie buns (1 per serving)

Trim and discard fat from roast. Place roast in the slow cooker, cutting roast if needed to make it fit. Trim and discard stems from the mushrooms. Place mushrooms on top of the roast. Sprinkle 1 packet of dry soup mix over all. Pour in 2 cups of water. Cover and cook on low for 8-9 hours, or on high for 4-5 hours.

Remove roast from pan. Cover and let stand for 10 minutes. Meanwhile, check the cooking broth to see if you will need more juice to dip your sandwiches in (like a French Dip). If you are serving a lot of sandwiches, you will want to prepare the other packet of mushroom onion soup mix according to package directions and add it to the broth in the slow cooker.

Grill or toast the hoagie bread if desired. Thinly slice the roast beef. Slice the mushrooms in half. To assemble the sandwiches, arrange meat on the buns and top with each with 2 mushroom halves. Top with remaining half of hoagie. Slice sandwich in half and serve with broth to dip the sandwich in.

Each sandwich with sauce has 496 calories, 11g fat, 86g carbohydrate, 18g protein, 2g fiber

Grilled Steak Salad

No side dish needed

½ tsp dried thyme
¼ tsp salt
½ tsp pepper
1 lb. flank steak
1 Tbsp fresh chives, chopped+
1 Tbsp olive oil
1 Tbsp lemon juice
½ tsp Dijon mustard
⅛ tsp salt
6 cups spinach or arugula, coarsely chopped
¼ cup Parmesan cheese, grated or shaved

Trim obvious fat from edges of steak. Rub thyme, ¼ tsp salt, and ¼ tsp pepper over both sides of steak. Grill over med-high heat 4-5 minutes per side or until desired doneness (remember that flank steak gets tough when cooked too much). Remove from heat and let stand for 3-5 minutes before slicing.

Meanwhile, combine ¼ tsp pepper, chives, olive oil, lemon juice, mustard, and ⅛ tsp salt in a small bowl. Pour over greens and toss. Divide salad on serving plates.

Thinly slice steak across the grain. Arrange over the salad and sprinkle with Parmesan.

4 servings, each serving has 272 calories, 14g fat, 2g carbohydrate, 35g protein, 1g fiber

Pepper Steak CROCK POT

Side dish suggestion: Good served over brown rice

1 lb. beef steak, trimmed of fat & cut into strips
1/4 cup soy sauce
1 clove garlic, minced
1 large green pepper, sliced
1 large red pepper, sliced
1 large onion, sliced
2 large stalks celery, sliced
1Tbl cornstarch
½ cup water

Put steak, vegetables, soy sauce, and garlic into the crock pot. Cook on high for 3½ hours. Mix together water and cornstarch and stir into crock pot. Cook an additional ½ hour or until thickened.

4 servings, each serving has 235 calories, 7 g fat, 8 g carbohydrate, 33 g protein, 2g fiber
Each serving with 1 cup brown rice has 451 calories, 9g fat, 53 g carbohydrate, 38 g protein, 6g fiber

Swiss Steak Strips

Serve over rice or noodles. Include a side dish of vegetables or a salad.

¼ cup flour
¼ tsp Paprika
1½ lbs. Round steak, cut into 3/4" strips
2 Tbsp olive oil
1 clove garlic
½ tsp. Salt, divided
dash pepper
1 onion, thinly sliced
1½ cups water
2 tsp beef bouillon granules
¼ tsp Thyme
1 small bay leaf

Preheat oven to 325°. Combine flour, ¼ tsp salt, paprika, and pepper. Reserve 1 ½ Tbsp of flour mixture. Coat meat with remaining flour mixture & brown meat in 1 Tbsp hot oil. Remove meat from pan and transfer to a 8x8 baking dish.

Sauté onion and garlic in remaining oil 1 Tbsp for about 3 minutes. Mix in reserved flour. Add bouillon, ¼ tsp salt, thyme, and bay leaf. Mix well & pour over meat. Cover and bake for 1 hour.

4 servings, each serving has 394 calories, 17g fat, 5g carbohydrate, 53g protein, 1g fiber

Hungarian Goulash   *SLOW COOKER*

Side dish suggestion: green beans

1½ lbs beef top round steak, cut into strips
1 medium onion, chopped
2 Tbsp flour
1 ½ tsp paprika
1 tsp garlic salt
½ tsp pepper
1 can (15 oz) diced tomatoes, undrained
1 bay leaf
1 cup fat free sour cream
16 oz wide egg noodles

Place beef and onion in a slow cooker. Combine the flour, paprika, garlic salt and pepper; sprinkle over beef and stir to coat. Stir in tomatoes. Add bay leaf. Cover and cook on low for 8-10 hours.

Discard bay leaf. Just before serving, stir in sour cream; heat through. Cook & drain egg noodles according to package directions. Serve goulash over noodles.

6 servings, each serving has 548 calories, 10g fat, 67g carbohydrate, 46g protein, 4g fiber

Steak & Lime Pasta

No side dish needed

16 oz Rotini or other medium pasta
1½ lbs boneless beef top sirloin steak
3 Tbsp lime juice
1 (15 oz) can diced tomatoes with green chilies, un-drained
1 (15 oz) can black beans, rinsed and drained
1 green pepper, chopped
1 cup frozen corn, thawed and drained
4 green onions, sliced
½ cup loosely packed cilantro leaves, chopped
2 cloves garlic, minced
½ tsp ground cumin
½ tsp salt

Cook pasta according to package directions. While pasta is cooking, trim fat from steak and cut into ⅛" thick strips.

Spray a large nonstick skillet with cooking spray and heat over medium-high heat. Add steak and cook to desired doneness. Remove steak and set aside.

In same skillet, add lime juice, tomatoes, black beans, green pepper, corn, onion, cilantro, garlic, cumin, and salt. Cook and stir until heated. Add cooked meat and cook until heated through. Serve with steak mixture over pasta.

6 servings, each serving has 426 calories, 8g fat, 43g carbohydrate, 14g protein, 6g fiber

Marinated London Broil   *Grill or Broil*

Start the day before or in the morning. Side dish suggestion: baked potatoes

½ cup fat free mayonnaise
⅓ cup soy sauce
¼ cup lemon juice
2 Tbsp mustard
1 tsp garlic powder
½ tsp ground ginger
¼ tsp pepper
1 London broil (round steak), 1-2 inches thick

Whisk together all ingredients except the beef. Pour into a shallow dish. Trim fat from edges of beef. Add beef and turn to coat. Marinate in the refrigerator for 6 to 24 hours. Broil or Grill 6-8 inches from heat to desired doneness. To serve, slice diagonally against the grain.

4-6 servings, each 4 oz serving has 212 calories, 7 g fat, 0 g carbohydrate, 34 g protein, 0 g fiber

Marinated London Broil II

You can marinade the meat in as little as 15 minutes or up to overnight. Side dish suggestion: Greek or green salad with feta cheese

1 lb. London broil or sirloin steaks
¼ cup red wine vinegar
1 Tbsp olive oil
1 medium onion, sliced
1 red pepper, sliced
8 oz mushrooms, sliced
2 garlic cloves, minced
1 (15oz) can quartered artichoke hearts, packed in water, drained
½ cup water
½ tsp chicken bouillon granules
2 Tbsp red wine
1 tsp cornstarch
½ tsp dried basil leaves

Place meat in a glass bowl and pour red wine vinegar on the top. Turn meat to coat and allow to marinate (marinate in the refrigerator if soaking for longer than 30 minutes).

Heat oil in a nonstick skillet. Add onions, pepper, mushrooms and garlic and sauté until pepper is crisp-tender, about 3-4 minutes. Stir in artichokes. Reduce heat, cover and cook for 5 minutes.

Preheat broiler. Spray a broiling rack with nonstick cooking spray, and place meat on rack, reserving marinade. Broil until done to taste, 6-10 minutes on each side.

Meanwhile, combine water, bouillon, wine, cornstarch, basil, and reserved marinade in a small bowl. Pour over vegetable mixture and cook, stirring constantly until mixture comes to a boil. Set aside and keep warm.

To serve, thinly slice steak diagonally across the grain and arrange on a plate. Top with vegetable mixture.

4 servings, each serving has 293 calories, 11 g fat, 7 g carbohydrate, 38 g protein, 3 g fiber

Pot Roast &Gravy CROCKPOT

Side Dish Suggestion: Mashed potatoes and a vegetable of your choice

Lean Beef Roast (cut of your choice, up to 5 lbs)
1 can Cream of Mushroom Soup
1 package dry onion soup mix

Trim fat off of the edges of the roast. Place the roast into your crockpot. Top with soup and spread it out over the top of the roast. Sprinkle the dry soup mix on top. Cover and cook on low setting approx. 8 hours. Stir gravy before serving.

Servings: 4-10, depending on the size of the roast, serving size: 3 oz with 3 Tbsp gravy
Each serving has 229 calories, 9g fat, 8g carbohydrate, 27g protein, 0g fiber

Stuffed Flank Steak SLOW COOKER

Side dish suggestion: mixed vegetables

1 can (4oz) mushrooms, un-drained
2 Tbsp water
1 package (6oz) stuffing mix, any flavor
1 (1½ -2 lbs) flank steak
1 envelope dry brown gravy mix
¼ cup green onions, chopped
1¼ cups water
¼ tsp beef bouillon granules

In a bowl, stir together the un-drained mushrooms, water, and stuffing mix. Spread the mixture over the steak to within 1 inch of the edges. Roll up, jelly-roll style. Place it into a slow cooker that has been sprayed with cooking spray. Combine remaining ingredients and pour over the meat. Cover and cook on low for 8-10 hours.

6 servings, each serving has 360 calories, 13 g fat, 24 g carbohydrate, 34g protein, 1g fiber

Grilled Polenta & Steak

This dish is pretty when "plated" correctly. Be careful not to overcook the flank steak, as it will make it tough. No side dish needed

4 tsp olive oil, divided
¾ tsp sea salt, divided
½ tsp ground cumin
½ tsp chipotle chili powder
¼ tsp pepper
1 lb. flank steak, trimmed of edge fat
1 tube plain polenta, cut into 8 slices
1 large ripe avocado, sliced
½ cup chopped cilantro
2 oz cotija cheese, crumbled
½ cup salsa

Preheat grill. Meanwhile, combine 1 teaspoon oil, ½ tsp salt, cumin, chili powder, and pepper. Rub evenly on both sides of steak. Grill 6 minutes per side or until desired doneness. Remove from heat and let stand 5 minutes. Cut steak into thin diagonal slices when ready to serve.

Brush olive oil over the polenta slices and sprinkle with salt. Place in a grill basket and grill 3 minutes on each side until grill marks begin to show.

To plate: Arrange each plate with 2 polenta slices. Place avocado slices next to the polenta. Top with steak slices. Sprinkle with cilantro and cheese. Top with 2 Tablespoons of salsa.

4 servings, each serving has 396 calories, 22g fat, 21g carbohydrate, 31g protein, 5g fiber

Beef with Potatoes & Greens

Side Dish Suggestion: None needed, but good served with hot breadsticks or bread

1 lb. round steak
1½ tsp paprika
1½ tsp oregano
½ tsp chili powder
¼ tsp garlic powder
¼ tsp black pepper
⅛ tsp cayenne pepper
¼ tsp dry mustard
8 small red or white potatoes, halved
2 cups finely chopped onion
2 cups water
2 tsp beef bouillon granules (or cubes)
2 large garlic cloves, minced
2 large carrots, peeled, cut into thin 2-1/2-inch strips
1 bunch mustard greens, kale, or turnip greens, stems removed, coarsely torn

Thinly slice beef across the grain into strips 1/8" thick. Combine paprika, oregano, chili powder, garlic powder, black pepper, red pepper, and dry mustard. Coat strips of meat with the spice mixture.

Spray a large skillet with nonstick spray coating. Preheat pan over med-high heat. Add meat; sauté for 5 minutes.

Add potatoes, onion, water, bouillon, and garlic. Cook covered, over medium heat for 20 minutes.

Stir in carrots, place greens over top, and cook, covered, until carrots are tender, about 15 minutes.

6 servings, each serving has 246 calories, 5 g fat, 25 g carbohydrate, 25 g protein, 4g fiber

Steak Verde GRILL

Side dish suggestion: Spanish rice

1½ tsp paprika
½ tsp pepper
¼ tsp ground cumin
⅛ tsp cayenne pepper
4 sirloin steaks
4 slices Havarti cheese
1 cup green chili salsa, room temperature

Combine seasonings in a bowl and rub onto both sides of steak. Grill, covered, over medium heat for 8-12 minutes per side or until desired doneness.

Top with cheese. Cover and grill 1-2 more minutes or until cheese melts. Top with salsa.

4 servings, each 6 oz serving has 381 calories, 14g fat, 4g carbohydrate, 56g protein, 0 g fiber

Beef or Chicken Fajitas

You can make it spicier by increasing the chili powder if you want. There really doesn't need to be a side dish with this, but if you'd like, simple canned refried beans and/or Spanish rice works fine.

1 tsp garlic powder
1 ½ tsp zesty seasoning salt
1 ½ tsp ground cumin
½ tsp chili powder
½ tsp crushed red pepper flakes
2 Tbsp olive oil
2 Tbsp lemon juice
1 ½ lb. lean beef or chicken breasts
1 Tbsp olive oil
1 large onion, thinly sliced
1 green pepper, seeded and sliced
1 red pepper, seeded and sliced
8 (8") flour tortillas

Optional Toppings
Avocado slices
Shredded cheddar cheese
Fat free sour cream
Salsa

Combine the first 7 ingredients to make the marinade. Slice Chicken or beef into thin strips. Add to marinade and marinate covered in refrigerator for 2 hours.

Heat 1 Tbsp olive oil in a large skillet. Quickly sauté onions and peppers in oil until crisp tender. Remove from pan and keep warm.

Sauté marinated meat until cooked through. Add vegetables back to the pan and toss to combine with the meat. Spoon into flour tortillas and serve with optional toppings, if desired.

8 servings, each serving with beef has 434 calories, 15g fat, 39g carbohydrate, 31g protein, 3g fiber
8 servings, each serving with chicken has 418 calories, 13g fat, 39g carbohydrate, 30g protein, 3g fiber

Decrease the amount of total fat eaten. Fat has more than twice the calories of carbohydrates or protein. Dietary fat is also easily converted and stored as body fat. Limit dietary fat to no more than 30% of your daily intake.

Pot Roast w/Veggies CROCK POT
No side dish needed

1 can cream of mushroom soup
1 pkg dry onion mushroom soup mix
⅓ cup red wine (optional)
1 tsp dried rosemary
3 lb boneless beef chuck roast
4 carrots, cut into 2 inch pieces, thick pieces halved
2 parsnips, cut into 2 inch pieces, thick pieces halved
5 medium red potatoes, unpeeled, sliced ½ inch thick

Stir together soup, dry soup mix, wine (optional), and rosemary in a slow cooker. Trim fat off the edges of the beef and place in slow cooker. Turn once to coat. Arrange vegetables on the top and around the beef. Cover and cook for 8-10 hours on low, or until vegetables are tender.

6 servings, each serving has 659 calories, 18g fat, 49g carbohydrate, 69g protein, 6g fiber

Creamy Mushroom Steaks
Side dish suggestion: mashed potatoes

4 beef top sirloin steaks
Salt & pepper
1 Tbsp butter or margarine

Sauce:
8 oz fresh mushrooms, sliced
1 Tbsp butter or margarine
¼ cup chopped onion
2 Tbsp flour
1 ½ cups fat free half & half
1 tsp soy sauce
Salt, to taste
Pepper, to taste

Trim beef steaks. Sprinkle with salt & pepper. Let sit at room temperature for about 30 minutes.

In a saucepan, sauté the mushrooms and onions in butter until they are lightly browned. Sprinkle with flour, stir to blend well. Gradually add half-and-half, stirring & simmering until thickened. Add soy sauce, and salt and pepper to taste.

Meanwhile, heat 1 Tablespoon butter in a skillet. Add steaks. Brown lightly on both sides. Reduce heat. Cover. Let steaks simmer for a few minutes. Add mushroom sauce to skillet. Let steaks simmer in the sauce until they are tender and cooked to your desired doneness.

4 servings, each serving has 269 calories, 12g fat, 11g carbohydrate, 30g protein, 1g fiber

Mexican Stewed Beef

Serve as is, on rice, or inside warm tortillas.

2 ½ lbs round roast, trimmed of fat and cut in bite-sized pieces
¼ cup flour
1 Tbsp olive oil
1 large onion, chopped
3 cloves garlic, diced
2-3 jalapeno peppers, seeded and minced
3 cups water
3 tsp beef bouillon granules
2 Tbsp tomato paste
4 tsp cumin
1 tsp chili powder

Preheat oven to 350°. Toss meat pieces with flour, then brown in oil in an ovenproof Dutch oven. Add onion, garlic, jalapeño, water, bouillon, tomato paste, cumin and chili powder; bring to a simmer on the stove. Cover Dutch oven and place in the preheated oven, baking for 2 to 2-1/2 hours, until meat is very tender.

6 servings, each serving has 360 calories, 10g fat, 8g carbohydrate, 56g protein, 1g fiber

Italian Pepper Steak

No side dish needed suggestion

9 oz fresh refrigerated fettuccini
1 lb. lean beef sirloin, cut into very thin, bite sized pieces
½ tsp crushed red pepper, divided
1 Tbsp olive oil
1 green pepper, chopped
1 red pepper, chopped
1 small onion, sliced
2 Tbsp balsamic vinegar
1 (15oz) can Italian diced tomatoes, drained
½ tsp salt
¼ - ½ tsp pepper

Combine steak with ¼ tsp crushed red pepper. Set aside.

Cook pasta according to package directions. Drain and keep warm. Meanwhile, sauté onions and peppers in olive oil over medium-high heat, 2-3 minutes or until crisp-tender. Stir in vinegar and remove vegetables from skillet. Add steak to skillet and cook 2-3 minutes or until desired doneness. Drain, if needed.

Return vegetables to pan. Add tomatoes, salt, and ¼ teaspoon pepper. Toss with steak and heat through. Add additional black pepper and crushed red pepper to taste. Toss mixture with warm pasta. Serve immediately.

4 servings, each serving has 392 calories, 11g fat, 31g carbohydrate, 40g protein, 3g fiber

Steaks with Mushroom Sauce

Side dish suggestion: baked potatoes & steamed broccoli spears

4 beef tenderloins
Salt
pepper
1 Tbsp olive oil
8 oz sliced mushrooms
¼ cup water
½ tsp beef bouillon granules
¼ cup half & half

Sprinkle steaks with salt & pepper on one side. In a large skillet sprayed with cooking spray, cook steaks until desired doneness, turning once. Transfer steaks to a plate and keep warm.

Add oil to the same skillet and heat. Add mushrooms and sauté until almost tender. Stir in water, bouillon, and half & half. Bring to a simmer and cook for 2 minutes (sauce will be thin). Season with additional salt & pepper if desired. Spoon mushrooms and a little bit of sauce on top of the steaks before serving.

4 servings, each serving has 292 calories, 20g fat, 2g carbohydrate, 24g protein,1g fiber

Beef Stew *SLOW COOKER*

Side dish suggestion: dinner rolls

1 ½ lbs lean stew meat
1 packet dry onion soup mix
1 ½ tsp beef bouillon granules
4 potatoes, cut into chunks
6 carrots, cut into 2 inch pieces
1 (28 oz) can tomatoes, un-drained
2 garlic cloves, chopped
¼ tsp pepper
Salt, to taste
2 Tbsp cornstarch
¼ cup cold water

Put all ingredients except cornstarch and water in a slow cooker on low heat for 8 hours or until vegetables and meat are tender.

Stir cornstarch into water and stir into stew. Turn heat to high and cook another 5-10 minutes or until thickened.

6 servings, each serving has 410 calories, 8g fat, 46g carbohydrate, 41g protein, 7g fiber

Crock Pot Roast

Adjust the size of the roast and the amount of carrots you want to use according to how many people you'd like to feed. Side dish suggestion: mashed potatoes or egg noodles

1 beef roast, any type
1 package dry brown gravy mix
1 package dry Italian salad dressing mix
½ package dry ranch dressing mix
½ cup water
5 carrots, cut into 3 inch pieces

Place beef roast in crock pot. Mix the dried mixes together in a bowl and rub into roast on all sides. Sprinkle any extra mix over the roast. Pour the water around the roast. Set carrots around the roast. Cook on low for 7-9 hours.

4-12 servings, each 3 oz serving of meat plus 1 carrot has 234 calories, 10g fat, 8g carbohydrate, 23g protein, 2g fiber

Beef & Snow Pea Stir-Fry

No side dish needed

12 oz lean top round steak, trimmed of fat
2 Tbsp cornstarch, divided
2 Tbsp soy sauce
1 Tbsp dry sherry
½ tsp Sugar
½ tsp Salt
1 cup uncooked rice
2 green onions, thinly sliced
½ red bell pepper, diced
1 Tbsp olive oil
¾ cup water
1 can (8 oz) sliced Water chestnuts, drained
6 oz pea pods

Cut meat diagonally across grain into very thin slices; place in shallow baking dish. Combine 1 Tbsp cornstarch, soy sauce, sherry, sugar and salt; pour over meat. Marinate at room temperature 30 minutes.

Prepare rice according to package directions. Stir green onions and bell pepper into cooked rice and set aside. Meanwhile, drain meat, reserving marinade. Heat oil in large nonstick skillet until hot. Add meat. Cook and stir until lightly browned. Combine remaining 1 Tbsp cornstarch and water with meat marinade; mix well. Add to skillet with water chestnuts and pea pods. Cook and stir until sauce boils, thickens, and pea pods are heated through. Serve over rice.

4 servings, each serving has 338 calories, 8g fat, 44g carbohydrate, 23g protein, 3g fiber

Sesame Beef

Serve with brown rice

1 lb. boneless sirloin steak
2 Tbsp sugar
2 Tbsp soy sauce
4 green onions, chopped
5-6 cloves garlic, minced
3 Tbsp olive oil, divided
¼ tsp pepper
1 Tbsp sesame seeds, toasted

Trim fat from beef & cut into 1/8" slices. Mix sugar, 2 tablespoons oil, soy sauce, pepper, onions, and garlic in glass bowl. Mix in beef until well coated. Cover and refrigerate 30 minutes.

Remove beef from marinade and discard marinade. Cook beef in 1 tablespoon oil over medium-high heat until brown, 3-4 minutes. Sprinkle with seeds and serve over rice.

4 servings, each serving (without rice) has 260 calories, 12g fat, 0g carbohydrate, 35g protein, 0g fiber
4 servings, each serving (with 1 cup rice) has 466 calories, 13g fat, 45g carbohydrate, 39g protein, 1g fiber

Herb-Marinated Steak *(Start in the morning or the night before)*

Side dish suggestions: Green beans & mashed potatoes

1 lb boneless beef chuck shoulder steak, 1" thick
¼ cup minced onion
2 Tbsp chopped parsley
2 Tbsp vinegar
1 Tbsp olive oil
1 Tbsp Dijon mustard
1 clove garlic, minced
½ tsp dried thyme leaves

Combine onion, parsley, vinegar, oil, mustard, garlic, thyme. Place beef chuck shoulder steak in plastic bag; add marinade, spreading evenly over both sides.

Close bag securely and marinate in refrigerator 6 to 8 hours (or overnight, if desired), turning at least once. Pour off marinade and discard. Preheat broiler. Place steak on rack in broiler pan so surface of meat is approximately 6-8 inches from heat.

Broil 16-18 minutes to desired doneness (rare to medium-rare), turning once. Carve steak into thin slices to serve.

4 servings, each serving has 212 calories, 7g fat, 1g carbohydrate, 35g protein, 0g fiber

Chicken Fried Steak

I was given the challenge of creating a chicken fried steak that was less fattening than the typical restaurant version. I tried cooking it various ways. The lowest fat version was baked, and while it was crispy, the meat was tough in comparison to the fried versions. So, I used olive oil and cooked it longer with a lid in a skillet in order to get the tenderness without submerging it in fat. The result was that it was still a bit oily, but had 50% less fat and calories than the restaurant version, which averaged 800 calories and 40 grams of fat (without gravy)! Obvious side dish suggestions are mashed potatoes and gravy. Use packaged gravy mix and make the mashed potatoes without butter in order to keep the fat and calories down. Serve with some carrots the side and you'll see that even chicken fried steak can be done sensibly.

1 ½ lb thin lean round steak or cube steak
1 beaten egg
1 Tbsp skim milk
1 cup finely crushed saltine crackers
¼ tsp pepper
¼ cup olive oil

Trim fat from meat. Cut steak into individual sized pieces. Pound steak to ¼ inch thickness (unless using cubed steak). If the steak is already cut thin, pound it slightly on both sides to tenderize.

Heat the oil in a large skillet over med-high heat. Meanwhile, stir together the egg & milk and pour into a pie plate or other flat bowl. In another pie plate (or flat bowl) combine the cracker crumbs and the pepper. Dip the steak pieces into the egg mixture, then the cracker mixture, making sure to coat both sides. Cook the meat in the oil until brown on both sides. Reduce heat. Cover and cook 45-60 minutes, turning once during the cooking process. Remove the lid during the last 5 minutes of cooking, if you want it crispier.

4 servings, each serving has 413 calories, 20g fat, 3g carbohydrate, 53g protein, 0g fiber

Beef Caesar Kabobs

Side dish suggestion: rice

½ cup light Caesar salad dressing
½ tsp pepper
1 lb. beef steak, cut into 1" cubes
16 cherry tomatoes
8 small mushrooms
1 zucchini, sliced in half, then cut into 1" think chunks
1 large green pepper, cut into 1" pieces

Stir together dressing and pepper in a glass bowl. Add remaining ingredients and toss gently to coat. Cover and marinate in the refrigerator for 1-8 hours. Thread ingredients on skewers (discard marinade) and grill or broil until meat is cooked to your liking.

4 servings, each serving has 208 calories, 8g fat, 7g carbohydrate, 28g protein, 2g fiber

Carne Asada Tacos   GRILL

The salsa makes these tacos great, so don't substitute jarred in this case. No side dish needed unless you can't resist beans & rice.

For carne asada
2 lbs. flank steak or thin round steaks, trimmed of edge fat
⅓ cup lime juice
2 tsp garlic powder
2 Tbsp crushed red pepper flakes
½ tsp pepper
1 Tbsp oregano

Salsa
4 Roma tomatoes, chopped
1 jalapeno pepper, (discard seeds unless you like it hot) diced
1 clove garlic, minced
2 green onions, chopped
¼ - ½ cup chopped cilantro
2 Tbsp lime juice
½ tsp salt

Serve with:
Shredded lettuce
Corn or flour tortillas, warmed

In a glass bowl, marinate the steak in lime juice, garlic, red pepper, pepper, and oregano. Marinate in refrigerator, covered, for at least 20 minutes and up to 24 hours, turning occasionally.

For salsa, mix all ingredients in a bowl and set aside.

When grill is hot, remove steaks from marinade and sprinkle lightly with salt. Grill steaks on each side for 2-5 minutes, or until desired doneness (flank steak is tough when overcooked).
Meat is thin and cooks quickly. Let meat rest for 2 minutes then cut into thin strips against the grain. Serve immediately in warm tortillas. Top with salsa and lettuce.

8 servings, each serving (not counting tortillas) has 213 calories, 7g fat, 1g carbohydrate, 35g protein, 0g fiber

Avoid glass and marble cutting boards. They will destroy your knives. Instead opt for wood or plastic. Having several available in different sizes will speed up your cooking time by avoiding the extra washings and help keep foods from accidentally becoming contaminated when cutting raw meats.

Steak Tampiquena

Start to finish time: 15 minutes
Side dish suggestion: Mexican (yellow) rice

2 quality cuts of steak (1 lb. each), about ½" - ¾ " thick
Seasoning salt
1 tsp olive oil
1 small onion, minced
2 Roma tomatoes, chopped
3 cloves garlic, minced
1 (7oz) can whole roasted green chilies, drained
4 oz Monterey Jack cheese, sliced

Preheat oven to broil. Heat olive oil in pan. Sauté onion, garlic and tomato for 2- 3 minutes or until tender. Set mixture aside. Cut green chilies into halves and set aside.

Sprinkle seasoning salt on both sides of steak. Broil steaks about 5-8 minutes on one side. Turn steaks over and broil the other side another 5-8 minutes or until almost done.

Remove from oven and place onion mixture evenly on one side of steaks. Top with strips of green chili. Place cheese slices evenly over the top. Broil until steak is done and cheese is melted, about 2-3 more minutes. Let sit for 2 minutes. Slice each steak into 3 pieces.

6 servings, each serving has 376 calories, 17 g fat, 4 carbohydrate, 51 g protein, 1 g fiber

Deviled Beef Rolls

Side dish suggestion: green salad and peas

2 Tbsp dry onion soup mix
3 Tbsp horseradish mustard
4 beef cubed steaks
4 oz can mushrooms
1 Tbsp butter, melted
Pepper
toothpicks

Mix dry soup mix and 4 tsp. water. Let stand 5 minutes. Stir in mustard.

Sprinkle steaks with pepper. Spread one side of each steak with the mustard mixture. Top steaks with the mushrooms. Roll steaks and fasten with toothpicks. Brush lightly with butter.

Broil 6-8" from heat source about 6 minutes. Turn and brush again with butter. Broil 6 more minutes.

4 servings, each serving has 250 calories, 10 g fat, 2g carbohydrate, 35 g protein, 1g fiber

Fish

Shrimp Tacos

You can also cook the shrimp in a skillet, if you don't want to grill. No side dish needed

1 lb. large or extra-large shrimp, peeled
2 tsp chili powder
2 tsp olive oil
3 cups bagged coleslaw mix
⅓ cup light ranch dressing
¼ cup chopped cilantro
4 large soft, flour tortillas, warmed
1 large avocado, peeled and diced

Heat grill. Meanwhile, toss first 3 ingredients in a bowl. In another bowl, mix next 3 ingredients. Place shrimp on grill (sprayed with non-stick spray) & cook until shrimp is opaque. Top tortillas with slaw, then shrimp and avocado, and roll up. Serve with salsa

4 servings, each serving has 432 calories, 19g fat, 36g carbohydrate, 30g protein, 8g fiber

Shrimp Newberg

No side dish needed

16 oz bowtie or other medium pasta
1 bunch asparagus, trimmed & cut into 1 inch pieces
1 lb shrimp, peeled and deveined
½ cup dry Sherry
⅓ cup green onions, thinly sliced, divided
15 oz bottled light Alfredo sauce
1 can (14 ½ oz) diced tomatoes

Cook pasta according to package directions, adding asparagus 6 minutes before pasta will be done. Meanwhile, spray a large nonstick skillet with cooking spray and heat over medium-high heat. Add shrimp and sauté 3-4 minutes or until shrimp is cooked through. Remove shrimp from skillet and set aside.

Add sherry, and half of the green onions to the skillet. Bring to a boil. Simmer uncovered for 5 minutes. Add Alfredo sauce and tomatoes. Stir until heated.

Drain pasta and asparagus. Return to pot. Add shrimp, tomatoes, and sauce. Toss thoroughly to coat. Sprinkle servings with remaining green onion.

6 servings, each serving has 413 calories, 15g fat, 39g carbohydrate, 25g protein, 4g fiber

Shrimp Pasta Primavera *Microwave*

No side dish needed

1¼ Cups water
1½ tsp chicken bouillon granules
¼ - ½ tsp garlic salt, to taste
2 Tbsp cornstarch
1 Tbsp Olive oil
12 oz shrimp, shelled and deveined
1 medium onion, cut into thin wedges
2 cloves garlic, minced
2 medium carrots, cut into matchsticks
1 red pepper, cut into thin strips
½ cup snow peas
2 Tbsp lemon juice
2 tsp dried basil
⅛ tsp crushed red pepper, optional
8 oz medium shell pasta (or other)

Whole wheat pasta is good for you, but has a different texture. If you don't like the texture, try making a blend of ½ whole wheat pasta & ½ regular pasta.

Cook shells according to package directions; drain. Meanwhile, in a small bowl stir water, bouillon, garlic salt, and cornstarch, and set aside. In large microwavable casserole dish or bowl combine oil, onion, garlic, carrots, red pepper, snow peas, lemon juice, basil, and crushed red pepper. Cover; microwave on High stirring once, for 3 minutes or until vegetables are tender-crisp. Re-stir cornstarch mixture. Stir into vegetables. Cover; microwave stirring once, for 5 minutes or until slightly thickened. Add shrimp. Cover; microwave for 2 minutes or until shrimp are cooked through. Stir in drained pasta.

4 servings, each serving has 255 calories, 6g fat, 29g carbohydrate, 22g protein, 3g fiber

Smoked Salmon Pizza

Side dish suggestion: green salad

1 pre-baked Italian bread shell crust
⅓ cup reduced-fat ranch salad dressing
2 Roma tomatoes, sliced
½ cup crumbled reduced-fat feta cheese
1 package (3 oz) smoked cooked salmon
4 slices provolone cheese, cut in strips

Preheat oven to 425°. Place crust on an un-greased pizza pan. Spread with ranch dressing; top with tomato, feta cheese and salmon. Arrange provolone cheese over top. Bake for 15-20 minutes or until cheese is melted.

8 slices, each slice has 242 calories, 10g fat, 27g carbohydrate, 12g protein, 1g fiber

Spicy Baked Fish

This really is spicy, because of the pepper. You can tone it done simply by using less.
Side dish suggestion: mixed vegetables

1 Tbsp Butter, melted
½ tsp rosemary
½ tsp basil
¼ tsp salt
1 tsp pepper
⅛ cayenne pepper
¼ tsp garlic powder
2 Tbsp lemon juice
1 lb firm boneless whitefish fillets

Preheat oven to 400°. Melt butter in a baking dish. Add spices and lemon juice. Stir to evenly coat bottom of dish. Place fish fillets in dish. Turn to coat. Bake uncovered for 10 minutes. Carefully turn fish over. Bake another 10 minutes or until fish tests done.

4 servings, each serving has 162 calories, 8g fat, 0g carbohydrate, 22g protein, 0g fiber

Scallops Bonne Femme

Serve over pasta or rice

2 Tbsp butter
¼ cup chopped onion
1 lb sea scallops (or bay scallops)
8 oz sliced mushrooms
½ cup dry white wine
1 Tbsp lemon juice
3 Tbsp flour
½ tsp salt
¼ tsp pepper
1 cup fat-free half & half
2 Tbsp fresh parsley, chopped
Parmesan Cheese (optional)

Dried herbs last a long time, but they should still have good color and smell. If not, it's time to re-stock.

In a large skillet over med high heat melt butter and cook onion until tender. Add scallops and mushrooms, wine, and lemon juice. Reduce heat to medium low. Cover and cook until scallops are almost tender (about 12-15 minutes for sea scallops or 3-5 minutes for bay scallops) Stir occasionally.

In a small bowl whisk flour, salt, pepper, and half and half. Gradually stir into scallop mixture. Cook until thickened. Serve over the top of pasta or rice. Sprinkle with parsley and parmesan (optional) on top.

4 servings, each serving has 243 calories, 8g fat, 15g carbohydrate, 23g protein, 1g fiber

Pistachio Fish Fillets

Side dish suggestion: rice pilaf and steamed broccoli

1 egg white, beaten
1 tsp water
½ cup pistachios, finely chopped
⅓ cup dry bread crumbs
¼ cup fresh parsley, minced
½ tsp pepper
¼ tsp salt
4 thin, mild white fish fillets (like orange roughy or cod)
4 tsp butter, melted

Preheat the oven to 450°. Whisk together egg white and water in a shallow bowl and set aside. In other bowl mix the nuts, bread crumbs, parsley, salt, and pepper. Dip fish into the egg and then into the nut mixture to coat. Put fish on a cookie sheet that has been sprayed with non-stick cooking spray. Drizzle fillets with butter. Bake for 8-10 minutes or until fish flakes easily.

4 servings, each serving has 248 calories, 12 g fat, 11 g carbohydrate, 24 g protein, 2g fiber

Snapper Veracruz

Side dish suggestion: green beans

4 snapper fillets (or other firm white fish)
1 (14½ oz) can Mexican style diced tomatoes
1 (4 oz) can sliced olives, drained
2-3 drops hot pepper sauce (optional)
1 (8-10 oz) pkg. seasoned yellow rice mix

Preheat oven to 300°. Mix tomatoes and olives in a baking dish that is just large enough to hold the fish without overlapping. Add hot pepper sauce to taste, if desired.

Rinse fish and pat dry. Top tomato mixture with fish fillets. Bake uncovered for 15 minutes. Spoon some of the tomato mixture over the fish and bake another 15 minutes or until fish flakes easily when tested with a fork.

Meanwhile, prepare rice according to package directions, but omitting any oil. Serve fish and sauce over the rice.

4 servings, each serving has 267 calories, 8g fat, 27g carbohydrate, 20g protein, 1g fiber

Invest in extra set of measuring spoons. It will make cooking faster since you won't have to wash them out when changing ingredients.

Basil Shrimp

Side dish suggestion: rice and broccoli

1 ½ lbs. shrimp, peeled and deveined
3 Tbsp Dijon mustard
¼ cup butter, melted
3 cloves garlic, minced
½ cup chopped fresh basil
2 Tbsp olive oil
¼ cup lemon juice
½ tsp salt
¼ tsp pepper

Stir together all ingredients in microwave safe bowl, except shrimp. Whisk mixture well then stir in shrimp. Cover and marinate in the refrigerator for 1-12 hours.

Vent lid (or plastic wrap) and microwave for 5-10 minutes, stirring every couple of minutes, until shrimp are cooked through.

6 servings, each serving has 234 calories, 14g fat, 3g carbohydrate, 23g protein, 0g fiber

Grilled Salmon & Spinach

Side dish suggestion: Rice pilaf or yams

4 salmon fillets (about 6 oz each)
1 lemon, halved
2 tsp olive oil
8 oz sliced mushrooms
10 oz spinach leaves

Squeeze half of the lemon over the salmon fillets, then brush with olive oil. Begin cooking salmon on either an indoor or outdoor grill until opaque throughout (about 5 minutes per side). Remove skin when done cooking.

Meanwhile, spray a pan with cooking spray, add mushrooms, and begin to sauté mushrooms, for 3 minutes or until they begin to get tender. Add spinach to pan (gradually, if needed), and sauté with mushrooms until wilted.

Divide spinach mixture between the plates and then top with salmon fillets. Squeeze remaining lemon over all.

4 servings, each serving has 233 calories, 8 g fat, 4g carbohydrate, 36 g protein, 2g fiber

To store fresh herbs for a week: Wash & refrigerate in a re-sealable bag with two paper towels, or put stems in a glass of water & cover loosely.

Crab Stir-Fry

Side dish suggestion: good served over brown rice

2 tsp cornstarch
1 tsp chicken bouillon granules
¾ cup water
½ tsp soy sauce
2 carrots, sliced
1 cup snow peas
1 red pepper, sliced
1 tsp grated ginger root
2 cloves garlic, minced
1 lb. Imitation crab

In a small bowl, combine the cornstarch, bouillon, water, and soy sauce until well blended; set aside. Spray a large skillet with cooking spray and sauté carrots, over medium-high heat for 1-2 minutes. Stir in the peas, red pepper, ginger and garlic and stir-fry 2 minutes longer or until vegetables are crisp tender. Add cornstarch mixture to the pan. Bring to a boil; cook and stir for 1-2 minutes or until thickened. Stir in crab and heat through.

4 servings, each serving (without rice) has 144 calories, 2g fat, 18g carbohydrate, 15g protein, 2g fiber

Scallops & Spinach

Side dish suggestion: cous cous or brown rice

1 lb. sea or bay scallops
2 Tbsp flour
2 tsp blackened steak seasoning or Cajun seasoning
1 Tbsp olive oil
10 oz fresh spinach
1 Tbsp. water
2 Tbsp. balsamic vinegar
6 slices turkey bacon, cooked and broken into small pieces

In a plastic bag or a bowl, combine flour and seasoning. Add scallops; toss to coat. In a large skillet cook scallops in hot oil over medium heat about 6 minutes or until browned and opaque, turning once. Remove scallops.

Add spinach and water to skillet. Cook, covered, over medium-high heat about 2 minutes or until spinach is wilted. Add vinegar; toss to coat evenly. Return scallops to skillet and toss to heat through. Sprinkle with bacon.

4 servings, each serving has 184 calories, 6g fat, 8g carbohydrate, 23g protein, 2g fiber

Tuna Spaghetti

Side Dish Suggestion: salad

1 pkg. (8 oz) Spaghetti
2 cloves, garlic, diced
1 Tbsp margarine or butter
¾ cup fat free half-and-half
1 Tbsp chopped fresh or 1 tsp Dried basil leaves
¾ tsp chopped fresh or 1/4 tsp Dried oregano leaves
1 can (9¼ oz) Tuna (in water), drained
½ cup sliced pimiento-stuffed olives (optional)
¼ cup grated Parmesan cheese

Cook spaghetti as directed on package. Meanwhile, heat margarine in a saucepan until melted. Cook garlic in margarine over medium heat, stirring occasionally, until garlic is golden. Stir in half-and-half, basil and oregano. Heat to boiling. Stir in tuna, olives and cheese; heat to boiling. Simmer and stir 1 minute. Drain spaghetti. Toss with tuna mixture. Sprinkle with chopped fresh parsley or basil if desired.

4 servings, each serving has 276 calories, 9 g fat, 23g carbohydrate, 23 g protein, 1g fiber

Honey Glazed Salmon & Asparagus

Side dish suggestion: Rice Pilaf

¼ cup honey
2 Tbsp Dijon mustard
1 tsp Butter Buds
1 tsp Worcestershire sauce
Dash of salt
Dash of pepper
4 (4oz) salmon fillets
1 lb fresh asparagus spears, ends trimmed
½ cup chopped walnuts

Preheat the oven to 400°. Line a 9x13" baking pan with aluminum foil.

In a small bowl, stir together the honey, mustard, Butter Buds, Worcestershire sauce, salt, and pepper.

Place the salmon fillets in the center of the pan and arrange the asparagus around the salmon. Sprinkle with the walnuts and drizzle with the honey-mustard sauce.
Bake for 20 to 22 minutes, or until salmon flakes when tested with a fork.

4 servings, each serving has 242 calories, 6g fat, 22g carbohydrate, 26g protein, 2g fiber

Tuna Casserole II

Side dish suggestion: cauliflower

2½ cups hot cooked elbow macaroni, rinsed and drained
½ cup chopped onion
¼ cup chopped green bell pepper
1 can Cream of Celery or Mushroom Soup
⅓ cup skim milk
¾ cup shredded reduced-fat cheddar cheese
½ cup canned sliced mushrooms, drained
¼ cup jarred chopped pimiento
1 (6 oz) can white tuna, packed in water, drained and flaked

Cook pasta according to package directions. Preheat oven to 350°. Spray and 8 x 8 inch baking dish with cooking spray. In a large skillet sprayed with cooking spray, sauté onion and green pepper 8-10 minutes or just until tender. Stir in soup, milk, and cheese. Continue cooking, stirring often, until cheese melts. Add mushrooms, pimiento, and tuna. Mix well to combine. Stir in macaroni. Spread mixture into prepared baking dish. Bake 20 to 25 minutes. Let stand 5 minutes before serving.

4 servings, each serving has 280 calories, 4g fat, 33g carbohydrate, 23g protein, 3g fiber

Shrimp and Scallop Teriyaki

This is good served over rice.

¼ cup teriyaki sauce
¾ tsp ginger
3 Tbsp dry sherry
2 cloves garlic, minced
1½ tsp cornstarch
8 oz scallops
8 oz Medium shrimp, peeled & cleaned
6 oz snow pea pods
8 oz mushrooms
5 green onions, cut into 2" lengths
2 Tbsp olive oil

Mix teriyaki, sherry, ginger, garlic, and cornstarch in glass bowl. Add shrimp and scallops. Cover and refrigerate at least 30 minutes.

Heat 1 tablespoon oil over medium-high heat. Add pea pods & cook and stir until bright green. Remove from pan. Add another 1 tablespoon oil to pan. Add mushrooms and cook until soft. Add shrimp mixture and onions. Cook until shrimp turns pink. Stir in pea pods.

4 servings, each serving has 211 calories, 8g fat, 9g carbohydrate, 24g protein, 1g fiber

Fish & Potato Casserole

Side dish suggestion: green salad

12 oz. frozen loose-packed hashed browns, thawed
1 Cup egg substitute
2 Cups skim milk
1 Tbsp minced dry onion
1¼ tsp seasoned salt
1 tsp dried dillweed
⅛ tsp pepper
1 cup shredded reduced fat cheddar cheese
14 oz frozen fish sticks

Preheat oven to 350°. Meanwhile, in a large bowl, combine eggs, milk, onion, seasoned salt, dill weed, and pepper. Stir in potatoes and cheese. Pour into a 12 X 7 inch baking pan that has been sprayed with cooking spray. Arrange fish sticks on top. Bake for 55-60 minutes or until center is nearly set. Let stand 10 minutes before serving.

6 servings, each serving has 314 calories, 12 g fat, 32 g carbohydrate, 19 g protein, 2 g fiber

Greek Shrimp & Beans

No side dish needed

Aluminum foil
Cooking spray
1 lb shrimp, peeled & deveined
1 can (15 oz) cannellini beans, rinsed and drained
8 oz grape tomatoes, halved
8 oz fresh green beans, trimmed
¼ cup pitted Kalamata olives, chopped
2 tsp olive oil
½ tsp dried lemon peel
3 cloves garlic, minced
¼ tsp pepper
¼ tsp oregano
¼ cup reduced fat feta cheese

Preheat oven to 500° or preheat grill. Spray 4 big pieces of foil (about 16 inches long) with cooking spray.

Mix all ingredients, except feta cheese in a large bowl. Divide equally into the center of each piece of foil. Fold the top and sides of the foil to make a packet and seal. Bake for 15 minutes or grill for 10 minutes or until shrimp are opaque. Carefully unfold (watch out for steam) one packet to make sure that the shrimp are cooked though. When finished cooking, sprinkle with feta.

4 servings, each serving has 348 calories, 10g fat, 30g carbohydrate, 35g protein, 8g fiber

Scallop Lo Mein

No side dish needed

6 oz vermicelli
1 Tbsp olive oil
1 lb. asparagus, cut into 1-inch pieces
1 red bell pepper, cut into thin rings
3 green onions, chopped
2 cloves garlic, minced
1 lb. sea scallops, halved crosswise (bay scallops are fine to substitute)
2 Tbsp soy sauce
1 tsp Hot pepper sauce
1 tsp Sesame oil
juice of ½ lime (about 1 Tbsp)

Cook noodles according to package directions. Meanwhile, heat olive oil in wok or large skillet over med-high heat. Add asparagus, red pepper, onions, and garlic. Stir-fry 2 minutes. Add scallops; stir-fry until scallops turn opaque. Stir in soy sauce, hot pepper sauce, sesame oil and lime juice. Add noodles and toss to coat.

4 servings, each serving has 239 calories, 5 g fat, 23 g carbohydrate, 24 g protein, 4 g fiber

Seared Scallops

Side dish suggestion: rice pilaf

1 lb Sea scallops
2 Tbsp flour
1-2 tsp blackened steak seasoning
1 Tbsp olive oil
10 oz fresh spinach
1 Tbsp water
2 Tbsp balsamic vinegar
¼ cup cooked turkey bacon pieces

To make shopping easier, attach your grocery list to a clip board. It will be easier to mark items off as you go along. You can also attach any coupons you might be using that day too.

Rinse scallops & pat dry. In a plastic bag, mix flour & seasoning. Add scallops & toss to coat. Cook scallops in hot oil over medium heat for about 6 minutes or until browned & opaque, turning once. Remove scallops.

Add spinach & water to pan. Cover & cook for about 2 minutes or until spinach is wilted. Add vinegar & toss to coat. Return scallops to pan & heat through. Sprinkle with bacon.

4 servings, each serving has 164 calories, 6g fat, 5g carbohydrate, 22 protein, 2g fiber

"Fried" Scallops

These scallops are actually baked, but still have a crispy coating. Side dish suggestion: Mashed Potatoes Florentine

1 lb. Sea scallops
¼ cup buttermilk
½ cup seasoned dry bread crumbs
½ tsp ground thyme
Butter flavored non-stick cooking spray

Preheat oven to 450°. Soak scallops in a bowl with the buttermilk at room temperature for 15 minutes.

In a small bowl, combine the bread crumbs and the thyme. Toss each scallop into the crumb mixture and turn to coat. Place on baking sheet that has been coated with cooking spray. Repeat with each scallop. Spray the tops of scallops with cooking spray.

Bake 7-10 minutes. Carefully turn scallops over. Spray tops with cooking spray again. Bake another 7-10 minutes or until browned and cooked through.

4 servings, each serving has 144 calories, 2g fat, 3g carbohydrate, 27g protein, 0g fiber

Crab Enchiladas   MICROWAVE

You can also bake this in your oven for 20-30 minutes at 375° if you choose. Side dish suggestion: yellow rice

1 (10¾ oz) can cream of mushroom soup
½ cup chopped onion
3-5 drops hot pepper sauce (like Tabasco)
dash of ground nutmeg
⅛ tsp black pepper
1 (10 oz) pkg. frozen chopped spinach, thawed and drained
8 oz real or imitation crab meat, chopped
1 cup shredded Monterey Jack cheese
8 small flour tortillas
1 cup skim milk
½ cup chopped cilantro (optional)

In a mixing bowl, stir together soup, onion, hot pepper sauce, nutmeg, and pepper. In another bowl, stir together half of the soup mixture, spinach, crab, and ½ cup of the cheese; set aside. Warm tortillas slightly in the microwave so they are pliable. Put ⅓ cup of crab mixture on each tortilla and roll up. Place seam side down in a 12x7" glass baking dish that has been sprayed with cooking spray. Stir milk into the reserved soup mixture; pour over the enchiladas. Cover and cook on high power for 12-15 minutes, or until hot. Uncover and sprinkle with remaining cheese. Microwave for 30 seconds. Let stand for 5 minutes. Sprinkle with cilantro (optional) and serve.

4 servings, each serving has 465 calories, 19g fat, 50g carbohydrate, 25g protein, 6g fiber

Greek Shrimp

Serve over orzo or cous cous

2 cloves garlic, minced
1 lb. shrimp, peeled and deveined
2 tsp olive oil
1 (15oz) can diced tomatoes, un-drained
½ tsp oregano
¼ cup pine nuts, toasted
⅓ cup reduced-fat feta cheese

Sauté garlic and shrimp in olive oil until shrimp are almost cooked. Stir in tomatoes and oregano, Heat until shrimp are cooked through. When ready to serve, top with pine nuts and feta.

4 servings, each serving has 231 calories, 11g fat, 6g carbohydrate, 28g protein, 2g fiber

Seafood Pasta

Start to finish time: 15 minutes. No side dish needed.

2 Tbsp cornstarch
¼ cup cold water
16 oz thin spaghetti
½ onion, chopped
3 cloves garlic, minced
1 tsp olive oil
2 tsp chicken bouillon granules
1¾ cups water
1 (14 oz) can Italian seasoned diced tomatoes
1 tsp seafood spice
½ tsp marjoram
1 tsp basil leaves
¼ tsp pepper
8 oz imitation crab
8 oz shrimp, peeled & deveined
Red pepper flakes (optional)

Prepare pasta according to package directions. In a small bowl, stir together the cornstarch with ¼ cup cold water and set aside. Meanwhile, sauté garlic and onion in oil for 1-2 minutes. Add bouillon, water, and seasonings and bring to a simmer. Add seafood and simmer for 1 minute. Stir in cornstarch mixture and simmer until thickened and shrimp turn pink. Serve with red pepper flakes on the side if you like it spicy.

6 servings, each serving has 240 calories, 3g fat, 36g carbohydrate, 18 g protein, 2g fiber

Shopping in the bin food section can save a lot of money. Items like nuts and spices are often 3-4 times less expensive when purchased this way, plus you can buy only what you need.

Dijon Salmon

This recipe is for 1 serving. Start out with as much salmon as you'd like, and top each piece with the mustard and spices. Side dish suggestion: spinach salad

1 piece (6 oz) salmon **for each person** you want to serve

Top each serving with:
1 Tbsp Dijon Mustard
¼ tsp garlic powder
⅛ tsp black pepper

Preheat oven to 375 °. Spread 1 tablespoon of mustard on each piece of salmon and sprinkle garlic and pepper. Put on a baking dish lined with foil and spray with cooking spray. Bake for 30 minutes or until fish flakes.

Each serving has 212 calories, 6 g fat, 0 g carbohydrate, 34 g protein, 0 g fiber

Salmon with Lime Butter

Side dish suggestion: Serve with brown rice and Sautéed Asparagus

1 Tbsp. butter, divided
1 ½ lbs salmon fillet
4 tsp. lime juice, divided
½ tsp. sea salt, divided

Spray a large skillet with nonstick cooking spray and heat it over medium-high heat. When the pan is hot, add half of the butter and let it melt. Add the salmon, skin side down, and sprinkle it with half of the lime juice and half of the salt. Sear the salmon (cook it without moving it) for about 5 minutes. Add the remaining butter to the pan, and carefully flip the salmon. Reduce the heat slightly. Top the salmon with the remaining lime juice and salt. Cook it for 3-5 more minutes until the salmon flakes easily and is cooked through.

4 servings, each serving has 279 calories, 10g fat, 0g carbohydrate, 44g protein, 0g fiber

Asparagus 6 Ways

Grill. *Toss with olive oil & salt. Grill, turning once, about 5 minutes.*

Broil. *Same as above.*

Roast. *Same as above, but bake at 450° for 15 minutes.*

Steam: *Place in steamer for 12-15 minutes.*

Stovetop: *Boil ½ inch of salted water in a large pan. Simmer asparagus in a single layer, covered, about 5 minutes.*

Microwave: *Cover with plastic wrap (vented), and cook for 5-10 minutes or until tender.*

Blackened Salmon

Adjust the cayenne pepper according to whether or not you like things spicy. Side dish suggestion: broccoli

1 ½ tsp garlic powder
1 ½ tsp dried parsley flakes
1 ½ tsp dried basil
¾ tsp thyme
½ - 1 tsp cayenne pepper
½ tsp sea salt (or 1 tsp table salt)
¼ tsp pepper
1 Tbsp olive oil
4-8 serving size salmon filets

Mix seasonings together. Rub the seasonings into the salmon fillets, coating on all sides. Heat the oil over med-high heat. Cook salmon flesh side down for 3 minutes or until seared. Carefully turn over the fish, and continue cooking another 3-5 minutes or until cooked through.

4-8 servings, each 3 oz serving has 118 calories, 5g fat, 0g carbohydrate, 17g protein, 0g fiber

Linguine with Tuna Sauce

Side dish suggestion: bread sticks

16 oz linguine
4 large tomatoes, chopped
1 Tbsp olive oil
½ cup chopped fresh parsley
1 bunch green onions, chopped
½ tsp dried basil
1 lemon
12 oz canned tuna in water, drained
1 tsp pepper
½ tsp salt

Cook linguine according to package directions. Meanwhile, cook tomatoes, parsley, green onion, and basil in hot oil for 5 minutes.

Grate the lemon rind and add the rind to the tomatoes mixture. Stir in tuna, salt, and pepper. Adjust salt and pepper to taste. Squeeze in some of the lemon juice, to taste, if desired. Cook another 5 minutes. Toss over drained pasta.

6 servings, each serving has 230 calories, 4g fat, 29g carbohydrate, 20g protein, 3g fiber

Save up to 70% on your produce by buying apples, citrus fruits, potatoes, and onions in bulk bags

Seafood & Yellow Rice

Side dish suggestion: green salad

1 large onion, chopped
2 garlic cloves, minced
1 Tbsp olive oil
1 cup uncooked rice
½ tsp turmeric
2 ¼ tsp chicken bouillon granules
2 ½ cups water
8 oz uncooked shrimp, peeled & deveined
8 oz bay scallops
1 cup frozen peas
¼ tsp salt
⅛ tsp pepper

In a large non-stick skillet, sauté onion & garlic in oil until tender. Add rice and turmeric & toss until coated. Stir in water and bouillon granules. Bring to a boil. Cover and simmer for 15 minutes. Add remaining ingredients and stir. Cover, and simmer another 4-7 minutes or until shrimp are pink.

4 servings, each serving has 291 calories, 5 g fat, 33 g carbohydrate, 26 g protein, 3 g fiber

Tilapia & Tomatoes

This dish is fast & easy, but looks fancy. Side dish suggestion: rice

1 Tbsp olive oil
4 serving size portions tilapia fillets (or other thin white fish)
salt
pepper
1 pint cherry or grape tomatoes, halved
¼ cup fresh chopped parsley
½ cup pitted kalamata olives, halved
1 Tbsp lemon juice

In a non-stick skillet, heat the oil over medium-high heat. Add fish and sprinkle with salt and pepper. Cook the fish, gently turning once, until done (it should turn white and flake easily). Transfer the fish to serving platter and keep warm.

In the same skillet, sauté the tomatoes, parsley, and olives for 2-4 minutes until the tomatoes are softened. Stir in the lemon juice. Add salt and pepper to taste, if desired. Pour the sauce over the fish.

4 servings, each serving has 240 calories, 14 g fat, 8 g carbohydrate, 24 g protein, 3 g fiber

Garlic Shrimp Pasta

Great with salad & breadsticks

1 lb spaghetti
¼ tsp garlic seasoned salt
¾ tsp lemon pepper seasoning
¼ tsp black pepper
¼ tsp paprika
¼ tsp Italian seasoning
⅛ tsp garlic salt
¼ cup olive oil
2 Tbsp butter
½ cup onion, chopped
6 cloves garlic, diced
1 ½ lbs. shrimp, shelled and deveined
¾ cup shredded part-skim mozzarella cheese
½ cup shredded Parmesan cheese

Cook spaghetti following package directions. Reserve 1/4 cup of the cooking water and drain. Return pasta to pot. Meanwhile, heat oil and butter in a large skillet over medium-high heat. Add onion and garlic and sauté for 3 minutes. Stir in shrimp and seasonings. Sauté for about 4 minutes, or until shrimp are pink. Pour everything from the skillet into the hot, drained pasta & toss. Add the reserved ¼ cup of the pasta water if needed. Stir in cheeses and stir immediately.

6 servings, each serving has 423 calories, 19 g fat, 25g carbohydrate, 35g protein, 2g fiber

Sesame Flounder

Watch these carefully while broiling, so they don't burn. Side dish suggestion: rice & vegetables

3 Tbsp low fat buttermilk
2 tsp soy sauce
1 tsp lemon juice
½ cup dry plain bread crumbs
2 Tbsp sesame seeds
1 Tbsp sesame oil
4 flounder fillets

Preheat broiler. Meanwhile, in shallow mixing bowl, combine buttermilk, soy sauce, and lemon juice. In another shallow bowl, combine bread crumbs, sesame seeds, and sesame oil. Mix the bread crumb mixture thoroughly with a fork until oil is mixed in evenly.

Dip fillets in buttermilk mixture, then in crumb mixture to coat on both sides. Place fillets on a broiling rack or non-stick cookie sheet. Broil 10 inches from heat for 5-6 minutes. Carefully turn fish over. Broil another 3-5 minutes or until fish flakes easily when tested with a fork.

4 servings, each serving has 186 calories, 7g fat, 7g carbohydrate, 23g protein, 1g fiber

Maryland Fish Fillets

Side Dish Suggestion: rice pilaf & green salad

4 sole, flounder, or other skinless thin, white fish fillets
1 Tbsp margarine or butter
1 Tbsp flour
1 cup skim milk
salt and pepper to taste
1 oz Gruyere cheese, grated
2 oz Monterey Jack cheese, grated, divided
1 ½ Tbsp fresh chopped chives

Melt margarine in a saucepan over low heat. Stir in flour, blending well. Gradually pour in milk, whisking constantly until the sauce comes to a light boil. Reduce heat. Simmer on low for 15 minutes, stirring occasionally. Season to taste with salt and pepper. Add chives, Gruyere, and half of the Monterey Jack cheese. Stir over low heat just until the cheeses melt. Remove from heat.

Meanwhile, rinse fillets. Pat dry with paper towel. Place fillets on a broiling pan that has been sprayed with cooking spray. Top each fillet with 3- 4 tablespoons of sauce, spreading to coat evenly. Sprinkle with remaining Monterey Jack cheese. Broil 8 inches from heat, about 5 minutes or until fish tests done by flaking easily with a fork.

4 servings, each serving has 210 calories, 11g fat, 3g carbohydrate, 24g protein, 0g fiber

Foil Fish Bake

Start to finish time: 30 minutes
Side dish suggestion: rice

4 fresh lake trout (about 8 oz each) or other whole white fish
2 Tbsp margarine or butter
½ cup fresh parsley, diced
½ cup fresh dill sprigs, diced
¼ cup fresh chives, diced
¼ cup diced onion
2 Tbsp lemon juice
¼ tsp black pepper

Preheat the oven to 400°. Meanwhile, clean and rinse fish; allow to drain.

Make the stuffing by mixing together margarine, parsley, dill sprigs, chives, onion, lemon juice, and pepper. Divide evenly among fish and stuff and wrap each fish separately in aluminum foil, sealing the edges carefully. Bake for 20 minutes.

4 servings, each serving has 319 calories, 16g fat, 0g carbohydrate, 41g protein, 0g fiber

Stir-Fried Scallops & Vegetables

Side dish suggestion: Serve with brown rice

1 Tbsp soy sauce
1 Tbsp cornstarch
1 lb. scallops
4 slices turkey bacon, chopped
8 oz mushrooms
1 Red pepper, cut into thin strips
6 oz snow pea pods
2 Tbsp water
Pepper

In a medium bowl, mix soy sauce, and cornstarch. Add scallops and toss.

Cook bacon over medium heat. Remove scallops from the bowl with a slotted spoon and then add the scallops to the bacon. Use cooking spray if needed. Cook until scallops are opaque. Remove bacon & scallops from pan.

Add mushrooms, red pepper, and pea pods to the pan & stir-fry 2-3 minutes. Return bacon and scallops. Add water and fry until hot. Sprinkle with pepper.

4 servings, each serving has 160 calories, 2 g fat, 10 g carbohydrate, 23 g protein, 2g fiber
With 1 cup brown rice each serving, 376 calories, 4 g fat, 55 g carbohydrate, 28 g protein, 6g fiber

Shrimp Linguine

Side dish suggestion: spinach salad

8 oz linguine
1 lb medium shrimp, shelled and deveined
½ cup dry white wine
1 Tbsp lemon juice
1 Tbsp lime juice
¼ lb fresh snow peas
6 green onions, thinly sliced
1 Tbsp chopped fresh parsley
¾ tsp dried basil
½ tsp Lemon pepper
2 cloves garlic, minced
1 bay leaf

Prepare linguine according to package directions; drain. Meanwhile, in large skillet, combine shrimp, wine, lemon juice, and lime juice. Bring to a boil. Reduce heat to low; cover and simmer 3 minutes. Add remaining ingredients. Cook, stirring constantly, until snow peas are tender and shrimp are opaque, about 3-5 minutes. Remove bay leaf from shrimp mixture. Combine shrimp mixture with hot linguine; toss to coat.

4 servings, each serving has 362 calories, 3 g fat, 48 g carbohydrate, 31g protein, 3g fiber

Stuffed Sole

Side dish suggestion: wild rice and green beans

½ tsp onion powder
¼ tsp celery salt
1 Tbsp parsley
¼ cup dry bread crumbs
1 can crab meat, drained and flaked
1 Tbsp Lemon Juice
⅛ tsp Cayenne Pepper
6 thin sole fillets
1 Tbsp butter, melted
1 tsp paprika

Preheat oven to 400°. Combine first 7 ingredients in a bowl. Divide the crab meat mixture evenly amongst the sole fillets and roll them up. Place the stuffed sole on a broiling pan or cooking sheet that has been sprayed with cooking spray, seam side down.

Sprinkle melted butter and paprika over the stuffed sole. Bake for 20-25 minutes or until fish tests done.

6 servings, each serving has 153 calories, 4 g fat, 4 g carbohydrate, 26g protein, 0g fiber

Balsamic Glazed Salmon   GRILL

If you don't have a grill basket, you can also spray the grilling rack and the salmon with cooking spray to prevent it from sticking. You can leave the salmon in one fillet or pre-slice it into serving sized pieces. Side dish suggestion: spinach

2 tsp olive oil
3 cloves garlic, minced
1 Tbsp balsamic vinegar
1 tsp Dijon mustard
2 tsp fresh chives, minced
1-3 lb. salmon fillet *(4 oz = 1 serving)*
1 tsp sea salt (or ½ tsp table salt)
¼ tsp pepper

Preheat the grill to medium-high heat. Meanwhile, in a small bowl or measuring cup, whisk together the oil, garlic, vinegar, mustard and chives.

Sprinkle the salmon the salt and pepper. Place salmon in a grill basket that has been coated with nonstick cooking spray. Grill the salmon flesh side down for 3-4 minutes, with the lid closed. Turn the salmon over and baste the fish with the vinegar mixture. Reduce the grill's heat and cook (covered) for 10 more minutes until it is cooked through.

4-12 servings, each 4 oz serving has 143 calories, 5g fat, 0g carbohydrate, 23g protein, 0g fiber

Thai Pot Rice (Shrimp Version)

Side dish suggestion: sautéed fresh green beans

6 cups hot cooked rice (preferably brown)
2 Tbsp olive oil
2 cloves garlic, minced
4 green onions, sliced
1 green pepper, chopped
1 ½ cups frozen peas
2 cups drained pineapple chunks
1 lb. shrimp, peeled
½ tsp ground ginger
¼ cup soy sauce
¼ tsp pepper
⅓ cup peanuts

Heat the oil in a large skillet over medium-high heat. Cook the garlic for 1-2 minutes, until just starting to brown. Add the green onions and stir-fry for 1 minute. Add the peas and pineapple and cook for another minute.

Push the vegetables to one side of the skillet and add the shrimp to the other side. Cook Until the shrimp is almost cooked. Combine the shrimp with the vegetables and continue to cook until the shrimp is fully cooked.

Stir in the cooked rice, soy sauce, ginger, and pepper. Top with the peanuts.

6 servings, each serving has 458 calories, 11g fat, 65g carbohydrate, 25g protein, 7g fiber

Load up on the veggies! They are packed full of nutrients and are usually low in calories and fat. We need about 5 servings per day, and most people can eat unlimited amounts of daily vegetables without the concern of weight gain. Just be careful what you put ON your vegetables...that's where the calories can get out of hand.

Poultry

Lemon Rice & Chicken

Start to finish time: 20 minutes. Side dish suggestion: green beans

2 boneless, skinless chicken breast halves, cut into thin strips
3 cloves garlic, minced
1 carrot, grated
Grated rind from 1 lemon
1 ¾ cups water
1 ¾ tsp chicken bouillon granules
1 Tbsp parsley
1 (4oz) can sliced black olives, drained
2 cups instant white rice

In a large skillet sprayed with cooking spray, cook chicken until no longer pink, adding the garlic during the last couple of minutes. Stir in remaining ingredients. Bring to a boil. Reduce heat to a simmer; cover for 5 minutes, or until rice is soft and liquid is absorbed.

4 servings, each serving has 299 calories, 5 g fat, 43 g carbohydrate, 17 g protein, 1 g fiber

Turkey Chili CROCK POT

Side dish suggestion: corn bread

1 onion, chopped
1 red pepper, chopped
1 Tbsp garlic, minced
1 lb. Ground turkey
1 ½ tsp Sea salt
½ tsp Red chili flakes
¼ tsp Black pepper
1 (15 oz) can red kidney beans, rinsed and drained
1 (15 oz) can black beans, rinsed and drained
1 (15 oz) can tomato sauce
1½ cups water
2 tsp chicken bouillon granules
1 Tbsp chili powder
 2 tsp cumin
1 tsp oregano

Brown turkey in non stick skillet until cooked. Put into crock pot with other ingredients and stir. Cook for 8 hours on low, or 3-4 hours on high.

4 servings, each serving has 346 calories, 2g fat, 43g carbohydrate, 42g protein, 11g fiber

Spanish Chicken & Rice

Side dish suggestion: warm tortillas

3 boneless, skinless chicken breast halves
1 pkg. Spanish rice mix
1¾ cups water
1 (15oz) can black beans, rinsed and drained
1 (15oz) can diced tomatoes, un-drained (or use seasoned Mexican style tomatoes)
Sharp reduced fat cheddar cheese (optional)
Fat free sour cream (optional)
Salsa (optional)

Trim fat from chicken and cut into bite sized pieces. Spray a non-stick skillet with cooking spray and sauté chicken until lightly browned (it doesn't need to be cooked through). Stir in rice from package and sauté until rice begins to turn golden brown. Stir in water, rice seasoning, beans, and tomatoes. Bring to a boil. Reduce heat, cover, and simmer for 20 minutes or until rice is tender and chicken is cooked through. Serve with optional toppings and salsa, if desired.

4 servings, each serving (without optional toppings) has 348 calories, 2g fat, 57g carbohydrate, 29 g protein, 10g fiber

Texas Stuffed Potatoes

Side Dish Suggestion: Tossed green salad

2 large baking potatoes, baked and cooled to the touch
8 oz ground turkey
½ cup chopped onion
1 clove garlic, minced
1 cup canned stewed tomatoes, un-drained
1 tsp Chili powder
¼ tsp Dried oregano, crushed
¼ tsp Ground cumin
¼ tsp Crushed red pepper
¼ tsp Salt
½ cup Shredded reduced-fat Cheddar cheese

Slice potatoes lengthwise in half. Scoop out center of each potato to within ¼ - ½ inch of potato skin.

In medium skillet, over medium-high heat, combine turkey, onion, and garlic. Cook until turkey is no longer pink; drain if needed. Add tomatoes, chili powder, oregano, cumin, crush red pepper and salt. Simmer 15 minutes or until most of liquid has evaporated.

Spoon turkey mixture evenly into potato shells and sprinkle with cheese. Place shells in a baking pan. Bake at 375° for 15 minutes or until cheese melts.

4 servings, each serving has 274 calories, 7 g fat, 37g carbohydrate, 18 g protein, 4g fiber

Pizza Potatoes *Microwave Meal*

Sometimes you just need to take a break. This dish is quick & easy. Side dish suggestion: green salad

4 baking potatoes
1 (26-28 oz) can spaghetti sauce, meatless
6 oz Turkey pepperoni, diced
1 green pepper, diced
¾ cup shredded part skim mozzarella cheese

Wash potatoes thoroughly. Poke them several times with a fork. Place in microwave and cook until done. Meanwhile, heat spaghetti sauce in a saucepan and keep warm.

Slice each cooked potato, and press the ends in order to open. Slightly mash the inside of the potato. Top each potato evenly with sauce, green pepper, pepperoni, then mozzarella cheese. Put potatoes back into the microwave for 30 to 60 seconds or until cheese melts.

4 servings, each serving has 393 calories, 10 g fat, 50 g carbohydrate, 25 g protein, 9 g fiber

Thai Rice

Side dish suggestion: egg rolls

1 tsp peanut or olive oil
3 bell peppers (preferably different colors), cut into strips
8 oz sliced fresh mushrooms
4 carrots, matchstick cut
1 lb. lean ground turkey
¾ cup dry white rice (not instant)
2½ Cups water
1 Tbsp Chicken bouillon granules
3 Tbsp soy sauce
¾ tsp salt
½ tsp black pepper
4 green onions, chopped
¼ cup chopped cilantro
2 Tbsp lime juice

In a medium skillet, heat 1 teaspoon oil over medium-high heat. Add the peppers, carrots, and mushrooms and sauté for 3-5 minutes. Set aside.

Meanwhile, brown meat in a Dutch oven. Drain & rinse meat. Return it to pan and add the rice, bouillon, water, soy sauce, salt and pepper. Bring it to a boil, reduce the heat. Cover and simmer 15 minutes. Stir in the sautéed vegetables and the green onions. Cover and cook another 5 minutes, or until rice is cooked. Stir in the cilantro and lime juice and serve.

5 servings, each serving has 211 calories, 2g fat, 26g carbohydrate, 26g protein, 6g fiber

Cumin Chicken

Side dish suggestion: yellow rice

½ cup picante sauce
¼ cup water
1 tsp chicken bouillon granules
2 tsp ground cumin, divided
½ tsp dried oregano
¼ tsp garlic salt
4 boneless, skinless chicken breast halves

Combine the picante sauce, water, bouillon, and 1 teaspoon cumin in a bowl and set aside.

In a separate small bowl, combine 1 teaspoon cumin, oregano, and garlic salt and sprinkle both sides of the chicken. Spray a large nonstick skillet with cooking spray and brown chicken on both sides. Pour picante sauce mixture over the chicken and bring to a boil. Reduce heat. Cover and simmer for 10 to 12 minutes or until chicken is no longer pink. Remove chicken and keep warm. Cook and stir the sauce over medium-high heat for several minutes or until slightly thickened. Serve the sauce over the chicken.

4 servings, each serving has 144 calories, 1 g fat, 5 g carbohydrate, 26 g protein, 1 g fiber

Chicken in Wine Sauce

Side dish suggestion: cous cous

4 skinless chicken breast halves
½ tsp salt
¼ tsp pepper
2 tsp butter
2 tsp olive oil
1 cup white wine (or use chicken broth)
4 thin slices deli ham, diced
1 green onion, chopped
1 tsp dried sage leaves
1 garlic clove, minced

Sprinkle chicken with salt and pepper. In a large skillet, brown chicken in butter and oil. Add remaining ingredients, stirring to loosen any brown bits on the bottom. Bring to a boil. Reduce heat. Cover and simmer for 20-25 minutes or until chicken is cooked through. Remove chicken and keep warm.

Bring sauce to a boil. Cook uncovered 8-12 minutes or until liquid is reduced to ¾ cup. Serve sauce with chicken.

4 servings, each serving has 218 calories, 6g fat, 2g carbohydrate, 33g protein, 0g fiber

Chicken Bonne Femme

This classic French recipe is a cinch to make. Side dish suggestion: green salad

4 boneless skinless chicken breast halves
salt
2 Tbsp flour
2 tsp olive oil
1 medium onion, sliced
8 oz sliced mushrooms
1½ cups water
1 tsp chicken bouillon granules
¼ cup white wine
¼ tsp tarragon
¼ tsp pepper
2 medium potatoes, peeled and cut into ½ inch thick slices

> *"Luck is when an opportunity comes along and you're prepared for it."*
>
> *~Denzel Washington*

Sprinkle chicken breasts lightly with salt and coat in flour. Heat oil over medium-high heat and cook chicken until brown on both sides, 3-5 minutes. Remove chicken and set aside.

In the same skillet, sauté onions and mushrooms for 1-2 minutes. Stir in water, bouillon, wine, tarragon and pepper. Top with potato slices. Return chicken to pan, placing on top of the potato slices. Reduce heat, cover and simmer until chicken is cooked through, and potato is soft, about 20 minutes.

4 servings, each serving has 253 calories, 4g fat, 22g carbohydrate, 30g protein, 2g fiber

Crispix Chicken

If you can't find cutlets in your store, you can use boneless, skinless breasts and pound or slice them to be 1/4" thick. Side dish suggestion: mashed potatoes, gravy, and a veggie of your choice.

2 cups Crispix cereal, crushed
½ cup nonfat buttermilk
4 thinly sliced chicken (or turkey) cutlets (about 1 lb. Total)
½ tsp salt
¼ tsp black pepper
2 Tbsp olive oil

Put the cereal in a re-sealable bag and smash it until it is crushed, but not ground. Put the cereal in a shallow bowl. Put the buttermilk in a separate shallow bowl. Dip each cutlet in the buttermilk, then the cereal. Sprinkle the culets with salt & pepper.

In a large nonstick skillet, heat the oil over medium heat. Cook the chicken until it is brown on each side and cooked through, about 3-5 minutes per side for thin cutlets.

4 servings, each serving has 220 calories, 7 g fat, 10 g carbohydrate, 27 g protein, 0 g fiber

Crockpot Chicken

Side dish suggestion: steamed broccoli

4 skinless boneless chicken breasts
2 cans Cream of Chicken Soup
1 can Cream of Mushroom Soup
1 box Rice-a-Roni Chicken Flavor Rice

Put soups in the crockpot and stir. Add chicken, turning to coat. Cover & cook on low for 8-10 hours.

Before serving, cook the packaged rice according to package directions. Serve the chicken and gravy over rice.

4 servings, each serving has 442 calories, 14 g fat, 46 g carbohydrate, 33 g protein, 3 g fiber

Chicken & Sesame Noodles

No side dish is needed, but it does need to marinade for 2-3 hours before it's time to cook.

Marinade
¼ cup soy sauce
¼ cup teriyaki sauce
3 garlic cloves, minced
¼ cup unpacked brown sugar
1 tsp ground ginger
4 boneless, skinless chicken breast halves

Sesame Noodles
1 lb thin spaghetti
½ cup soy sauce
3 Tbsp sesame oil
¼ cup sugar
3 green onions, thinly sliced
3 Tbsp sesame seeds, toasted

Mix the soy sauce, teriyaki sauce, garlic, brown sugar and the ginger in a glass bowl. Stir well. Add the chicken, making sure it's all coated with the sauce. Marinate in the fridge for 2-3 hours.

To make the noodles, mix the soy sauce, sesame oil, sugar, and green onion in a bowl or jar. Set aside. Cook the spaghetti according to package directions. Drain. Pour the sesame oil mixture over the noodles and keep warm.

Meanwhile, remove the chicken from the marinade, and toss out the marinade left at the bottom of the bowl. Cook the chicken on a grill or cook in a skillet until cooked through. Slice the chicken diagonally into thin strips.

To serve, put the pasta in a serving bowl. Top with the chicken, and sprinkle with sesame seeds.

4 servings, each serving has 518 calories, 17 g fat, 53g carbohydrate, 38 g protein, 3 g fiber

Chicken & Dumplings

This dish takes a while, but is classic, yummy comfort food. No side dish needed

1 large chicken, cut up
4 stalks celery, sliced
6 carrots, peeled and cut into 2 inch chunks
1 medium onion, chopped
8 cups water
3 Tbsp chicken bouillon granules
2 Tbsp dried parsley
½ tsp salt
1 tsp pepper
2 cups flour
4 tsp baking powder
¾ tsp salt
3 Tbsp olive oil
¾ cup skim milk
1 Tbsp cornstarch

Combine chicken, celery, carrots, onion, water, parsley, chicken bouillon granules, salt and pepper in a large pot or Dutch oven. Add additional water if needed to cover chicken. Bring to a boil; reduce heat, cover and simmer for 2 hours.

Remove chicken and let stand until cool enough to handle. Remove skin from chicken and tear meat away from bones.

Strain fat from broth, and return broth and vegetables to the pot. Add chicken meat to the broth and discard skin and bones. Add more salt and pepper to taste, if desired. Return to a simmer.

To make dumplings, combine flour, baking powder, and salt in a mixing bowl. Cut in the olive oil. Add the skim milk and mix until it forms a dough. Shape into golf-ball sized balls and set aside.

Mix corn starch with ½ cup cold water. Stir into simmering broth. Drop dough balls into the broth. Cover and simmer for 20 minutes. Serve immediately.

5 servings, each serving has 448 calories, 14g fat, 51g carbohydrate, 28g protein, 4g fiber

The next time you find yourself snacking, ask yourself if you are hungry. You might discover that you are just snacking out of habit or boredom. If that's the case, decide to do something else. Read a book, paint, go for a walk, give yourself a manicure, start building your dream (insert your own ideas here).

Chicken Cordon Bleu

Side dish suggestion: green salad

4 thin chicken (or turkey) cutlets
4 slices deli style ham
4 slices reduced fat Swiss cheese
2 Tbsp Dijon mustard
2 tsp honey
½ cup plain dry bread crumbs
toothpicks
Cooking spray

Preheat oven to 375°. Top each piece of chicken with a slice of ham and cheese. Roll up, jelly-roll fashion, and secure with toothpicks.

In a small bowl, mix the mustard and honey. Baste the chicken rolls with the mustard mixture, then roll in bread crumbs to coat on all sides. Place chicken rolls on baking sheet that has been sprayed with cooking spray. Lightly spray the tops of the chicken rolls with cooking spray. Bake for 30 minutes or until chicken is cooked through.

4 servings, each serving has 206 calories, 3 g fat, 8 g carbohydrate, 34g protein, 0g fiber

Latin Chicken

Side dish suggestion: Mexican rice

2 - 8 boneless, skinless chicken breast halves
¼ cup lime juice
3 Tbsp soy sauce
2 Tbsp honey
2 Tbsp chipotle chilies in a adobe sauce, minced

Combine lime juice, soy sauce, honey, and chipotle chilies in a large bowl. Add chicken and toss to coat. Marinate 15 minutes at room temperature.

Remove chicken (reserve marinade) and bake in a 400° oven for 15 minutes or grill over med-high heat, turning once during cooking. Meanwhile, place the reserved marinade in a saucepan and boil. Cook for 2-3 minutes.

Brush the chicken with cooked marinade. Cook chicken an additional 10 minutes or until cooked through (thermometer should reach 165°).

2-8 servings, each serving has 153 calories, 3g fat, 3g carbohydrate, 27g protein, 0g fiber

Chicken Carne Asada Tacos

Don't be afraid of the Cotija cheese, if you are unfamiliar with it. It's inexpensive and tastes a little like a dryer, salty, mozzarella. It's perfect on these tacos. It can usually be found in the dairy section, next to the salsa. Side dish suggestion: Black beans

1 medium red onion, sliced thin
¼ cup orange juice
3 Tbsp lime juice
½ tsp sugar
½ tsp ground cumin
3 boneless, skinless chicken breast halves, cut into thin strips
1 tsp oregano
1 tsp ground cumin
¾ tsp salt
½ tsp pepper
8 corn tortillas
1 avocado, diced
½ cup crumbled Cotija cheese

Place the sliced onion in a pan of boiling water. Boil for 1-2 minutes. Drain onion in a colander and rinse with cold water. Put the cooled onion into a bowl. Add orange juice, lime juice, sugar, and ½ tsp cumin. Mix well and set aside.

Spray a large non-stick skillet with cooking spray and heat to med-high heat. Add chicken. Sprinkle with remaining spices and cook until no longer pink.

To serve, heat corn tortillas on a griddle (or use your microwave) until warm and pliable. Make tacos with the chicken, avocado, cheese, and onion mixture.

4 servings, each serving has 336 calories, 13g fat, 28g carbohydrate, 28g protein, 6g fiber

Tuscan Chicken

Side dish suggestion: cous cous

4 boneless, skinless chicken breasts
1 tsp Italian seasoning
½ cup pitted Kalamata olives
½ cup white wine (or use chicken broth)

Spray a large skillet with cooking spray. Brown chicken on both sides over medium heat, about 10 minutes. Sprinkle Italian seasoning on the chicken. Add wine (or broth) and olives to the skillet. Bring to a boil. Reduce heat to a simmer. Cover and simmer for 20-25 minutes or until chicken is no longer pink.

4 servings, each serving has 211 calories, 7g fat, 3g carbohydrate, 27g protein, 0g fiber

Deluxe Chicken Breasts

Side Dish Suggestion: Cauliflower & Brown Rice

4 boneless, skinless chicken breast halves
2 egg yolks, plus 2 Tbsp water
½ cup flour
dash salt
dash black pepper
dash paprika
¼ cup dry bread crumbs
3 Tbsp Parmesan cheese
2 Tbsp butter or margarine

Cheese Sauce:
2 Tbsp butter or margarine
2 Tbsp all-purpose flour
1 cup skim milk
1-2 tsp Worcestershire sauce
1 Tbsp Parmesan cheese
¾ cup grated reduced fat Cheddar cheese

Slice chicken breast half lengthwise, so they are between ¼- ½ inch thick. (You should now have eight pieces of chicken)

Whisk egg yolk with water & set aside.

In separate bowl, combine flour, salt, pepper, paprika, bread crumbs, and Parmesan cheese.

Dip chicken breasts in egg yolks. Roll in flour-crumb mixture. Brown chicken breasts in butter or margarine on both sides. Place in shallow baking dish. Bake at 350°for 20 minutes or until cooked through. Keep warm until ready to serve.

In the meantime, prepare sauce: melt butter in a saucepan. Stir in flour. Slowly add the milk, stirring until the sauce thickens. Add Worcestershire sauce, Parmesan cheese, and cheddar cheese. Stir until cheese melts.

Transfer chicken to a serving dish. Pour sauce over the chicken.

8 servings, each serving has 175 calories, 8 g fat, 6g carbohydrate, 18 g protein, 0g fiber

Save money by buying blocks of cheese and shredding it yourself. Plus, the cheese tastes better.

Roast Turkey Breast with Rosemary Gravy

Side dish suggestion: stuffing, carrots, & cranberries

1 Red Apple, sliced
2 sliced leeks (white portions only)
2 cups water, divided
2 tsp chicken bouillon granules, divided
1 bone-in Turkey breast
2 tsp olive oil
1 tsp dried Rosemary, crushed, divided
2 Tbsp butter
3 Tbsp flour

Arrange apples and leeks in a small roasting pan. Add 3/4 cup water, and 1 teaspoon chicken bouillon granules. Set aside.

With fingers, carefully loosen skin from the turkey breast. In a small bowl, combine oil with half of the rosemary. Rub the rosemary mixture under the turkey skin. Place the turkey on top of the apple mixture. Cover and cook according to the times listed on the turkey breast packaging. Uncover during the last 30 minutes so that the turkey can brown. Remove turkey to a platter. Loosely cover with foil and let stand for 15 minutes. Discard apples, and leeks. Reserve ¼ cup pan drippings.

To make the gravy, melt the butter in a saucepan. Stir in flour. Gradually whisk in 1 cup water 1 teaspoon chicken bouillon granules, remaining Rosemary, and reserved pan drippings. Stir constantly until thickened.

Servings vary. Each 4 oz skinless serving (with 2 Tbsp gravy) has 238 calories, 6 g fat, 7 g carbohydrate, 35 g protein, 0 g fiber

Chicken & Cheesy Potatoes

Side dish suggestion: green beans

3 boneless, skinless chicken breast halves
1 pkg. Julienne potatoes mix
1 tsp dried parsley
1 cup shredded reduced fat sharp cheddar cheese
⅔ cup skim milk

Boil chicken breasts in a saucepan of water until cooked through, about 15 minutes. Remove chicken from water and set aside to cool. Shred using two forks.

Preheat oven to 400°. Meanwhile bring 2¼ cups water to a boil. In a large bowl, combine the potato mix (including cheese sauce packet), boiling water, parsley, and shredded chicken. Stir in the milk and half of the cheese. Pour mixture into a 2 quart baking dish that has been sprayed with cooking spray. Bake for 35 minutes. Sprinkle with remaining cheese and bake an additional 5-10 minutes. Let stand for 5 minutes before serving.

4 servings, each serving has 297 calories, 8g fat, 24g carbohydrate, 30g protein, 1g fiber

BBQ Fajitas

Side dish suggestion: baked corn chips

9x13 disposable foil pan
2 boneless, skinless chicken breast halves, cut into thin, bite-sized pieces
1 green pepper, cut into strips
1 red pepper, cut into strips
1 onion, sliced
½ cup BBQ sauce (spicy is good, but any will work)
8 (8 inch) flour tortillas, warmed
1 cup cojita cheese, crumbled
Fat free sour cream

Mix chicken and veggies with BBQ sauce and set aside. Using a fork, poke several holes in the bottom of the foil pan. Place chicken and veggies in the pan. Place the pan on the grill. Close the lid and cook over medium heat for 20 minutes or until chicken is cooked, stirring occasionally. Spoon onto tortillas and top with cheese and sour cream.

4 servings, each serving has 420 calories, 13g fat, 51g carbohydrate, 26g protein, 5g fiber

Chinese BBQ Chicken Legs CROCKPOT

This is super economical, & you can add more chicken if need more servings. Side dish suggestion: Rice

18 Skinless chicken legs
1 can (8oz) tomato sauce
½ cup soy sauce
¼ cup packed brown sugar
3 cloves garlic, minced
3 Tbsp cornstarch
¼ cup cold water

In a small bowl, stir together the tomato sauce, soy sauce, brown sugar, and garlic. Pour enough sauce to cover the bottom of the slow cooker. Add legs. Pour remaining sauce over legs. Cover and cook on high for 5 hours, or until chicken is tender and cooked through.

Remove chicken and keep warm. Pour cooking juices into a sauce pan and bring to a boil. In a cup, stir the cold water and the cornstarch until blended. Whisk into the boiling sauce and stir until thickened. Pour some of the sauce over the chicken, and serve the extra sauce on the side.

6 servings, serving size: 3 legs, each serving has 298 calories, 12g fat, 12g carbohydrate, 38g protein, 1g fiber

The road to wellness isn't straight, clear, or predictable.
It's a path you forge yourself.

Chicken & Artichoke Pasta

Side dish suggestion: green salad

12 oz bowtie pasta
2 boneless skinless chicken breast halves
8 oz fresh mushrooms, sliced
½ cup chopped green onions
2 Tbsp white wine or chicken broth
1 can (15 oz) diced tomatoes, un-drained
¾ tsp garlic powder
1 can (14 oz) water packed, quartered artichoke hearts, drained
¼ tsp salt
1 tsp dried basil
2 tsp cornstarch
2 tsp cold water
½ cup shredded Parmesan cheese

Cook pasta according to package directions. Meanwhile, in a large skillet sprayed with cooking spray, sauté chicken until cooked through. Remove and keep warm.

In the same skillet, sauté mushrooms and onions until tender, re-spraying the skillet with cooking spray as needed. Stir in the wine (or chicken broth), tomatoes, garlic powder, artichokes, salt, basil and chicken. Cook and stir for 4 to 5 minutes or until heated through.

Stir together cornstarch and water in a small cup until smooth. Gradually stir into the pan. Bring to a boil and cook until thickened, stirring constantly. Serve chicken mixture over drained pasta, and sprinkle with Parmesan cheese.

4 servings, each serving has 325 calories, 6g fat, 43g carbohydrate, 27g protein, 6g fiber

Turkey Cordon Bleu

Side dish suggestion: steamed broccoli or asparagus

4 turkey cutlets
½ teaspoon dried oregano
Pepper (optional)
4 ham slices (deli style)
4 provolone cheese slices

Place turkey between sheets of plastic wrap; pound to 1/4-inch thickness. Remove plastic wrap. Sprinkle turkey with oregano. Spray large skillet with cooking spray & heat over medium heat. Cook turkey 8-10 minutes (turning after 4-5 minutes) or until no longer pink in center, but being careful not to overcook. Sprinkle with pepper if desired.

Top each cutlet with ham and cheese; cover. Continue cooking 3 to 5 minutes or until cheese is melted.

4 servings, each serving has 264 calories, 10g fat, 2g carbohydrate, 40g protein, 0g fiber

Japanese Noodles

These can be served hot or chilled. No side dish needed.

12 oz Japanese noodles (or chow mein or spaghetti noodles)
2 boneless, skinless chicken breast halves, cut in ¼ " strips
2 Tbsp olive oil
1 red bell pepper, cut in ½" strips
3 carrots, sliced on the diagonal
1 small onion, sliced
2 cloves garlic, minced
4 green onions, chopped
¼ tsp red pepper flakes
2 Tbsp soy sauce
2 Tbsp teriyaki sauce
1 Tbsp sesame seeds, toasted (only if serving hot)

Cook noodles according to the package directions. Meanwhile, heat oil over medium-high heat in a large skillet. Add the chicken and cook until the chicken is cooked through. Remove the chicken to a large bowl and keep warm. Add peppers, carrots, onions, garlic, green onions, and red pepper flakes. Sauté until vegetables are crisp-tender. Add the drained noodles, chicken, soy sauce, and teriyaki sauce and toss. Top with sesame seeds, if serving immediately. Otherwise, omit seeds.

4 servings, each serving has 324 calories, 10g fat, 38g carbohydrate, 20g protein, 4g fiber

Chicken with Rosemary & Onion Sauce

Side dish suggestions: mashed potatoes & baby carrots

4 boneless, skinless chicken breast halves
½ tsp salt
¼ tsp pepper
1 medium onion, chopped
1 garlic clove, minced
4 tsp flour
½ cup water
½ tsp chicken bouillon granules
½ cup fat-free milk
1 tsp dried rosemary, crushed

Preheat oven to 350°. Sprinkle chicken with salt and pepper. Coat a nonstick skillet with cooking spray and brown chicken. Transfer to an 11x7 inch baking dish coated with nonstick cooking spray. In the same skillet, sauté onion and garlic until tender, re-spraying pan if needed. Stir in flour until blended. Gradually stir in water, milk, bouillon, and rosemary. Bring to a boil; cook and stir for 1-2 minutes or until thickened. Pour sauce over chicken. Cover and bake for 20-25 minutes or until chicken juices run clear.

4 servings, each serving has 147 calories, 1g fat, 4g carbohydrate, 28g protein, 0g fiber

Pecan Chicken

The sauce is optional, but it's a nice touch. Side dish suggestion: green beans

4 boneless skinless chicken breast halves
¼ tsp salt
⅛ tsp pepper
¼ cup flour
1 tsp dried rosemary, crushed
¼ cup butter, melted
1 Tbsp brown sugar
¾ cup pecans, finely chopped

*Sauce:
¾ cup fat free half-and-half
⅓ cup crumbled blue cheese
2 green onions, finely sliced
¼ tsp salt
¼ tsp pepper

Preheat oven to 375°. Sprinkle chicken with salt and pepper. Combine flour and rosemary in a bowl and set aside. In another bowl, combine the butter and brown sugar. Put pecans in another bowl. Coat chicken with flour mixture, then dip in butter mixture, then coat with pecans. Put chicken on a cookie sheet or broiling pan that has been coated with cooking spray. Bake on a center rack for 25 minutes or until juices run clear.

Meanwhile, place the ½ & ½ in a small saucepan and bring to a simmer for 3-4 minutes. Stir in the cheese, onion, salt, and pepper and cook for 1 minute longer. Serve with chicken.

4 servings with 2 Tbsp sauce, each serving has 399 calories, 27 g fat, 10 g carbohydrate, 30 g protein, 2 g fiber
4 servings without sauce, each serving has 375 calories, 25 g fat, 8 g carbohydrate, 29 g protein, 2 g fiber

Kielbasa Lime Chili

Side dish suggestion: warm corn bread

12 oz turkey kielbasa, cut into ¼ inch slices
2 (15oz) cans chili beans in sauce
1 ¼ cups salsa
4 tsp lime juice
⅓ cup green onions, sliced (optional)

In large saucepan sprayed with cooking spray, sauté sausage until brown. Stir in beans with sauce, salsa, and lime juice. Heat through. Sprinkle with green onions if desired.

4 servings, each serving has 318 calories, 8 g fat, 37 g carbohydrate, 23 g protein, 9g fiber

Chicken Chili

Side dish suggestion: baked tortilla chips

8 oz ground chicken or turkey
1 (4 oz) can mushrooms (drained)
¼ cup chopped green pepper
¼ cup chopped onion
1 small can tomato paste
1 (14 oz) can diced tomatoes
1 (15 oz) can red kidney beans, drained
¾ cups water
¾ tsp sea salt
¼ tsp chili powder
¼ tsp oregano
¼ tsp black pepper
¼ tsp basil

Cook green pepper, onion, and ground turkey until brown. Add remaining ingredients. Heat to boiling and then simmer for 25-30 minutes.

4 servings, each serving has 146 calories, 1g fat, 20g carbohydrate, 18g protein, 6g fiber

Smothered Chicken GRILL

Side dish suggestion: Green salad

4 boneless skinless chicken breast halves
½ tsp rotisserie chicken seasoning
10 oz fresh spinach
8 oz sliced fresh mushrooms
4 green onions, sliced
2 Tbsp chopped pecans
1 tsp olive oil
2 slices reduced-fat provolone cheese, halved

Green onions are also called scallions.

Coat grill rack with cooking spray before starting the grill. Sprinkle chicken with seasoning. Grill, covered, over medium heat for 4-5 minutes on each side or until a meat thermometer reads 170°.

Meanwhile, in a large skillet, sauté the spinach, mushrooms, onions and pecans in oil until mushrooms are tender. Carefully spoon the spinach mixture evenly over each cooked chicken breast. Top with cheese. Cover and grill 2-3 minutes longer or until cheese is melted.

4 servings, each serving has 249 calories, 10g fat, 5g carbohydrate, 34g protein, 2g fiber

Chicken Chipotle Tacos

Adjust the spiciness by the salsa that you choose. Black bean and corn salsa works nicely, but any will work. In spite of the name of this recipe, you don't actually have to use the chipotle chili, if you want to save money. If you decide to use them, chipotle has a nice smoky flavor & you might even want to use more then two. Side dish suggestion: baked tortilla chips

2 boneless, skinless chicken breast halves
1 (15oz) can pinto beans, rinsed and drained
2 chipotle peppers in adobe sauce, diced
1 (16oz) jar salsa
6 (8 inch) flour tortillas, warmed
1 ½ cups Monterey Jack Cheese, shredded
Shredded lettuce

Cook chicken breasts in boiling water until cooked through, about 15 minutes. Remove from water and shred chicken using 2 forks. Put shredded chicken in a sauce pan. Add beans, peppers, and salsa. Bring to a boil. Reduce heat and simmer on low for 15-20 minutes, stirring frequently. To serve, put some chicken mixture down the center of a warm tortilla. Top with cheese & lettuce.

6 servings, each serving has 378 calories, 13 g fat, 41 g carbohydrate, 24 g protein, 6 g fiber

Creamy Chicken & Bacon Pasta

No side dish needed (unless you're craving a salad, of course)

16 oz spaghetti noodles
2 boneless, skinless chicken breast halves, cut into ½ inch cubes
7 strips of turkey bacon, diced
1 small onion, chopped
4 garlic cloves, diced
3 Tbsp flour
1 ¼ cups water, divided
1 ¼ tsp chicken bouillon granules
½ cup white wine (or chicken broth)
⅓ cup fat free half & half
½ tsp salt
¼ tsp pepper
1 tomato, chopped
1 can (2 ¼ oz) sliced black olives, drained

Cook pasta according to package directions. Drain & set aside. Meanwhile, cook chicken in a large skillet that has been coated with cooking spray until chicken is no longer pink. Remove chicken and set aside. In the same pan, cook the bacon & onion until bacon is crisp, adding the garlic during the last minute. Put the chicken back into the pan & stir.

In a cup, stir together the flour and ½ cup water. Mix well and set aside. Add the wine, half & half, chicken bouillon, salt, pepper, and ¾ cups water to the skillet with the chicken. Bring to a simmer. Add the tomato and olives. Gradually stir in the flour/water mixture, stirring constantly until thickened, about 3-4 minutes. Pour mixture over warm pasta & toss.

4 servings, each serving has 380 calories, 7 g fat, 48 g carbohydrate, 23 g protein, 3 g fiber

Turkey Pecan Enchiladas

If you don't wish to use your oven, you can cover and heat in the microwave at 75% power until heated through. Side dish suggestion: Yellow Mexican rice

1 medium onion, chopped
6 oz reduced-fat cream cheese
1 Tbsp water
1 tsp ground cumin
¼ tsp pepper
¼ tsp salt
4 cups cubed cooked turkey breast
¼ cup chopped pecans
8 (8 inch) flour tortillas, warmed
1 can (10-3/4 ounces) condensed cream of chicken soup
1 cup fat free sour cream
1 cup skim milk
4 oz can chopped green chilies
¾ cup shredded reduced-fat cheddar cheese

Preheat oven to 350°. In a small nonstick skillet coated with cooking spray, cook and stir onion over medium heat until tender. Set aside. In a large bowl, beat the cream cheese, water, cumin, pepper and salt until smooth. Stir in the onion, turkey and pecans.

Divide the turkey mixture amongst the tortillas and spoon down the center of each tortilla. Roll up and place seam side down in a 13 X 9 inch baking dish coated with cooking spray. Combine the soup, sour cream, milk and chilies; pour over enchiladas.

Cover and bake for 40 minutes. Uncover; sprinkle with cheese. Bake 5 minutes longer or until heated through and cheese is melted.

8 servings, each serving has 328 calories, 13g fat, 29g carbohydrate, 23g protein, 4g fiber

Wooden Spoons are great because they don't scratch pans and they are cheap. Even though they are not supposed to go into the dishwasher (as with all wooden materials), they actually stand up to dishwasher use anyway, and they still last for years.

Oriental Chicken with Stir-Fry Vegetables

Side dish suggestion: Brown Rice

½ cup water
½ tsp Chicken bouillon granules
¼ cup soy sauce
1 Tbsp pineapple juice
1 Tbsp dry sherry
½ tsp Ground ginger
1 Tbsp cornstarch
2 boneless, skinless chicken breasts, sliced into strips
½ tsp Garlic powder
½ cup chopped red or green pepper
2 stalks celery, sliced
1 cup thinly sliced mushrooms
6 oz snow peas
2 cups bean sprouts

Combine water, chicken bouillon, soy sauce, pineapple juice, sherry, ginger, and cornstarch. Set aside. Coat a large skillet with cooking spray and heat over medium-high heat. Brown chicken & garlic and cook until chicken is no longer pink inside. Remove. Stir-fry peppers, celery, mushrooms, and snow peas for 2 minutes. Add soy mixture and chicken and continue cooking for 2 minutes. Add sprouts just before serving and heat through.

4 servings, each serving has 111 calories, 1 g fat, 8 g carbohydrate, 18 g protein, 3 g fiber

Now & Again Chicken Stuffing Casserole

Note : this recipe makes 2 casseroles. Serve one tonight. Freeze the other casserole for up to 3 months.
Side dish suggestion: cranberry sauce

2 packages (6 oz each) chicken (or Turkey) stuffing mix
2 cans cream of mushroom soup, undiluted
1 cup skim milk
4 cups cubed cooked chicken (or Turkey)
10 oz frozen corn
2 cans (8 oz each) mushrooms, drained
3 cups reduced fat cheddar cheese, shredded

Preheat oven to 350°. Prepare stuffing mix according to package directions, omitting butter. Set aside. Meanwhile, in a large bowl, combine soup and milk. Spread the stuffing into two 8x8 square baking dishes that have been sprayed with nonstick cooking spray. Layer with chicken (or turkey), corn, mushrooms, soup mixture, and cheese. Cover and bake for 30 to 35 minutes or until cheese is melted. Cover and freeze the remaining casserole *(be sure to attach a note on how to cook the frozen casserole to the pan, so you will have the directions when you are ready to bake it.*

To use the frozen casserole, remove from the freezer 30 minutes before baking. Bake at 350° for 90 minutes. Uncover and bake 10 to 15 minutes longer or until heated through.

Each casserole has 6 servings. Each serving has 316 calories, 8 g fat, 31 g carbohydrate, 28 g protein, 2 g fiber

Cheesy Spaghetti

You can heat this in the oven or microwave. Side dish suggestion: green salad

12 oz spaghetti
4 oz light Velteeta Cheese (or similar), cubed
2 boneless, skinless chicken breast halves
2 cups jarred spaghetti sauce
2 Tbsp grated Parmesan Cheese

If using the oven, preheat oven to 400°. Cook spaghetti according to package directions. Place chicken breasts in boiling water and cook for 10-15 minutes or until cooked through. Cut up chicken breasts into bite-sized pieces.

In a large bowl, combine drained pasta, chicken, Velveeta, and sauce. Place into a casserole dish and sprinkle with Parmesan. Bake for 20 minutes or until heated through. Alternately, microwave for 5 minutes or until heated through.

4 servings, each serving has 325 calories, 6g fat, 40g carbohydrate, 26g protein, 2g fiber

Now & Again Turkey Tetrazzini

This recipe makes two dinners. Serve one tonight and freeze the other one for future use. Side dish suggestion: green salad

16 oz spaghetti
8 oz sliced mushrooms
1 cup chopped onion
3 cloves garlic, minced
1 Tbsp olive oil
3 cans mushroom soup, undiluted
3 cups cooked turkey, cubed
1 ⅓ cups water
1 ½ tsp chicken bouillon granules
1 tsp Italian seasoning
¾ tsp pepper
1 ¾ cups grated Parmesan cheese, divided

Preheat oven to 400°. Cook pasta according to package directions and set aside. Meanwhile, in a Dutch oven, sauté onions, mushrooms, and garlic in oil until tender. Stir the soup, water, bouillon, and seasonings. Bring to a simmer. Add in the turkey, pasta, and 1 cup of cheese. Mix well.

Divide mixture between two 8x8 (or equivalent) baking dishes that have been coated with cooking spray. Sprinkle with remaining Parmesan. Bake 1 casserole for 20 minutes or until heated through Cover the remaining dish with foil, and freeze for up to 3 months.

To use frozen casserole: Thaw in refrigerator overnight. Remove from fridge 30 minutes before baking. Cook, covered in a 350° oven for 45 minutes. Remove cover and continue to bake for 5-10 minutes longer or until bubbly and heated through.

Makes 2 casseroles. Each casserole has 6 servings, each serving has 256 calories, 11g fat, 19g carbohydrate, 20g protein, 1g fiber

Glazed Chicken Breasts GRILL or BAKE

Side dish suggestion: Rice

4 boneless, skinless chicken breast halves
½ cup fat free Catalina salad dressing
½ cup Simply Fruit apricot spread (or similar)
3 Tbsp dry onion soup mix

Baking Instructions: Preheat oven to 350°. Spray a skillet with cooking spray and cook chicken 3- 4 minutes on each side or until brown. Remove from skillet and place in 2 quart baking dish.

Stir together salad dressing, apricot preserves, and soup mix in a small bowl and pour over the chicken. Bake 40-45 minutes or until chicken is cooked through. Serve chicken with extra sauce.

Grilling Instructions: Whisk together the salad dressing, apricot preserves, and soup mix in a small saucepan. Bring to a boil. Reduce heat and simmer while chicken is cooking. Meanwhile, cook chicken on grill 7-10 minutes per side or until no longer pink. Remove ¼ cup of sauce from saucepan. Baste chicken breasts with the sauce on each side during the last few minutes of cooking. Serve chicken with extra sauce.

4 servings, each serving has 269 calories, 3 g fat, 27 g carbohydrate, 27 g protein, 0 g fiber

Chicken & Vegetable Stir-Fry

Serve over rice

2 Tbsp cornstarch
¼ tsp ground ginger
1 can (14 oz) Vegetable broth
1 Tbsp soy sauce
2 boneless, skinless chicken breast halves, cut into strips
4 cups chopped broccoli
4 oz mushrooms, halved
4 carrots, peeled and sliced on the diagonal
4 stalks celery, sliced
4 green onions, chopped
1 clove garlic, minced

Stir together cornstarch, ginger, broth, and soy until smooth; set aside.

Spray large skillet with non-stick cooking spray and heat over med-high heat. Cook chicken until browned. Add in vegetables and garlic and stir-fry until tender-crisp.

Stir in reserved broth mixture. Cook until mixture boils and thickens, stirring constantly. Serve over rice.

4 servings, each serving has 153 calories, 1g fat, 19g carbohydrate, 18g protein, 5g fiber

Kielbasa & Roasted Vegetables

Side dish suggestion: pickled beets

1 large onion, cut into chunks
6 carrots, cut into 1 inch pieces
4 potatoes, cut into 1 inch chunks
1 Tbsp olive oil
¼ tsp salt
¼ tsp pepper
1 (14oz) turkey kielbasa, cut into 1 inch pieces

Mustard Sauce
½ cup fat free sour cream
2 Tbsp Dijon mustard
1 Tbsp water

Oven directions: Preheat oven to 500° Put vegetables in a bowl and toss with oil, salt, and pepper. Line a cookie sheet with foil & place veggies on it. Put in the middle of the oven and roast for 15 minutes. Add kielbasa and turn veggies. Move up one rack in the oven (getting closer to the heat source), and roast for another 15 minutes or until veggies are tender. Meanwhile, prepare mustard sauce. Serve along the side with roasted vegetables.

Grill directions: Preheat grill. Put vegetables in a bowl and toss with oil, salt, and pepper. Place veggies on a sheet of heavy-duty foil. Wrap foil over veggies and seal the edges. Put on a middle grill rack, close grill lid and roast for 15 minutes. Make another foil packet, this time containing the kielbasa. Add to the grill with the veggies and cook for another 15 minutes or until veggies are tender. Meanwhile, prepare mustard sauce. Serve along the side with roasted vegetables.

4 servings, each serving has 383 calories, 8g fat, 60g carbohydrate, 17g protein, 6g fiber

> "...the moments when you have truly lived are the moments when you have done things in the spirit of love."
> Henry Drummond

Southwest Creamy Chicken Crock Pot

Side dish suggestion: yellow rice

1 (15 oz) can black beans, drained
1 (15 oz) can corn, drained
2 cups salsa
4 frozen boneless skinless chicken breasts
8 oz reduced fat cream cheese

Place beans, corn, and salsa in the crock pot & stir. Place frozen chicken breasts on top. Cook on low for 6 hours or until chicken is cooked. Top with cream cheese (just throw it on top), cover, and cook for 15 minutes. Stir cream cheese into bean mixture and turn chicken breasts to coat. Cover and cook an additional 15 minutes.

4 servings, each serving has 492 calories, 13g fat, 51g carbohydrate, 45g protein, 8g fiber

Spinach Burgers

These are good served as-is with a side salad, or as a hamburger, complete with buns and the usual toppings.

Non-stick cooking spray
1 clove garlic, minced
1 medium red onion, chopped
10 oz frozen chopped spinach, thawed and squeezed dry
1 tsp oregano
⅓ cup reduced fat feta cheese crumbles
20 oz ground turkey
1 Tbsp Steak seasoning (I use Montreal Spicy Steak Seasoning)

Spray a large nonstick skillet with cooking spray and heat over med-high heat. Add garlic and red onion and cook 4-5 minutes. Transfer the onions and garlic to a bowl to cool. Return pan to heat. Thoroughly mix remaining ingredients with the cooled onions and garlic and form into 6 patties. Add patties to the pan and cook 6 min on each side, or until cooked through.

6 servings, each serving has 134 calories, 2 fat, 4g carbohydrate, 27g protein, 1g fiber

Creamy Chicken & Broccoli Pasta

Side dish suggestion: Green Salad

16 oz. Spaghetti
4 cups broccoli florets
1½ cups diced cooked chicken (or turkey) breast
1 med onion, diced
1 can (10-3/4 oz.) reduced fat condensed cream of chicken soup
½ cup skim milk
½ cup water
3 oz. Reduced fat cream cheese, cubed and softened
¾ cup Grated Parmesan cheese

Cook pasta according to package directions, adding broccoli to pasta cooking water during last 2 minutes; drain.

Meanwhile, in large skillet over medium heat, sauté onion for 2-3 minutes. Add chicken.

In medium bowl, whisk together soup, milk, water and cream cheese until smooth; add to chicken & onions. Heat to boiling; reduce heat to low. Simmer 1-2 minutes. Remove from heat; stir in Parmesan cheese. Toss hot pasta and broccoli with sauce.

6 servings, each serving has 323 calories, 9g fat, 35g carbohydrate, 25g protein, 4g fiber

Pot Au Feu

No side dishes needed. A nutritional powerhouse!

1 cut up chicken OR 6 chicken breast halves, skinless
4 cups water
2 stalks celery, coarsely chopped
1 onion, stuck with 4 cloves
⅓ cup chopped fresh parsley
1 clove garlic, halved
2 tsp chicken bouillon granules
1 bay leaf
½ tsp dried rosemary, crushed
¼ tsp salt
3 drops hot pepper sauce
4 carrots, cut into 1 inch pieces
4 parsnips, cut into 1 inch pieces
8 oz sliced fresh mushrooms
8 oz fresh spinach, washed and coarsely chopped

In a large saucepan or Dutch oven, combine chicken, water, celery, onion, parsley, garlic, bouillon cubes, bay leaf, rosemary, salt and hot pepper sauce. Bring to a boil; cover, simmer 30-40 minutes until chicken is tender. Remove chicken, and set aside. Strain broth and skim off any fat. Return broth to pan. Add carrots. Simmer, uncovered, 10 minutes. Add parsnips, simmer 10 minutes longer. Meanwhile, if you used the whole chicken, remove chicken from any bones and discard bones. If you used chicken breasts, cut chicken in large chunks. Add chicken, mushrooms and spinach to broth; cover, simmer 5 minutes longer.

6 servings using white meat, each serving has 202 calories, 4g fat, 13g carbohydrate, 30g protein, 4g fiber
*If using the white & dark meat from 1 chicken, you will still have 6 servings but they will be smaller as you will have less meat. Each serving has 179 calories, 5g fat, 14g carbohydrate, 22g protein, 4g fiber. Even though it looks like it's less calories to include dark meat, ounce per ounce the white meat version is the leanest choice.

When choosing mushrooms, the caps should be closed around the stems. Avoid black or brown gills.

Feta Turkey Patties

Side dish suggestion: steamed broccoli & a green salad

1 lb ground turkey (or chicken)
4 oz crumbled reduced fat feta cheese
2 tsp oregano
¼ tsp salt
¼ tsp garlic powder

Preheat grill or broiler (You can also use a George Foreman type grill).

Mix all ingredients well and form into 4 patties. Grill or broil patties until internal temperature of patties reach 165°, or until cooked through.

4 servings, each serving has 180 calories, 7 g fat, 1 g carbohydrate, 28 g protein, 1 g fiber

Chicken & Mushroom Pasta

Side dish suggestion: steamed asparagus

12 oz fettuccine
2 chicken breast halves
1 tsp olive oil
8 oz sliced mushrooms
3 cloves garlic, minced
¾ cup water
1 tsp chicken bouillon granules
½ cup canned evaporated skim milk
½ tsp pepper
½ cup shredded Parmesan cheese
2 Tbsp flour
¼ cup water

Cook pasta according to package directions. Meanwhile, trim fat from chicken. Slice lengthwise to make 4 thin pieces (like cutlets). Spray a nonstick skillet with cooking spray and cook chicken over med-high heat until lightly browned on both sides and cooked through. Remove from skillet and set aside. When cool, slice into thin bite-sized pieces.

In the same skillet, sauté the mushrooms and garlic in oil for 1-2 minutes. Stir in water, bouillon, milk, pepper, and sliced chicken. Cook until heated through. Stir in Parmesan. Heat until bubbling.

In a cup, mix the flour with ¼ cup water until smooth. Gradually stir flour mixture into the mushroom sauce. Stir until thickened, about 1 minute. Pour sauce over the hot, drained pasta. Mix to coat. Serve with additional Parmesan, if desired.

4 servings, each serving has 691 calories, 15 g fat, 80 g carbohydrate, 57 g protein, 4 g fiber

Mexican Chicken & Beans   SLOW COOKER

Serve over rice

3 boneless, skinless chicken breast halves
1 (16 oz) jar salsa Verde
2 (15 oz) cans black beans, drained
1 (15 oz) can corn, drained
1 (15 oz) can diced tomatoes, drained
1 ½ tsp ground cumin
½ tsp chili powder
½ tsp garlic salt
¼ tsp pepper
4 oz reduced fat cream cheese (optional)

Cut each chicken breast into 4 pieces. Place chicken breasts in the bottom of slow cooker. Combine remaining ingredients, except cream cheese, into a large bowl and stir. Pour over chicken. Cover and cook on low for 8-10 hours. Before serving, add cream cheese if desired. Stir until it melts.

6 servings, each serving without cream cheese has 300 calories, 2g fat, 48g carbohydrate, 22g protein, 8g fiber. Each serving with cream cheese has 344 calories,6g fat, 50g carbohydrate, 24g protein, 8g fiber

Braised Cornish Game Hens

Side dish suggestion: rice pilaf

2 Cornish games hens, skinned and cut in half
2 Tbsp flour
1 Tbsp olive oil
5 stalks celery, cut into 2 inch pieces
1 medium onion, coarsely chopped
1 lb. Baby carrots
2 cups water
½ cup cooking sherry
2 tsp chicken bouillon granules
1 tsp thyme leaves
¼ tsp pepper

Coat hens in flour, shaking off any excess. Heat oil over med-high heat in a Dutch oven and brown hens on each side. Remove from pan.

In the same pan, sauté onions, celery, and carrots until onions are lightly browned. Stir in water, sherry, bouillon, thyme, and pepper. Place hens on top. Reduce heat. Cover and cook for 30 minutes or until hens are cooked through.

4 servings, each serving has 337 calories, 12 g fat, 30 g carbohydrate, 27 g protein, 7 g fiber

Chicken Casserole Ole'

This has been a family favorite for years. It's easy, cozy, and tastes great.
Side dish suggestion: Yellow (Mexican) rice

1 can (10 ½ oz) Cream of mushroom soup
1 can (10 ½ oz) Cream of chicken soup
1 can (4 oz) diced green chilies
10 oz Monterey Jack cheese, grated
10 oz low fat cheddar cheese, grated
12 8-inch flour tortillas, torn into pieces
4 skinless, boneless chicken breast halves, cooked and cut into bite-sized pieces
1 can evaporated skim milk

Mix together soups and chilies in a small bowl and set aside. In another bowl, mix cheeses and set aside.

In a 13X9X2 " baking dish, sprayed with cooking spray, layer half of each ingredient in dish in the following order: tortillas, chicken, soup mixture, cheese mixture. Repeat. Pour evaporated skim milk evenly over top of casserole & let stand for one hour.

Bake in a 350°oven for 50 minutes. Let casserole sit for 5 minutes before serving.

8 servings, each serving has 458 calories, 20g fat, 40g carbohydrate, 26g protein, 4g fiber

Pepperoni Pizza Potatoes MICROWAVE!

You can toss in any of your other favorite diced pizza toppings! So be as creative as you want. Side dish suggestion: green salad

4 medium baking potatoes
1 can (16 oz) tomato sauce
1 tsp garlic powder
1 tsp oregano
¼ tsp pepper
⅓ cup fat free ricotta cheese
⅓ cup shredded part-skim mozzarella cheese, divided
15 slices turkey pepperoni, diced

Scrub potatoes. Pierce several times with a fork and cook in the microwave until done. Remove the potatoes from the microwave and set aside.

Combine all remaining ingredients into a bowl. Once the potatoes have cooled enough to handle, slice the potatoes lengthwise in half. Using a spoon, carefully scoop out the pulp, leaving a ¼ inch shell. Add potato pulp to the tomato sauce mixture and stir well to combine. Stuff the potatoes with the mixture. Top each potato with additional cheese if desired. Return back to microwave for 1-2 minutes, or until potatoes are warm and cheese is melted.

4 servings, each serving has 264 calories, 3 g fat, 48g carbohydrate, 12g protein, 6g fiber

Tuscan Chicken II

I like this recipe because you can cook it two ways. You can cook at as directed, or grill the chicken separately & make the sauce in a sauce pan. Then you just spoon the sauce over the top of the grilled chicken. Side dish suggestion: Sautéed zucchini

1 Tbsp olive oil
4 boneless, skinless chicken breast halves
½ cup finely chopped onion
2 large cloves garlic, minced
½ tsp salt
⅛ tsp pepper
½ cup white wine
1 (16 oz) can diced tomatoes
¼ cup pitted kalamata olives, chopped
1 tsp oregano
1 tsp parsley

Heat the oil over medium heat in a non-stick skillet. Add the chicken, onions, garlic, salt, and pepper. Sauté until chicken is lightly browned on both sides. Add the remaining ingredients and bring to a boil. Reduce heat, cover, and cook about 6-8 minutes, or until chicken is no longer pink.

Remove chicken to platter and keep warm If the sauce is too thin, turn up the heat on the sauce and cook, stirring frequently, another 2-3 minutes until it begins to thicken. Serve sauce over the chicken.

4 servings, each serving has 259 calories, 6 g fat, 6 g carbohydrate, 33 g protein, 1 g fiber

Olive-Stuffed Chicken

Note: An oven proof skillet has a handle that won't burn or melt. Side dish suggestion: green beans

4 boneless skinless chicken breast halves
4 oz reduced fat cream cheese
1 (4 oz) can sliced black olives, drained
¼ tsp oregano
⅛ tsp pepper
½ cup seasoned bread crumbs
¼ tsp salt
1 Tbsp olive oil
toothpicks

Preheat oven to 350°. Pound chicken to ¼ inch thickness and set aside. In a small bowl, combine the cream cheese, olives, oregano, and pepper. Spoon the cream cheese mixture down the center of each chicken breast. Fold chicken over the filling and secure with toothpicks. Combine bread crumbs and salt in a shallow dish. Roll chicken in the bread crumbs. Using a large ovenproof skillet, brown chicken in oil on all sides. Place the skillet in the oven for 20 to 25 minutes or until juices run clear.

4 servings, each serving has 269 calories, 14 g fat, 9 g carbohydrate, 27 g protein, 0 g fiber

Quick Mexi-Chicken & Rice

Side dish suggestion: Refried beans and baked tortilla chips

1 lb boneless, skinless chicken breast, cubed
1 tsp garlic powder
2 cups instant rice
1 (16-oz) jar Salsa
1¼ cups water
1 tsp chicken bouillon granules
2 green onions, chopped

Spray skillet with non-stick cooking spray. Add chicken and garlic powder; sauté until chicken is no longer pink.

Add rice, salsa, water, bouillon and green onions. Bring to a boil. Cover; reduce heat to low. Cook, stirring occasionally, for 10 to 12 minutes or until rice is tender and liquid is absorbed.

4 servings, each serving has 329 calories, 2 g fat, 43 g carbohydrate, 32 g protein, 1g fiber

Caraway Chicken

Use leftover dill in scrambled eggs, or dry it for future use. Side dish suggestion: pickled beets

¼ cup rye flour
1 tsp caraway seed
4 thin chicken cutlets
salt
2 tsp olive oil
3 oz smoked deli ham, diced
1 medium onion, chopped
1 Tbsp flour
½ cup water
½ tsp chicken bouillon granules
1 tsp Dijon mustard
2 tsp fresh dill, chopped
¼ cup plain low-fat yogurt

Mix rye flour and caraway seeds in a shallow bowl. Lightly sprinkle chicken with salt then coat chicken evenly with flour mixture.

Heat oil in a non-stick skillet over med-high heat. Add chicken and cook until cooked through, about 5 minutes on each side. Remove and keep warm.

In the same skillet, sauté onion and ham until onion is softened. Sprinkle with flour and stir to coat onion. Stir in water, bouillon, mustard and dill. Reduce heat and cook, stirring constantly, until mixture thickens. Stir in yogurt and remove skillet from heat. Serve sauce over the chicken.

4 servings, each serving has 153 calories, 4 g fat, 61g carbohydrate, 22g protein, 1g fiber

Oriental Orange Chicken

This has surprising low calories and fat compared to the restaurant version. Serve over rice.

Orange Sauce
1 ½ Tbsp soy sauce
1 ½ Tbsp water
5 Tbsp sugar
5 Tbsp white vinegar
1 tsp dried minced orange peel

4 boneless, skinless chicken breast halves, cut into bite-sized pieces
1 egg
1½ tsp salt
½ tsp pepper
Olive oil
½ cup + 1 Tbsp cornstarch
¼ cup flour
1 tsp ground ginger
2 cloves garlic, minced
½ tsp dried crushed red pepper
5 green onions, chopped
1 Tbsp rice wine vinegar
¼ cup water

Mix together ingredients for orange sauce in a small bowl and set aside.

Place chicken in large bowl. Stir in egg, salt, pepper, and 1 tablespoon oil and mix well. In another bowl, combine ½ cup cornstarch and flour together. Add chicken pieces, stirring to coat.

Heat enough olive oil to cover the bottom of a large skillet over med-high heat. Add chicken and fry 4-6 minutes or until golden crisp and cooked through. Remove chicken from skillet and drain on paper towels; set aside.

Add ginger, garlic, chilies, green onions, and rice wine to skillet and stir-fry about 15 seconds. Add Orange Sauce and bring to boil. Stir in cooked chicken.

Stir ¼ cup cold water into remaining 1 Tbsp cornstarch until smooth and add to chicken. Heat until sauce is thickened. Serve over rice.

4 servings, each serving without rice has 342 calories, 8g fat, 37g carbohydrate, 28g protein, 1g fiber

Cooking white rice in any amount is super easy with no added salt, butter or special rice cooker needed! Measure your rice, then add twice as much cold water to the saucepan. Turn to high and let it boil. Reduce heat; Cover and simmer for 20 minutes. Note: Brown rice is healthier but dies takes longer. Cooking times vary, so check the package.

"Fried" Chicken & Buttermilk Gravy

OK, so it's not actually fried… but this baked version comes close, and the gravy isn't really all that fattening either! Side dish suggestion: mashed potatoes & corn on the cob

⅓ cup dry plain bread crumbs
2 Tbsp grated Parmesan cheese
½ tsp paprika
¼ tsp pepper
½ tsp salt
4 boneless, skinless chicken breast halves
1 envelope dry chicken gravy mix
1 cup reduced fat buttermilk
¼ tsp dried sage

Combine bread crumbs, parmesan, paprika, pepper, and salt in a shallow bowl and set aside.

Pound the chicken breasts under a piece of waxed paper or plastic wrap with the smooth side of a mallet until flattened to be ½ inch thick. Dip chicken pieces in the crumb mixture to coat both sides. Place coated chicken on a broiling pan that has been coated with cooking spray.

Broil 8-10 inches away from the heat about 12-15 minutes or until cooked, turning once.

Meanwhile make gravy according to package directions but use the buttermilk instead of the water. Whisk in the sage. Serve gravy with the chicken.

4 servings, each serving has 215 calories, 3g fat, 12g carbohydrate, 31g protein, 0g fiber

BBQ Chicken Pizza

Leftover cooked chicken works in this recipe, if you happen to have some (skip the first part). Side dish suggestion: green salad

2 boneless, skinless chicken breast halves
⅔ cup barbeque sauce, divided
Store-bought pizza dough or Boboli bread
1 ½ cups part-skim mozzarella cheese, shredded
½ small red onion, thinly sliced
2 Tbsp fresh cilantro, chopped

Cook the chicken in boiling water for 20 minutes or until cooked through. Cool, and shred with two forks. Mix chicken with ½ cup BBQ sauce and set aside

Preheat oven to 425°. Follow the instructions to make pizza dough and roll into a crust. Place on baking sheet or pizza pan (or just set the Boboli bread on the pan). Spread the remaining barbeque sauce evenly over the crust. Sprinkle with ½ cup of the mozzarella. Add the barbeque chicken and red onion, then cover with remaining cheese. Sprinkle the cilantro on the top of the mozzarella. Bake for 10 minutes or until crust is done and cheese is melted.

8 slices, each slice using Boboli bread has 267 calories, 7g fat, 33g carbohydrate, 17g protein, 1g fiber. Each slice using Pillsbury pizza crust has 247 calories, 6g fat, 32g carbohydrate, 16g protein, 0g fiber

Smothered Chicken II

Side dish suggestion: Cauliflower

1 tsp dried oregano
½ tsp salt
½ tsp garlic powder
¼ tsp pepper
¼ tsp cayenne pepper
4 boneless, skinless chicken breast halves
8 oz sliced mushrooms
1 medium onion, thinly sliced
½ cup shredded part-skim mozzarella cheese
½ cup shredded reduced fat sharp cheddar cheese

Mix together spices in a small bowl. Sprinkle chicken breasts with spices. Spray a skillet with non-stick cooking spray and heat over medium heat. Add chicken breasts and cook until no longer pink, about 6-7 minutes per side. Remove from skillet and keep warm.

Re-spray skillet and add mushrooms and onion. Sauté until tender and browned. Remove from pan.

Return chicken to the skillet and spread the mushrooms and onions over the top. Sprinkle with cheeses. Cover and heat over med-low heat until cheese melts.

4 servings, each serving has 214 calories, 5g fat, 5g carbohydrate, 36g protein, 1g fiber

Chicken & Vegetable Medley

Note: All in one meal! No side dishes needed

4 skinless boneless chicken breast halves
½ cup water
2 tsp Chicken bouillon granules
½ tsp Thyme leaves
¼ tsp Onion powder
1 cup carrots, cut into strips
1 red bell pepper, sliced
1 med. yellow summer squash, sliced
1 med. zucchini, sliced

Spray large skillet with cooking spray & brown chicken. Add water, bouillon, thyme, onion powder and carrots. Cover; simmer 10 minutes. Add remaining vegetables; cover and cook 5 to 10 minutes longer or until tender.

4 servings, each serving has 159 calories, 2 g fat, 8g carbohydrate, 28 g protein, 3g fiber

Chicken & Corn Quesadillas

Side dish suggestion: green salad

1 cup fresh or frozen corn kernels, thawed
¾ cup salsa
2 Tbsp minced fresh cilantro
2 Tbsp lime juice
4 skinless, boneless chicken breast halves, cut into ½" pieces
1 Tbsp lime juice
½ tsp chili powder
½ tsp ground cumin
¼ tsp salt
⅛ tsp black pepper
2 tsp olive oil
2 garlic cloves, minced
4 (10 inch) flour tortillas
½ cup grated queso fresco cheese

For salsa, spray a nonstick skillet with cooking spray and heat over medium-high heat. Add corn; cook 5 minutes, stirring until lightly browned. Put corn into a bowl and allow to cool. Add salsa, cilatro, and 2 tablespoons lime juice and set aside.

Place chicken in a bowl with 1 tablespoon lime juice, chili powder, cumin, salt, and pepper. Stir. Heat oil in skillet over medium heat. Add chicken and cook 5 minutes or until cooked though. Add garlic and cook 1 minute more. Remove from skillet and set aside.

Place 1 tortilla in a heated clean skillet or griddle. Sprinkle 2 tablespoons cheese on top, followed by half of the chicken and salsa. Sprinkle 2 more tablespoons of cheese on top of the salsa. Top with remaining tortilla. Cook until lightly browned and carefully flip over until browned on both sides. Repeat with remaining quesadillas. Cut quesadillas into wedges when ready to serve.

4 servings, each serving has 394 calories, 12 g fat, 34 g carbohydrate, 36 g protein, 4g fiber

There are 4 main types of salt:

Kosher salt is a coarse salt.

Rock salt is an unrefined coarse salt and is not usually added directly to foods.

Sea salt is made by letting sale water evaporate and is preferred for its lack of chemicals.

Table salt is ground rock salt and is usually fortified with iodine.

Oriental Chicken

Side dish suggestion: brown rice

¼ cup soy sauce
2 Tbsp sherry
2 Tbsp honey or agave syrup
2 cloves garlic, minced
½ tsp ground ginger
¼ tsp Chinese five-spice powder
¼ tsp crushed red pepper
2 boneless, skinless chicken breast halves, sliced into thin, bite-sized pieces
1½ tsp peanut oil
1 red pepper, sliced
½ cup green onions, chopped
4 carrots, diagonally sliced
2 tsp sesame seeds, toasted

In a glass bowl, combine soy sauce, sherry, honey (or agave syrup), garlic, ginger, red pepper, and chicken. Stir to combine. Let stand for 15 minutes.

Heat the oil in a large non-stick skillet. Sauté chicken (reserve the marinade), until light golden brown. Push chicken to one side of the skillet. Add remaining vegetables and sauté until crisp-tender. Stir the chicken & veggies together and stir in reserved marinade. Bring to a boil and stir constantly for 1-2 minutes. Enjoy as is, or serve over rice. Sprinkle with sesame seeds right before serving.

4 servings, each serving has 191 calories, 3 g fat, 23g carbohydrate, 18g protein, 2g fiber

Shortcut: You can "toast" sesame seeds in the microwave.

Turkey Cutlets GRILL

You can grill these indoors or out, or you can even use your oven broiler if you like.
Side dish suggestion: green salad and corn.

2 tsp cornstarch
½ tsp salt, divided
Pepper
½ cup apple juice concentrate, thawed
¼ cup Dijon mustard
1½ tsp dried rosemary
4 thin turkey (or chicken) breast cutlets
cooking spray

In a small saucepan, combine the cornstarch, ¼ teaspoon salt and 1/8 teaspoon pepper. Whisk in the apple concentrate, mustard and rosemary until well blended. Cook and stir until thickened. Reduce heat and cook 2 minutes longer, stirring frequently. Remove from heat. Remove half of the sauce and set aside.

Spray Turkey (or chicken) with cooking spray. Sprinkle with ¼ teaspoon salt and ¼ teaspoon pepper. Grill, covered, over medium heat for 3-5 minutes on each side or until no longer pink, basting occasionally with half of the sauce. Before serving, brush with the other half of the reserved sauce using a clean basting brush.

4 servings, each serving has 191 calories, 1g fat, 11g carbohydrate, 28g protein, 0g fiber

Chicken and Broccoli with Mushroom Sauce

Side Dish Suggestion: Green salad

1 (10oz) pkg. frozen broccoli (florets or spears)
3 Tbsp margarine
3 Tbsp flour
1 cup water
1 tsp chicken bouillon granules
1 (4oz) can mushrooms, un-drained
Salt, to taste
Pepper, to taste
1 lb. cooked chicken breast, sliced
2 Tbsp chopped parsley
2 Tbsp dry bread crumbs

Cook broccoli according to package directions. Meanwhile, stir margarine and flour together in saucepan. Cook until melted and blended. Whisk in water, stirring constantly until thickened and smooth. Stir in bouillon, and un-drained mushrooms. Remove from heat. Season to taste with salt & pepper.

Place broccoli pieces in a shallow baking pan. Cover with sliced chicken and pour mushroom sauce over all. Top with parsley and bread crumbs. Bake uncovered at 375°, 15-25 minutes, or until bubbly.

4 servings, each serving has 303 calories, 13 g fat, 8g carbohydrate, 39 g protein, 2g fiber

Stuffed Chicken Breasts

Side dish suggestion: green salad

½ cup chopped onion
6 -7 cups fresh spinach, chopped
1 garlic clove, minced
1 Tbsp balsamic vinegar
¼ cup reduced fat feta cheese, crumbled
1 tsp grated lemon peel
¼ tsp salt
¼ tsp pepper
4 boneless skinless chicken breast halves
1 Tbsp olive oil
toothpicks

Trim fat from chicken and flatten each chicken breast to ¼ inch thickness and set aside.

Spray a large nonstick skillet with cooking spray. Sauté onion for 10-15 minutes or until onion is golden brown, re-spraying the pan as needed. Add the spinach, garlic, and vinegar. Cook until spinach is wilted and remove from heat. Allow to cool for at least 5 minutes. After the spinach mixture has cooled, stir in the feta cheese, lemon peel, salt and pepper. Next, spread the spinach mixture evenly amongst the chicken. Roll up and secure with toothpicks.

Heat the olive oil in a skillet and cook chicken 8-10 minutes on each side or until chicken is cooked through. Discard toothpicks before serving.

4 servings, each serving has 186 calories, 6g fat, 3g carbohydrate, 29g protein, 1g fiber

Super Joes *(turkey version)*

The smaller you dice the veggies, the less likely kids will notice them. Side dish suggestion: salad and/or baked French fries

1 lb. Ground turkey
½ onion, finely diced
1 red bell pepper, finely diced
1 large carrot, finely diced
1 can (15 oz) tomato sauce
2 Tbsp Worcestershire sauce
2 Tbsp ketchup
1 Tbsp brown sugar
Salt to taste
8 whole wheat buns

Brown the meat until cooked through. Drain off any fat or liquid, and add the diced vegetables to the skillet. Sauté for 2 more minutes. Stir in remaining ingredients, except buns. Bring to a boil. Reduce heat, cover, and simmer for 15 minutes or until the vegetables are tender. Serve in the buns.

8 servings, each serving has 242 calories, 6g fat, 27g carbohydrate, 19g protein, 4g fiber

Thai Pot Rice *(chicken version)*

Side dish suggestion: sautéed fresh green beans

6 cups hot cooked rice (preferably brown)
2 Tbsp olive oil
2 cloves garlic, minced
4 green onions, sliced
1 green pepper, chopped
1 ½ cups frozen peas
2 cups drained pineapple chunks
1 lb. boneless, skinless chicken breasts, cut into bite-sized pieces
½ tsp ground ginger
¼ cup soy sauce
¼ tsp pepper
⅓ cup peanuts

Heat the oil in a large skillet over medium-high heat. Cook the garlic for 1-2 minutes, until just starting to brown. Add the green onions and stir-fry for 1 minute. Add the peas and pineapple and cook for another minute.

Push the vegetables to one side of the skillet and add the shrimp or chicken to the other side. Cook for about two minutes or until the chicken is almost cooked through. Combine the chicken with the vegetables and continue to cook until the chicken is fully cooked.

Stir in the cooked rice, soy sauce, ginger, and pepper. Top with the peanuts.

6 servings, each serving has 458 calories, 11g fat, 65g carbohydrate, 25g protein, 7g fiber

Throw away the shortening & lard! Use cooking spray or olive oil instead. When choosing olive oil, go for a greener color over a yellow toned oil.

Rosemary Turkey Burgers

Side dish suggestion: potato salad

Sauce
¾ cup light mayonnaise
1 Tbsp dried rosemary leaves
2 garlic cloves, minced

Burgers
1 ½ lb ground turkey
½ tsp salt
¼ tsp pepper
6 burger buns
1 ½ cups fresh spinach leaves

For the sauce: mix together the mayonnaise, rosemary and garlic and set aside.

For the burgers: Preheat the grill, and spray a grilling rack with non-stick cooking spray.

In a large bowl, combine turkey, salt, pepper, and half of the mayonnaise mixture. Mix the ingredients and form in to 6 patties. Grill for about 7 minutes on each side, until cooked through.

Brush both sides of the buns with mayonnaise mixture. Grill for 1 to 2 minutes, until slightly brown. Top each bottom bun with a burger, ¼ cup of spinach, and the top bun. Serve with any remaining mayonnaise mixture.

6 servings, each serving has 350 calories, 14g fat, 24g carbohydrate, 32g protein, 1g fiber

To store herbs for up to 6 months: Wash, dry, and strip leaves from stems. Fill ice cube trays half up with herbs and add enough water just to cover. Freeze. Pop out the frozen herb-cubes and store in marked freezer bags.

To store herbs even longer: Wash and dry in a dehydrator, then store in plastic bags or spice jars. If you don't have a dehydrator, you can tie the herbs by the stems tightly with thick thread and hang upside down to dry out. Hang them somewhere that they will stay clean.

Pork

Pesto Pork & Pasta
No side dish needed

1 refrigerated package prepared pesto
12 Roma tomatoes, quartered
2-3 lb. pork roast
Salt
Pepper
16 oz rotini or spiral noodles

Preheat oven to 350°. Place tomatoes in a baking pan that has been sprayed with cooking spray. Sprinkle with salt & pepper. Place roast on top of tomatoes. Spread half of the pesto on top of the roast. Bake for 1½ -2 hours, uncovered, or until a meat thermometer reads 160°. Let stand 10 minutes before slicing.

A few minutes before the roast is done, prepare egg noodles according to package directions. Remove the baked tomatoes from the pan and add them to the drained cooked noodles. Stir in remaining pesto. Add additional salt & pepper to taste. Serve noodles with the pork.

8 servings, each serving has 571 calories, 23g fat, 49g carbohydrate, 42g protein, 4g fiber

Honey Spiced Pork Tenderloin   GRILL
Side dish suggestion: Rice & green salad

1 tsp chili powder
1 tsp garlic powder
1 tsp dry mustard
½ tsp paprika
⅛ tsp ground thyme
¼ cup fat free Catalina salad dressing
1 lb. pork tenderloin
1 Tbsp honey

Mix all of the dry spices together in a bowl and set aside. Brush all sides of the pork with half of the salad dressing. Rub spices all over the pork. Grill pork over medium heat for about 20 minutes, turning occasionally.

Mix remaining 2 tablespoons dressing with the honey. Brush the mixture onto the pork and continue to grill for an additional 10 minutes or until pork is cooked through (internal temperature of 160°). Remove from heat. Cover and let stand for 3-5 minutes before slicing.

4 servings, each serving has 217 calories, 6g fat, 8g carbohydrate, 32g protein, 0 g fiber

Sausage & Potato Tacos

This recipe is higher in fat than a typical Sensible Cook recipe, but is one of my husband's favorites, and he thought it should be shared. Splurge and buy fresh made tortillas from the specialty bread section if you can find them for a special treat. Side dish suggestion: yellow rice

2 tomatoes, diced
2 green onions, sliced
1 jalapeno, seeded and diced (leave seeds in if you like it hot)
⅓ cup chopped cilantro
salt
2 medium red potatoes
1 Tbsp olive oil
1 yellow squash or zucchini, cut into bite-sized cubes
Pepper
1 lb. lean ground sausage (mild or spicy, depending on your preference)
12 corn tortillas
6 oz queso fresco cheese, crumbled

In a small bowl, combine tomatoes, green onions, jalapeno, and cilantro. Season with salt to taste and set aside.

Pierce potatoes with a fork and place in a microwave proof bowl. Put ½ cup water in bowl and add ½ tsp salt. Cover and microwave for 5 minutes (potatoes should not be completely cooked).

Meanwhile, heat oil in skillet and add squash. Sprinkle with salt and pepper. Cook until browned and crisp-tender. Remove from skillet and set aside.

Add sausage to pan. Partially cook, browning for about 5 minutes. While the sausage is cooking, cut the potatoes into 1 inch cubes. Add potatoes to the sausage, and continue cooking until sausage is completely cooked, and potatoes are softened. Place in a colander to allow fat to drain. Once drained, return to skillet with the squash over med-high heat and sauté until hot.

Warm the tortillas to soften them. Fill with sausage mixture and top with cheese and salsa.

6 servings, each serving has 475 calories, 27g fat, 7g carbohydrate, 21g protein, 5g fiber

Honeyed Ham Steak *EASY & FAST*

Side dish suggestion: Brussels sprouts & yams

2 Tbsp Prepared mustard
1 Tbsp Butter or margarine
2 Tbsp Honey
1 fully cooked smoked ham, center slice, ½" thick

In large skillet over medium heat, heat mustard, honey, and butter until blended. Add ham; cook 5 minutes on each side or until heated through. Remove ham to platter; pour honey mixture over ham.

4 servings, each serving has 203 calories, 10g fat, 2g carbohydrate, 19g protein, 0g fiber

Ham with Fruit Sauce

Side dish suggestion: broccoli spears

1 fully cooked smoked ham slice, 3/4"thick
1 cup orange juice
¼ cup golden or dark raisins
2 Tbsp red currant jelly
1 Tbsp water
2 tsp cornstarch
1 (8oz) can peaches, drained and chopped

In a small pan, stir orange juice, raisins, and jelly. Heat to boiling; reduce heat to low. Cover and simmer 15 minutes.

Meanwhile, trim fat from ham steak. Spray pan with non-stick cooking spray. Add ham slice and cook until brown on both sides. Remove ham to platter and keep warm.

In cup, blend water and cornstarch until smooth. Stir into mixture in skillet and cook over medium heat, stirring constantly, until mixture thickens and boils. Boil 1 minute. Add peaches and heat through. Spoon sauce over ham.

4 servings, each serving has 242 calories, 5 g fat, 26 g carbohydrate, 23 g protein, 1g fiber

Costa Rican Beans

These portion sizes are a bit small. Nutritionally, it's pretty well rounded and doesn't really need a side dish. However, to make it a heartier meal, you may want to add cornbread and a vegetable on the side.

1 cup rice, uncooked
¼ cup diced onion
1 green pepper, seeded & diced
½ mild chili pepper (or use the whole thing if you want), seeded & diced
1 (15oz) can black beans, drained
⅔ cup water
1 tomato, chopped
3 oz cooked ham, diced
½ tsp salt
¼ tsp pepper

Cook rice according to package directions. Meanwhile, spray a non-stick skillet with cooking spray and sauté onions 1 minute. Stir in peppers and sauté until crisp-tender.

Pour beans into a bowl. Mash about ½ of the beans. Stir in remaining ingredients. Pour the bean mixture into the pepper mixture in the skillet. Cook until heated through. Serve over the rice.

4 servings, each serving has 257 calories, 3 g fat, 45 g carbohydrate, 13 g protein, 11g fiber

Mediterranean Pork   GRILL or BAKE

Side dish suggestion: garlic bread

Foil
1 Tbsp olive oil
1 tsp dried rosemary
3 Tbsp lemon juice
¾ tsp pepper
4 thin, boneless pork chops, trimmed of fat
1 large tomato, cut into large chunks
1 yellow squash, halved lengthwise and then sliced
1 zucchini, halved lengthwise and then sliced
1 can (15 oz) quartered artichoke hearts (packed in water), rinsed and drained
1 Tbsp capers, drained
½ tsp salt
8 basil leaves, thinly sliced

Tear off 4 large pieces of foil and set aside. In a large bowl, mix oil, rosemary, lemon juice, and pepper. Brush both sides of the pork with the mixture and set 1 piece of pork on each piece of foil. Add remaining ingredients to the bowl and stir to coat the vegetables. Divide the vegetables evenly on top of each piece of pork.

Make a foil packet by folding the foil at the top and sides to seal, leaving some space for steam. Place packets on a grill over medium heat for 20 minutes. Alternatively, you can bake in a preheated oven at 450° for 20 minutes. When ready to serve, carefully slice open the packets (the steam created will be hot).

4 servings, each serving has 206 calories, 9g fat, 7g carbohydrate, 24g protein, 3g fiber

Mexi-Pork Skillet

No side dish needed

2 Tbsp fat-free zesty Italian salad dressing
1 lb. Pork, cut into thin strips
1 envelope taco seasoning mix
1 green pepper, sliced
1 red pepper, sliced
2 cups instant brown rice
1¾ cups water
½ cup reduced fat cheddar cheese

Heat salad dressing in a large skillet over med-high heat. Add pork. Sprinkle ½ of the taco mix on the pork. Cook for 3-4 minutes.

Stir in peppers, rice, water, and remaining taco seasoning. Bring to a boil. Reduce heat to a simmer. Cover and simmer for 5 minutes. Sprinkle with cheese and cover. Turn heat off and let stand for 5 minutes.

4 servings, each serving has 396 calories, 8 g fat, 41 g carbohydrate, 39 g protein, 3 g fiber

Boiled Ham & Veggies

No side dish needed

6 carrots, cut into 1 inch pieces
2 large potatoes, and chopped into chunks
3 cups water
16 oz lean ham, cut into bite-sized pieces
1 med onion, chopped
½ tsp salt
½ tsp zesty seasoned salt
¼ tsp pepper
5 cups chopped cabbage
1 (15oz) can garbanzo beans (optional)

Combine all ingredients except the cabbage and garbanzo beans in a Dutch oven. Bring to boil. Cover and simmer for 10 minutes. Stir in the cabbage and optional garbanzo beans. Cover and cook for 10 to 15 minutes more, or until vegetables are tender.

6 servings, each serving has 228 calories, 3g fat, 35g carbohydrate, 17g protein, 6g fiber
With garbanzo beans, each serving has 313 calories, 5g fat, 51g carbohydrate, 21g protein, 10g fiber

> *"Laughter is brightest where food is best."*
> ~ Irish Proverb

Pork Medallions in Mustard Sauce

Side dish suggestion: Roasted vegetables

½ cup water
½ tsp chicken bouillon granules
1 tsp parsley
4 tsp spicy brown mustard
1 pound pork tenderloin, trimmed of fat and cut into half inch slices
¼ tsp salt
¼ tsp pepper
1 Tbsp olive oil
3 garlic cloves, minced
1 tsp cornstarch
2 Tbsp water

In a small bowl, combine the water, chicken bouillon, parsley, and mustard; set aside. Sprinkle pork with salt and pepper and brown pork in oil in a skillet. Remove and set aside. Add garlic to the pan and sauté for one minute. Stir in the chicken bouillon mixture and loosen any brown bits from the bottom of the pan. Bring to a boil, then reduce heat and simmer uncovered for 5 - 7 minutes. Return pork to the pan. Cover and simmer over low heat for 4-5 more minutes or until meat is cooked through. In a small cup, combine cornstarch with 2 tablespoons cold water and stir until smooth. Add to the pan and cook and stir for 1-2 minutes or until thickened.

4 servings, each serving has 205 calories, 7 g fat, 1 g carbohydrate, 32 g protein, 0 g fiber

Maple Pecan Pork Chops

Side dish suggestion: yams

4 boneless pork loin chops
Salt
Pepper
1 Tbsp butter or Smart Squeeze Butter Spread
2 Tbsp sugar free maple pancake syrup
⅓ cup chopped pecans

Trim fat from pork. Sprinkle with salt and pepper. Cook on a grill or in skillet until cooked through (160°). Keep warm.

Meanwhile, put pecans in a small bowl and microwave for 30 seconds. Stir in butter and pancake syrup. Microwave another 30 seconds or until bubbly. Serve pecan sauce over cooked pork chops.

4 servings (with butter), each serving has 328 calories, 20g fat, 2g carbohydrate, 33g protein, 1g fiber
4 servings (with Smart Squeeze), each serving has 303 calories, 18g fat, 2g carbohydrate, 33g protein, 1g fiber

Pork and Potato Supper

Side dish suggestion: green beans

4 Pork steaks (about 6 oz each), trimmed of fat
3 potatoes, peeled and sliced
¼ cup flour
1 tsp salt
⅛ tsp pepper
1 medium onion, sliced
1 Tbsp fresh parsley, minced
paprika
1¼ cup water
1½ tsp chicken bouillon granules

Spray large skillet with cooking spray and heat over med-high heat. Lightly coat steaks with a mixture of flour, salt and pepper. Brown pork on both sides, adding a small amount of olive oil, only if needed.

Add water & bouillon to skillet. Bring to a boil. Reduce heat, cover and simmer 25 minutes. Turn steaks over. Top with potatoes and onion slices. Cover and simmer 30-35 minutes. Sprinkle with parsley and paprika.

4 servings, each serving has 404 calories, 21g fat, 33g carbohydrate, 21g protein, 3g fiber

Ham Stuffed Potatoes

Side dish suggestion: green salad

2 large baking potatoes
1 cup non-fat cottage cheese
1 ½ cups cubed fully cooked lean ham
½ cup shredded part-skim mozzarella cheese
¼ cup finely chopped green pepper
¼ tsp pepper

Clean and pierce potatoes; place on a microwave safe plate. Microwave on high for 16-18 minutes or until tender, turning once. Let stand for 5 minutes. Cut a thin slice off the top of each potato and discard. Scoop out pulp and set aside, leaving a ¼ - ½ " shell.

In a large bowl, mash the potato pulp with the cottage cheese. Stir in the ham, mozzarella cheese and green pepper. Spoon into potato shells (shells will be full). Microwave, uncovered, on high for 2-4 minutes or until heated through.

4 servings, each serving has 289 calories, 6 g fat, 35 g carbohydrate, 28 g protein, 3g fiber

Chipotle Pork Sandwiches SLOW COOKER

Side dish suggestion: baby carrots

½ cup BBQ sauce
2 chipotle peppers in adobe sauce, chopped
16 oz pork tenderloin
1½ cups coleslaw mix
2 Tbsp fat free sour cream
2 Tbsp fat free mayonnaise
1 Tbsp Dijon mustard
4 whole wheat hamburger buns

Trim away any edge fat from the pork. Place pork in slow cooker. Top with BBQ sauce and peppers. Cover and cook on high for 4-6 hours or on low for 8 hours, or until pork is tender. Remove pork from crock pot, and shred using two forks. Return pork to crock pot and stir. Cover to keep warm.

In a bowl, mix the coleslaw mix, sour cream, mayonnaise, and mustard. To serve, put pork mixture on a bun, and top with coleslaw mixture.

4 servings, each serving has 418 calories, 8 g fat, 59 g carbohydrate, 31 g protein, 4 g fiber

Many recipes call for small amounts of chipotle chili peppers in adobe sauce. But what do you do with the rest of the can? Don't throw it out! Divide up the peppers in sauce (2 per bag) in small freezer bags & freeze. Defrost when needed. Use within 6 months.

113

Ranch Chops & Rice

Side dish suggestion: your favorite veggies.

4 boneless pork chops, 3/4" thick, trimmed of fat
1 can cream of mushroom soup
½ cup skim milk
1 pkg. (1 oz.) ranch salad dressing mix
Paprika
Rice

Prepare rice according to package directions to make 2 cups rice. Add ½ package of ranch dressing mix to water.

Meanwhile, spray skillet with cooking spray. Add chops and cook until brown on both sides.

In a small bowl, mix together soup, milk and remaining dressing mix. Add to the chops. Heat to a boil. Reduce heat, cover and cook 10 minutes or until done. Sprinkle lightly with paprika.

4 servings, each serving has 322 calories, 7 g fat, 29g carbohydrate, 29 g protein, 3g fiber

Balsamic Glazed Pork Chops

Note: You can decrease or increase the servings simply by changing the amount of pork chops that you use. Side dish suggestion: broccoli

2 Tbsp olive oil
4 lean pork chops
salt
pepper
1 small onion, chopped
1 tsp thyme
1 tsp rosemary
3 garlic cloves, chopped
¼ cup balsamic vinegar
2 Tbsp honey
1 cup water
1 tsp chicken bouillon granules
1 Tbsp butter

Heat a large skillet over medium-high heat. Add 1 tbsp of the olive oil. Season the chops with salt and pepper, then add to the hot skillet. Cook the chops for 5 minutes on each side, or until no longer pink.

Transfer the chops to a platter and cover with foil to keep warm. Return the pan to the heat and add the remaining 1 tbsp of olive oil. Add the onions, thyme, rosemary, and garlic. Sauté for 4-5 minutes. Add the balsamic vinegar, honey, water, and bouillon. Cook until the liquids have reduced by half, about 10 minutes.

Once reduced, add the butter. Stir the pan until the butter melts. Add the chops to the pan and coat them in the glaze. Serve topped with one teaspoon of glaze.

4 servings, each serving has 266 calories, 12g fat, 12g carbohydrate, 26g protein, 0g fiber

Baked Pork Chops

Side Dish Suggestion: Green beans and a salad

6 lean center-cut pork chops, 1/2" thick, trimmed of fat
1 egg white
1 cup evaporated skim milk
¾ cup cornflake crumbs
¼ cup fine dry bread crumbs
4 tsp paprika
2 tsp oregano
¾ tsp chili powder
½ tsp garlic powder
½ tsp black pepper
⅛ tsp cayenne pepper
⅛ tsp dry mustard
½ tsp salt

Preheat oven to 375°. Beat egg white with evaporated skim milk. Place pork chops in milk mixture and let stand for 5 minutes, turning once.

Meanwhile, mix together cornflake crumbs, bread crumbs, and remaining spices. Spray a 9x13-inch baking pan with nonstick spray coating.

Remove pork chops from milk mixture. Coat all sides evenly with crumb mixture. Place pork chops in pan and bake for 20 minutes. Turn chops and bake 15 minutes longer or until no longer pink.

6 servings, each serving has 157 calories, 3 g fat, 4 g carbohydrate, 27 g protein, 0g fiber

Marinated Pork Chops GRILL

Start the night before or in the morning so the chops can marinate at least 8 hours. Side dish suggestion: sliced tomatoes and corn on the cob

½ cup olive oil
¼ cup lime juice
4 tsp balsamic vinegar
2 tsp sugar
2 tsp Worcestershire sauce
1 tsp salt
1 tsp paprika
1 garlic clove, minced
6 boneless pork loin chops or steaks, trimmed of edge fat

In a large re-sealable plastic bag, combine the all of the ingredients, except pork. Close and mix. Add pork chops. Seal bag and turn to coat. Refrigerate for 8 – 24 hours.

Drain and discard marinade. Grill pork chops, covered, over medium heat for 4-5 minutes on each side or until juices run clear

6 servings, each serving has 294 calories, 16 g fat, 1 g carbohydrate, 33 g protein, 0 g fiber

> "As it turns out, now is the moment you've been waiting for."
>
> Lucinda Williams

Southwestern Pork Chops

No side dish needed

4 pork chops, ¾ -1" thick
¼ tsp pepper
1 onion, sliced
1 can (14 oz) stewed tomatoes
1 can (4 oz) green chilies, chopped
⅓ cup water
2 Tbsp packaged dry enchilada mix
1 can (4 oz) sliced black olives
1 green pepper, sliced
½ cup fat free sour cream
3 cups hot cooked rice

Prepare rice according to package directions (omitting butter) to make 3 cups. Meanwhile, spray a large non-stick skillet with cooking spray. Heat to med-high heat. Sprinkle pork with pepper and add pork chops to the hot skillet, browning on both sides. Remove to a plate (don't worry if they are not cooked through at this point).

In the same skillet, sauté onion, re-spraying pan with cooking spray if needed, until brown. Stir in the tomatoes, chilies, water, dry enchilada mix, and olives. Bring to a boil. Reduce heat and return pork to the pan. Cover and simmer for 7 minutes. Turn chops over and top with green pepper. Re-cover and cook an additional 5-10 minutes or until pork is cooked through.

Remove pork from pan. Stir in the sour cream until mixed. Serve pork and sauce over the hot cooked rice.

4 servings, each serving has 475 calories, 14g fat, 58g carbohydrate, 27g protein, 5g fiber

Vermont Ham & Cabbage

No side dishes needed

2 Tbsp butter
1 small head cabbage, coarsely sliced
1 fully cooked ham center slice, 1½ " thick, trimmed of edge fat
2 red apples, cut in wedges
2 Tbsp Sugar free pancake (or maple) syrup

Preheat oven to 325°. Heat butter in a skillet over medium-high heat. Cook cabbage until tender, about 5 minutes. Spoon into 9x13" baking dish. Place ham on cabbage & place apples around ham. Drizzle syrup over all. Bake, uncovered, for 50 minutes.

4 servings, each serving has 268 calories, 11g fat, 20g carbohydrate, 25g protein, 6g fiber

Pasta with Spinach & Sausage

You can adjust the spiciness by choosing either mild or spicy sausage. No side dish needed

16 oz. rotini or other pasta
14 oz spinach
1 onion, chopped
1 lb. Italian sausages, casings removed
1 cup water
1¼ tsp chicken bouillon granules
¼ tsp ground nutmeg
½ cup fat free half & half
Parmesan cheese (optional)

Cook pasta according to package directions, adding spinach during the last 30 seconds of cooking time (just so it wilts). Meanwhile, in a non-stick skillet over med-high heat, sauté onion and sausage, breaking up sausage into crumbles and cooking until cooked through. Remove to a colander and let fat drain.

Return sausage and onion to skillet. Stir in water, bouillon, nutmeg, and half & half. Heat for 1-2 minutes, or just until heated.

Combine the sausage sauce with the drained pasta and spinach mixture in a large bowl. Toss to combine. Serve with Parmesan cheese if desired.

6 servings, each serving has 575 calories, 22g fat, 66g carbohydrate, 27g protein, 4g fiber

Grilled Ham   GRILL

You can bake this in your oven, but baking it on your grill gives it a nice flavor and doesn't heat up your kitchen. You can use a regular bone-in ham, boneless, or a turkey-ham. Side dish suggestion: yams

1 fully cooked ham (choose the size according to how many servings you want)
½ cup sweet chili sauce

Pre-heat the grill to medium heat. Put ham on the grill and close the lid. Rotate ham to cook on all sides every 15 minutes. Grill for approximately 1 hour (more or less depending on how big your ham is).

Baste with chili sauce on all sides. Turn up heat to med-high, cover and cook for 5-10 minutes. Baste again on all sides. Turn ham over, cover and cook an additional 5 minutes.

Each 3 oz serving of regular ham (trimmed of fat) has 151 calories, 8g fat, 0g carbohydrate, 19g protein, 0g fiber. Each 3 oz serving of turkey ham has 96 calories, 3g fat, 0g carbohydrate, 15g protein, 0g fiber

Cuban Pork Sandwiches

If you need more sandwiches, you can keep the relish recipe the same but increase the other ingredients to serve up to 8. Side dish suggestion: carrot sticks

Relish
1 small red onion, thinly sliced
1 (8oz) jar roasted red peppers, chopped and drained
⅓ cup cider vinegar
2 garlic cloves, crushed
½ tsp oregano
¼ tsp salt
¼ tsp pepper
¼ tsp ground cumin

½ tsp garlic powder
1 tsp ground cumin
½ tsp salt
1 lb lean pork tenderloin
Cooking spray
8 slices sourdough bread
8 slices reduced fat Swiss cheese

In a small saucepan, cover onion slices with water. Bring to a boil. Cook for 1 minute and then drain. Add onion to a small bowl with remaining relish ingredients. Stir and let sit at room temperature for an hour.

Preheat oven to 425°. In a small bowl, combine garlic powder, cumin and salt. Cut away any outside visible fat from pork. Rub spices thoroughly into the pork until well coated on all sides. Bake uncovered for 30-35 minutes or until reaches an internal temperature of 160°. Let stand for 10 minutes. Thinly slice the pork.

Remove garlic from relish and discard garlic. To assemble the sandwiches, spray 1 side of each of the bread slices with cooking spray. Place 4 bread slices, sprayed side down onto a heated skillet or griddle. Top with pork slices, relish, cheese, and remaining bread slices. Grill until toasted on both sides.

4 servings, each serving has 498 calories, 9 fat, 55g carbohydrate, 48g protein, 2g fiber

When choosing onions, look for onions that feel heavy, with dry skins, no bruises, and no smell. Then store in a dark, cool, dry place with circulation. Don't store them in the produce bags from the store—they will rot.

Pork Chops with Mushroom Gravy

Side dish suggestion: mashed potatoes & cauliflower

5 tsp cornstarch
⅔ cup water
⅓ cup flour
½ tsp pepper
6 boneless pork chops
1 Tbsp olive oil
8 oz sliced mushrooms
⅓ cup chopped onion
3 turkey bacon strips, diced
1 clove garlic, minced
1 cup water
2 tsp chicken bouillon granules

In a small bowl, combine cornstarch with 2/3 cup water; set aside.

Place flour and pepper in a large re-sealable bag. Add pork, 1 piece at a time, and shake to coat. In a large skillet, cook pork in oil for 5-6 minutes per side, or until done (internal temperature of 160°). Remove, cover, and keep warm.

In the same skillet, sauté the mushroom, onion, garlic, and bacon until bacon is crisp. Add 1 cup water and the chicken bouillon, stirring to loosen any brown bits on the bottom. Stir in cornstarch mixture. Bring to a boil; cook and stir for 1-3 minutes or until slightly thickened. Serve with pork.

6 servings, each serving has 184 calories, 5 g fat, 5 g carbohydrate, 27 g protein, 1g fiber

Pasta with Ham & Tomatoes

No side dish needed

16 oz gemelli or other medium pasta
Aluminum foil
1 large onion, quartered & sliced
24 cherry or grape tomatoes, halved
½ tsp crushed red pepper (optional)
8 oz thinly sliced cooked lean ham
½ cup sliced fresh basil
3 Tbsp olive oil
1 tsp garlic powder

Cook pasta according to package directions. Meanwhile, line a cookie sheet or broiling pan with foil and spray with cooking spray. Broil onion slices about 6 inches from heat for about 5 minutes. Add tomatoes and broil 5 minutes more or until roasted (you want some brown on the edges).

Drain pasta and toss with roasted onions, tomatoes, and remaining ingredients.

4 servings, each serving has 365 calories, 13g fat, 44g carbohydrate, 18g protein, 4g fiber

Hawaiian Ham

Serve over rice.

3 cups lean cooked ham, diced
1 medium onion, sliced
1 green pepper, sliced in rings
8 oz can pineapple chunks
½ cup raisins
2 tsp Dry mustard
¼ cup brown sugar
1 Tbsp cornstarch
⅓ cup vinegar
1 tsp Worcestershire sauce
1 Tbsp soy sauce

Preheat oven to 350°. Put the cubed ham in a 2½ quart casserole dish. Arrange the onion and green pepper rings in the dish. Drain the pineapple cubes, but reserve the juice. Add enough water to the reserved juice to make 1 cup and set aside. Place the pineapple over the vegetables and sprinkle with raisins.

Blend the mustard, sugar, and cornstarch in a small saucepan. Stir in the pineapple juice and vinegar and cook, stirring constantly until the mixture boils and is clear. Blend in the Worcestershire and soy sauce. Pour over the ham and vegetables in the casserole dish. Bake for 45 minutes. Serve over rice.

4 servings, each serving has 315 calories, 10 g fat, 32 g carbohydrate, 25 g protein, 2g fiber

Chili Verde

Side dish suggestion: tortillas

1 lb. lean pork, cut into small cubes
1(16 oz) can kidney beans, rinsed and drained
1 (15 oz) can pinto beans, rinsed and drained
1 (15 oz) can chili beans with sauce, un-drained
1 (15 oz) can stewed tomatoes
1 to 2 cups green salsa, to taste
1 large onion, chopped
2 garlic cloves, minced
1Tbsp cilantro, minced
1½ tsp ground cumin
¾ cup reduced fat cheddar cheese (optional)

Spray a Dutch oven with cooking spray. Sauté pork cubes for 10 to 15 minutes, or until cooked through. Add all remaining ingredients. Bring to a boil. Reduce heat and simmer uncovered for 10 minutes. Sprinkle servings with reduced fat cheddar cheese, if desired.

8 servings, each serving has 264 calories, 4 g fat, 32 g carbohydrate, 25 g protein, 9 g fiber

Baked Ziti with Sausage

Side dish suggestion: green salad

1 lb. hot Italian turkey sausage
1 medium onion, chopped
3 large cloves garlic, chopped
1 (28 oz) can diced tomatoes, un-drained
¼ cup prepared pesto
Salt, to taste
Pepper, to taste
12 oz penne pasta, cooked
8 oz fresh spinach, chopped (stems removed)
8 oz shredded part-skim mozzarella cheese, divided
⅓ cup grated Parmesan cheese, divided

Preheat oven to 375°. Heat large saucepan over medium heat. Add sausage, onion, and garlic, and sauté until sausage cooked through, about 10 minutes. Drain fat and return to pan. Add tomatoes and simmer until sauce thickens slightly, stirring occasionally, about 10 minutes. Stir in pesto sauce. Season with salt and pepper to taste.

Spray a 13 x 9 baking dish with cooking spray. In a large bowl, combine pasta, spinach, 1½ cups mozzarella, and ¼ cup Parmesan cheese. Stir in hot tomato sauce. Mix to combine ingredients. Transfer mixture to prepared baking dish. Sprinkle remaining Parmesan cheese & mozzarella over top. Bake until sauce bubbles and cheese melts, about 20 minutes.

8 servings, each serving has 324 calories, 15g fat, 25g carbohydrate, 23g protein, 4g fiber

Chinese Pork Chops CROCKPOT

Side Dish Suggestion: Rice & broccoli

6 boneless pork loin chops (4 ounces each)
1 small onion, finely chopped
⅓ cup ketchup
3 Tbsp brown sugar
3 Tbsp water
3 Tbsp soy sauce
1 garlic clove, minced
1 tsp ground ginger

Place pork chops in a slow cooker coated with nonstick cooking spray. In a small bowl, combine the onion, ketchup, brown sugar, water, soy sauce, garlic and ginger. Pour over chops. Cover and cook on low for 4-6 hours or until meat is tender. Serve with rice and juices.

6 servings, each serving has 381 calories, 10g fat, 27g carbohydrate, 43g protein, 1g fiber

Southwestern Stir-Fry

You can roll these up like tacos with green chili salsa, serve it over rice, or enjoy it as is.

1 lb pork tenderloin
2 Tbsp dry sherry
2 Tbsp cornstarch
1 tsp Ground cumin
½ tsp garlic powder
½ tsp Seasoned salt
1 Tbsp olive oil
1 onion, thinly sliced
1 green bell pepper, cut into strips
12 cherry or grape tomatoes, halved

Cut pork tenderloin in to thin strips. Combine sherry, cornstarch, cumin, garlic, and seasoned salt in medium bowl. Add pork slices; stir to coat.

Heat oil in large skillet over medium-high heat. Add pork mixture; stir-fry 4-6 minutes or until cooked through. Stir in onion, bell pepper and tomatoes. Reduce heat to low; cover and simmer 3 to 4 minutes.

4 servings, each serving has 255 calories, 9g fat, 9g carbohydrate, 33g protein, 1g fiber

Balsamic Pork Chops

No side dish needed

4 cooked, smoked pork chops
1 (16oz) pkg frozen French cut green beans
¼ cup water
¼ tsp ground sage
½ cup balsamic vinegar

Cook pork chops in a large nonstick skillet until lightly browned on both sides. Remove from skillet. Stir together the water, beans, and sage in the skillet and place pork chops on top. Cover and cook over medium heat for 5 minutes.

Meanwhile in small saucepan, boil vinegar over med-high heat for 5 minutes (it will cook down to about ¼ cup). Pour vinegar evenly over pork chops and green beans.

4 servings, each serving has 168 calories, 3 g fat, 8 g carbohydrate, 28 g protein, 4g fiber

Potato & Ham Skillet

No side dish needed

6 medium red potatoes, cut into wedges
1 Tbsp olive oil
1 pkg.(16 oz) frozen broccoli florets
1 fully cooked ham steak, trimmed of fat and cut into cubes (about 1 ½ cups)
1 envelope dry mushroom and onion soup mix (or just onion soup mix will work too)

In a large skillet, cook potatoes in oil over med-high heat until potatoes are lightly browned, about 10 minutes. Stir in broccoli, ham, and dry soup mix. Reduce heat. Cover and cook for 25 minutes or until potatoes are soft.

4 servings, each serving has 424 calories, 7 g fat, 66g carbohydrate, 23g protein, 8g fiber

Pork and Broccoli Rotini

No side dish needed

16 oz Rotini, or Spiral Pasta
10 oz lean pork
1 medium onion, thinly sliced
2 tsp minced garlic
2 cups broccoli florets cut into small pieces
2 cups carrots, sliced
¼ cup soy sauce
1 ½ tsp molasses
2 Tbsp dry roasted peanut halves
¼ cup water

Prepare pasta according to package directions; drain and set aside. Meanwhile, cut the pork into ¼" strips. Spray a large skillet with non-stick cooking spray. Sauté pork over med-high heat until well done, remove and set aside.

Re-spray pan and add onion and garlic and stir until onion is lightly browned. Add broccoli, carrots and pork. Sauté until vegetables are crisp and tender, about 2 minutes.

In a small bowl, combine soy sauce, molasses and water. Add to skillet. Heat to boiling. Add pasta to the pork-broccoli mixture and toss until well mixed. Top with peanuts.

6 servings, each serving has 238 calories, 4 g fat, 34g carbohydrate, 18 g protein, 4g fiber

When using frozen vegetables, *make sure that the contents move around in the package. If they feel like one big chunk, they've likely thawed and re-froze, and will taste bad. Small 10 oz boxes won't apply to this rule.*

Slow Cooked Pork Roast Crock Pot

Side dish suggestions: mashed potatoes and carrots

1 (3 lb) boneless pork loin roast
½ cup flour
1 tsp onion powder
1 tsp dry mustard
1 Tbsp olive oil
2 cups water
2 tsp chicken bouillon granules
¼ cup cornstarch
¼ cup cold water

Trim all visible fat from roast and discard. In a large re-sealable bag, combine flour, onion powder, and dry mustard. Add roast and coat with flour mixture. Heat oil in a large skillet and brown roast over medium high heat.

Add 2 cups water and bouillon to crock pot. Add roast. Cover and cook on low for 8 hours, or on high for 4-5 hours or until tender.

Remove roast to platter and keep warm. Strain cooking juices into a sauce pan (skim fat if you have a fat separator) and heat to boiling. In a cup, combine cornstarch and cold water. Whisk cornstarch mixture into the cooking juices, stirring constantly until thickened. Serve gravy with roast.

8 servings, each serving has 266 calories, 12g fat, 5g carbohydrate, 33g protein, 0g fiber

Pork Chops & Apple Stuffing

Side dish suggestion: corn

4 pork chops
2 apples, sliced
1¾ cup water
1 small onion, sliced
1 package pork stuffing mix

Spray a large skillet with nonstick cooking spray. Brown pork chops 4 to 6 minutes on each side or until cooked through. Transfer to a plate and keep warm.

Meanwhile, bring apples, onions, and water to a boil. Stir in package stuffing mix. Cover, then remove from heat and let stand five minutes. To serve, arrange pork chops on top of the stuffing.

4 servings, each serving has 459 calories, 13 g fat, 43 g carbohydrate, 38 g protein, 4 g fiber

Cranberry Ham

Start to finish time: 10 minutes! You can serve this simple sauce with the ham steaks or with a whole baked ham. Side dish suggestion: Brussels sprouts and rolls

4 boneless, cooked ham steaks
1 can (15oz) jellied cranberry sauce
½ cup crushed pineapple, undrained
⅛ tsp ground cloves

In a large skillet, cook ham for 3 to 5 minutes on each side or until heated through. Set aside and keep warm. Meanwhile, in a medium saucepan, whisk together the cranberry sauce with the pineapple. Bring to a boil. Reduce heat. Cook, and simmer for 3 to 5 minutes. Serve with ham.

4 servings, each serving has 304 calories, 9 g fat, 28 g carbohydrate, 25 g protein, 1 g fiber

Breaded Pork with Dill Sauce

Side dish suggestion: mashed or baked potatoes

8 thin pork loin chops or tenderloins, trimmed of fat
⅓ cup flour
1 tsp seasoned salt
¼ tsp pepper
¼ cup egg substitute or 1 egg
2 Tbsp skim milk
¾ cup fine dry bread crumbs
1 tsp paprika
3 Tbsp olive oil
¾ cup warm water
1 tsp chicken bouillon granules
¼ tsp dried dill weed
1 Tbsp flour
½ cup fat free sour cream

Pound pork into ¼ - ⅛" thickness. Cut slits in edges to prevent curling.

In a bowl, combine flour, salt, and pepper. In another bowl combine egg and milk. In another bowl, combine the crumbs and paprika.

Heat oil in a skillet over medium-high heat. Dip pork into the flour mixture, followed by the egg mixture, then into crumbs and paprika. Cook in hot oil 2-3 minutes on each side, or until cooked. Remove to platter and keep warm.

Mix warm water & bouillon in a bowl. Pour into skillet & heat.

Stir 1 tablespoon of flour and ¼ teaspoon dill weed into sour cream. Stir sour cream mix into broth. Cook and stir until thick and bubbly. Serve with breaded pork.

8 servings, each serving has 160 calories, 9g fat, 7g carbohydrate, 12g protein, 0g fiber

Honey Garlic Pork Chops

Side dish suggestion: Corn on the cob

6 Tbsp honey
3 Tbsp soy sauce
6 garlic cloves, minced
6 boneless pork chops, fat trimmed

In a shallow dish, whisk together honey, soy sauce, and garlic. Coat chops in the mixture. Place pork chops on a grill that has been sprayed with nonstick cooking spray. Cook over medium-high heat for 7 to 10 minutes per side or until meat thermometer reaches 160°. Alternatively, you can broil pork chops in the oven, 8 to 10 inches from heat source, turning once, until done.

6 servings, each serving has 178 calories, 3 g fat, 12 carbohydrate, 26 g protein, 0 g fiber

Italian Pork Chops

Side dish suggestion: sautéed zucchini

6 pork chops, ½" thick, trimmed of all fat
½ tsp salt
¼ tsp pepper
1 (15oz) can tomato sauce
2 garlic cloves, minced
1½ tsp basil
1½ cups water
¾ cup rice
1 green pepper, chopped
6 slices part-skim mozzarella cheese
2 Tbsp Parmesan cheese

Spray a non-stick skillet with cooking spray and heat over medium-high heat. Add chops and cook until brown on both sides. Season with ¼ tsp salt and ¼ tsp pepper. Remove chops, drain.

Add ½ cup tomato sauce, garlic, basil, ¼ tsp salt, water, rice and green pepper. Heat over high heat to boiling. Place chops on top. Reduce heat to medium-low, cover, and simmer 20 minutes.

Put cheese slice on each chop, top with remaining tomato sauce and sprinkle with Parmesan cheese. Cover and simmer 8-10 minutes, or until cheese melts.

6 servings, each serving has 311 calories, 12g fat, 18g carbohydrate, 31g protein, 1g fiber

Grilled Marinated Pork

Start 8-24 hours ahead of time. Side dish suggestion: Potatoes, any way you like them!

¼ cup V-8 juice
1 Tbsp dried minced onion
1 Tbsp dried parsley
2 Tbsp white vinegar
2 Tbsp lemon juice
1 Tbsp olive oil
½ tsp garlic powder
¾ tsp salt
1 tsp basil
1 tsp marjoram
1 tsp thyme
½ tsp rosemary
½ tsp pepper
¼ tsp hot pepper sauce
4 pork chops or pork steaks
1 large resealable plastic bag

Put all of the ingredients, except pork, into a large resealable plastic bag. Mix well. Add pork to the bag, re-seal and turn to coat. Refrigerate 8-24 hours to marinate, turning bag occasionally.

Remove meat from marinade (discard marinade). Grill over medium heat 8-10 minutes per side or until a meat thermometer reads 160°.

4 servings, each 3 oz pork chop has 153 calories, 7g fat, 0g carbohydrate, 21g protein, 0g fiber
4 servings, each 3 oz pork steak has 193 calories, 11g fat, 0g carbohydrate, 23g protein, 0g fiber

Sea salt is the unrefined salt that is obtained by evaporating water from the seas or oceans. It is 98% sodium chloride, while the remaining 2% is other minerals like iron, sulfur, magnesium and other trace elements. This increases the nutritive value of sea salt compared to table salt. Sea salts may also boost the immune system of the body and don't cause high blood pressure like refined table salt.

One health concern is the fact that it is obtained from sea water that it could contain impurities. The sea water is neither boiled nor treated, as that would make it lose the its nutritive value. Sea salt can be coarse or fine grained. Due to the presence of the minerals, sea salt is about half as salty as table salt.

Vegetarian Meals

Ravioli in Garlic Oil

Side dish suggestion: green salad

20 oz cheese ravioli
¼ cup olive oil
3 large cloves garlic, minced
¼ tsp crushed red pepper flakes
2 Tbsp parsley, finely chopped
⅛ tsp pepper
¼ tsp onion powder
¼ tsp salt

Cook ravioli according to package directions. Gently drain.

Meanwhile, sauté garlic and red pepper in oil until garlic turns light brown. Remove from heat and stir in remaining spices. Pour seasoned oil over drained ravioli. Toss gently.

5 servings, each serving has 433 calories, 21g fat, 46g carbohydrate, 14g protein, 3g fiber

Gorgonzola and Vegetable Pasta

No side dish needed

16 oz rotini noodles
3 Tbsp olive oil
½ cup pine nuts
½ tsp salt
¼ tsp pepper
2 large tomatoes, diced
8 oz spinach, chopped
4 oz crumbled Gorgonzola cheese
1 Tbsp lemon juice

Cook the pasta according to package directions. Meanwhile, heat the olive oil in a large skillet over medium-high heat. Add the pine nuts, salt and pepper and cook it for about 2 minutes, until the pine nuts are lightly browned. Add the tomatoes and spinach and cook for 2 minutes.

Drain the pasta, reserving ¼ cup cooking water. In a large bowl, toss the spinach mixture with the pasta. Add the cheese and lemon juice and toss until the cheese is melted. Add some of the reserved cooking water, if needed.

6 servings, each serving has 502 calories, 21 g fat, 62 g carbohydrate, 17 g protein, 5 g fiber

Spaghetti with Vegetables

This is simple, inexpensive, and kid friendly! No side dish needed

2 zucchini, ends trimmed
4 carrots, peeled
16 oz spaghetti
¼ cup butter
3 cloves garlic, minced
1 Tbsp grated lemon peel
1 Tbsp lemon juice
½ tsp salt
¼ tsp pepper
Parmesan (optional)

Cook pasta according to package directions. Meanwhile, use a peeler to shave the zucchini and carrots into long strips. Toss the veggies strips in with the pasta 1 minute before noodles are done cooking. Reserve 1 cup pasta cooking water.

Meanwhile, sauté garlic in butter until lightly brown. Remove from heat and stir in remaining ingredients (except cheese). Pour over drained pasta and toss. Gradually stir in reserved pasta water until a thin sauce is formed. Top with Parmesan, if desired.

6 servings, each serving has 214 calories, 9g fat, 29g carbohydrate, 6g protein, 3g fiber

Pasta with No-Cook Sauce

No side dish needed

16 oz elbow macaroni or other medium pasta
1 cup celery, thinly sliced
7 large Roma tomatoes, cut into bite sized pieces
½ cup chopped fresh basil
4 oz part-skim mozzarella cheese, diced
1 can (15oz) artichoke hearts packed in water, drained and quartered
2 Tbsp olive oil
2 Tbsp lemon juice
1 Tbsp Dijon mustard
¾ tsp salt
¼ tsp pepper

Cook pasta according to package directions. Meanwhile, toss remaining ingredients in a large bowl. When pasta is done, drain and add it to mixture and toss to mix. Let stand 1-2 minutes.

6 servings, each serving has 240 calories, 8g fat, 31g carbohydrate, 10g protein, 4g fiber

Pierogies & Cabbage

No side dish needed

32 oz Potato & Cheddar Pierogies
1 small head of cabbage, shredded
1 can (15oz) diced tomatoes, un-drained
¼ tsp pepper

Cook Pierogies according to package directions. Meanwhile, spray a large non-stick skillet with cooking spray. Sauté cabbage until tender and starting to brown. Stir in tomatoes and pepper and heat through. Serve cabbage mixture over the drained Pierogies.

4 servings, each serving has 407 calories, 5g fat, 78g carbohydrate, 15g protein, 8g fiber

Vegetable Chili

This chili can be spicy. Start with less seasoning and gradually add more to taste. Side dish suggestion: crackers. Optional toppings: fat free sour cream, and/or reduced fat shredded cheddar cheese

1 Tbsp olive oil
1 medium onion, chopped
1 medium carrot, thinly sliced
1 green pepper, chopped
1 zucchini, sliced
8 oz fresh mushrooms, sliced
5 garlic cloves, minced
1 (16 oz) can diced tomatoes, undrained
2 cans (16 oz each) kidney beans, rinsed and drained
1 (16 oz) can tomato sauce
1 (4 oz) can diced green chilies
1-3 Tbsp chili powder (to taste)
1 Tbsp oregano
1 tsp ground cumin
1 tsp paprika
¼ tsp crushed red pepper flakes (optional)
2 tsp sea salt (or use 1 tsp table salt), or to taste

In a Dutch oven, sauté onion, carrot, green pepper, mushrooms and zucchini in olive oil until just tender. Add garlic and cook one minute more. Add the tomatoes, kidney beans, tomato sauce, green chilies, and seasonings *(start out with smaller amounts of chili powder, salt, and dried pepper flakes and add more if you like it spicier)*. Bring to a boil. Reduce heat and simmer for 30 minutes, stirring occasionally.

6 servings, each serving has 213 calories, 4 g fat, 38 g carbohydrate, 11 g protein, 10 g fiber

Fettuccine with Mushrooms

Side dish suggestion: steamed baby carrots

8 oz fettuccine
1 Tbsp olive oil
1 lb fresh white mushrooms, sliced
½ cup sliced green onions
2 cloves garlic, minced
2 medium tomatoes, diced
¼ cup chopped fresh basil or 1 Tbsp dried basil
1 tsp salt
½ cup reduced fat ricotta cheese
½ cup reduced fat feta cheese

Cook pasta according to package directions. Reserve ¼ cup of cooking liquid, then drain. Return pasta to pot. Meanwhile, in a large skillet heat oil until hot. Add mushrooms, green onions and garlic; cook, stirring frequently, until mushrooms are tender, 5 to 6 minutes. Stir in tomato, basil and salt; cook until tomato is just warm, about 1 minute.

Add ricotta cheese to the drained pasta in the pot. Add reserved cooking liquid to make it creamier, if desired. Add mushroom mixture and toss. Sprinkle servings with feta cheese.

4 servings, each serving has 219 calories, 8 fat, 27g carbohydrate, 13g protein, 3g fiber

Polenta & Chili Bake

No side dish needed

1¼ cups yellow cornmeal
½ tsp salt
4 cups boiling water
2 cups shredded reduced fat cheddar cheese, divided
3 cans (15 oz each) fat-free vegetarian chili
1 package (16 oz) frozen mixed vegetables, thawed and well drained

Preheat oven to 350°. Bring water to a boil. Combine cornmeal and ½ tsp salt in a saucepan. Gradually whisk in boiling water. Cook and stir over medium heat for 3 to 5 minutes or until thickened. Remove from heat and stir in ¼ cup cheddar cheese. Spread the cornmeal mixture into a 13 x 9 baking dish that has been sprayed with nonstick cooking spray. Bake uncovered for 20 minutes.

Remove baked cornmeal from oven and spread vegetables over the top. Sprinkle lightly with salt, if desired. Pour the chili over the vegetables and sprinkle with remaining cheese. Bake 15 minutes longer or until cheese is melted. Let stand for five minutes before serving.

8 servings, each serving has 344 calories, 6g fat, 44g carbohydrate, 19g protein, 13g fiber

Pasta with Tomatoes & Asparagus

Side dish suggestion: green salad

16 oz penne pasta
1 bunch asparagus, cut into 1 inch pieces
1 Tbsp olive oil
6 cloves garlic, minced
1 pint cherry or grape tomatoes, halved
Salt, to taste
black pepper, to taste
1 ½ Tbsp lemon juice
15 fresh basil leaves, chopped
1 cup shredded or diced smoked Gouda cheese (or Swiss cheese)

Cook the pasta according to package directions, reserving ½ cup of cooking water before draining. Meanwhile, heat the oil in a large skillet over medium-high heat. Add the asparagus, garlic, and tomatoes, and cook for several minutes. Season with salt and pepper to taste. Add the reserved cooking water, drained pasta, lemon juice, and basil to the skillet and toss gently. Transfer it to a large serving bowl and add the cheese. Toss the noodles and cheese to melt the cheese slightly.

6 servings, each serving has 229 calories, 8 g fat, 28 g carbohydrate, 11 g protein, 3 g fiber **Creamy**

Creamy Bean Burritos

Side dish suggestion: baked tortilla chips

½ cup instant Brown Rice
1 green pepper, chopped
2 tsp olive oil
1 can (15 oz) Pinto beans, rinsed and drained
1 cup canned diced tomatoes
4 oz reduced fat cream cheese, cubed
¾ tsp chili powder
1/4 tsp ground cumin
1/8 tsp ground coriander
1/4 tsp oregano
6 (10 inch) flour tortillas, warmed
1 cup reduced fat cheddar cheese
Salsa (optional)

Cook rice according to package directions and set aside. Meanwhile, in a large nonstick skillet, sauté green pepper in oil until tender.

In a bowl, coarsely mash the pinto beans. Add the beans, tomatoes, cream cheese, chili powder, cumin, coriander, and oregano to the skillet. Cook and stir until heated through and cream cheese is melted. Stir in the cooked rice. Spoon bean mixture into the center of each tortilla and top with cheese. Fold in sides and roll up. Serve with salsa, if desired.

6 servings, each serving has 338 calories, 11 g fat, 46 g carbohydrate, 15 g protein, 6 g fiber

Moroccan Stew

Side dish suggestion: good served on top of plain couscous

1 large onion, chopped
3 garlic cloves, crushed
1 tsp curry powder
1 tsp ground cumin
1 can (15 oz) garbanzo beans, rinsed and drained
1 can (15 oz) stewed tomatoes
1 ¾ cups water
1 ¾ tsp chicken bouillon granules
2 large carrots, sliced diagonally into half inch thick slices
1 zucchini, sliced into half inch slices and quartered
⅓ cup golden raisins
2 Tbsp cilantro, chopped

Spray a nonstick Dutch oven with cooking spray and heat over medium-high heat. Add onion and cook five minutes or until lightly browned, stirring frequently. Stir in garlic, curry powder, and cumin. Add beans, tomatoes, water, bouillon, and carrots. Heat to boiling. Reduce heat; cover and simmer for 5 minutes. Stir in zucchini in raisins. Cover and cook 5 more minutes or until zucchini is tender. Stir in cilantro and cook uncovered for 1 minute.

4 servings, each serving has 214 calories, 2g fat, 46g carbohydrate, 8g protein, 8g fiber

Eggplant Pasta

No side dish needed

16 oz spaghetti
1 Tbsp olive oil
4 cloves garlic, minced
1 small onion, diced
1 red pepper, chopped
1 eggplant, diced
4 tomatoes, coarsely chopped
2 tsp chicken bouillon granules
1¾ cups water
1-2 Tbsp capers
1 tsp balsamic vinegar
¼ tsp pepper, to taste
¼ tsp salt, to taste

Cook pasta according to package directions. Meanwhile, heat oil in a medium pan over medium-high heat. Sauté garlic for 1-2 minutes. Add onion, pepper, eggplant, and tomatoes. Cook 10 minutes, stirring occasionally. Add bouillon, water, capers, vinegar, salt, and pepper. Simmer 30 minutes more or until thickened. Serve over pasta.

4 servings, each serving has 183 calories, 3 g fat, 25g carbohydrate, 5g protein, 4g fiber

Pasta with Broccoli & Tomatoes

No side dish needed

12 oz penne pasta
3 ½ cups broccoli florets
2 tsp olive oil
2 to 4 garlic cloves, minced
1 (28 oz) Can crushed tomatoes, un-drained
¼ cup red wine
1 Tbsp chopped fresh basil or 1 teaspoon dried basil leaves
1 tsp sugar
½ tsp salt
Parmesan cheese (optional)

Cook penne according to package directions, adding broccoli during last 4 minutes of cooking time.

Meanwhile, in large skillet, heat oil over medium heat until hot. Add garlic; cook and stir 2 to 3 minutes or until tender. Stir in tomatoes and remaining ingredients; simmer 15 to 20 minutes, stirring occasionally.

To serve, drain penne and broccoli; arrange on serving platter. Top with sauce. Sprinkle with Parmesan cheese, if desired.

4 servings, each serving has 255 calories, 4g fat, 47g carbohydrate, 10g protein, 7g fiber

Tomato & Cheese Spaghetti

Side dish suggestion: garlic bread

16 oz spaghetti
6 med tomatoes, chopped & drained
12 oz part-skim mozzarella cheese, cut into small cubes
1 cup chopped fresh basil
1 can (2 oz) sliced black olives, drained
4 tsp balsamic vinegar
½ tsp salt
½ tsp pepper
4 garlic cloves, minced
2 Tbsp olive oil

Cook spaghetti according to package directions. Meanwhile, in a large bowl, combine remaining ingredients & stir. Drain spaghetti. Add to tomato mixture and toss to combine.

6 servings, each serving has 354 calories, 16 g fat, 32 g carbohydrate, 20 g protein, 3 g fiber

Summer Vegetable Stew

Side dish suggestion: breadsticks

1 Tbsp olive oil
1 large onion, quartered and thinly sliced
4 garlic cloves, minced
½ tsp dried thyme
1 small eggplant, cut into ½ inch cubes
1 zucchini, halved lengthwise and cut into slices
1 red bell pepper, cut into strips
1 can (15 oz) diced tomatoes, un-drained
½ tsp salt
½ tsp black pepper
1 cup fresh basil leaves, shredded

Heat the olive oil in a large skillet over medium heat. Add the onion and garlic and cook for 5 minutes. Stir in remaining ingredients, except basil. Cover; reduce heat, and simmer 20 minutes or until vegetables are tender. Stir in the basil and serve.

4 servings, each serving has 113 calories, 4g fat, 19g carbohydrate, 4g protein, 8g fiber

Ravioli & Brown Butter

This is one of those "once in a great while" recipes. It doesn't get the seal of approval for being the healthiest choice ever, but its simplicity and taste find it worthy of repeating. Just watch the portions and serve it with a giant salad.

24 -28 oz fresh or frozen cheese ravioli
6 Tbsp butter (*no substitutions*)
2-3 green onions, sliced
16-18 fresh sage leaves
1/4 tsp sea salt
1/4 tsp pepper
3/4 cup Parmesan, grated or shaved

Cook ravioli according to package directions. Meanwhile heat butter in large skillet over medium heat until it melts. Add onion and cook for 1-2 minutes. Increase heat to medium-high and add sage. Cook until leaves begin to crisp, about 1 ½ minutes. Remove from heat. Stir in salt and pepper. Return the back to the burner, turning the heat up until the butter foams (this usually takes less than a minute, so watch it closely).

Put the drained ravioli in a large bowl. Top with butter mixture, half of the cheese, and toss gently. Sprinkle remaining cheese on top.

6 servings, each serving has 548 calories, 27 g fat, 54 g carbohydrate, 22g protein, 4 g fiber

Black Beans & Rice *Fast! Easy! Cheap!*

This is perhaps not the most elegant of dishes, but it is great for those days when you're in a hurry or you're not in the mood to cook. Serve as is or top with shredded cheddar cheese, diced green onions, and extra salsa. Side dish suggestion: warm tortillas

4 cups cooked rice
2 cans (15 oz) black beans, un-drained
1 can (4 oz) diced green chilies
½ cup salsa
¼ - ½ tsp garlic salt, to taste

Cook rice according to package directions to make 4 cups. Meanwhile, heat remaining ingredients in a saucepan. Serve beans over the rice.

4 servings, each serving has 384 calories, 1g fat, 76g carbohydrate, 15g protein, 10g fiber

Enchilada Bake

Side dish suggestion: green salad

1 can (15 oz) beans (pinto or kidney beans), drained
1 onion, chopped
2 cloves garlic, minced
5-6 mushrooms, sliced
1 green pepper, chopped
1 (15oz) can stewed tomatoes
1 Tbsp chili powder
1 tsp ground cumin
½ cup dry red wine
8 (8 inch) wheat flour tortillas
¼ cup grated skim Mozzarella cheese
½ cup fat free ricotta cheese
¼ cup fat free plain yogurt
1 can (2 oz) sliced black olives

Preheat oven to 350°. Sauté onion, garlic, mushrooms, and pepper. Add the beans, tomatoes, spices, and wine. Simmer gently for about 20 minutes.

Mix ricotta cheese and yogurt. In an 1½ quart casserole dish that has been sprayed with cooking spray, put a layer of tortillas, a layer of sauce, 1½ Tbsp of mozzarella cheese and 4 Tbsp of yogurt mixture. Repeat until all ingredients are used, ending with a layer of sauce. Top with yogurt mixture and black olives. Bake for 15 to 20 minutes.

6 servings, each serving has 334 calories, 7g fat, 50g carbohydrate, 13g protein, 8g fiber

Penne Puttanesca

Start to finish time: 20 minutes! This is mostly vegetarian, although it does use anchovy paste. Side dish suggestion: bread sticks

16 oz penne pasta
1 ½ Tbsp olive oil
1 small onion finely chopped
4 cloves garlic, minced
1 can (28 oz) diced tomatoes, liquid reserved
2 Tbsp anchovy paste
1 cup pitted kalamata olives, coarsely chopped
2 Tbsp capers, drained
¼ tsp red pepper flakes (optional)
grated Parmesan cheese, to taste (optional)

Cook the pasta according to the package directions. Meanwhile, in a saucepan, heat the oil over medium heat. Sauté the onions and garlic until the onions are slightly browned, about 5 minutes. Stir in the tomatoes, anchovies, olives, capers and red pepper flakes (optional), adding reserved tomato liquid, if needed. Simmer for 15 minutes. Drain the penne and toss it with the sauce. Top it with Parmesan cheese, if desired.

4 servings w/out cheese, each serving has 394 calories, 15 g fat, 56 g carbohydrate, 11 g protein, 6 g fiber

Tomato Baguette Pizza

Side dish suggestion: Green salad

8 oz sliced fresh mushrooms
1 medium onion, sliced
1 tsp olive oil
2 garlic cloves, minced
½ tsp Italian seasoning
½ tsp garlic salt
¼ tsp pepper
1 French bread baguette (10-12 oz), halved lengthwise
1 ½ cups shredded part-skim mozzarella cheese
¾ cup thinly sliced fresh basil leaves
3 medium tomatoes, chopped

Preheat oven to 400°. Meanwhile, sauté mushrooms, onions, and oil in a large skillet until tender. Add the garlic, Italian seasoning, garlic salt and pepper. Sauté 1-2 minutes more.

Place baguette halves on a baking sheet; sprinkle with half of the cheese. Top with the basil, mushroom mixture, tomatoes and remaining cheese. Bake at 400° for 10-15 minutes or until cheese is melted. Cut each piece into three slices.

6 servings, each serving has 239 calories, 7 g fat, 32g carbohydrate, 14 g protein, 2 g fiber

Pesto Ravioli with Artichokes

The fat content is higher than a typical Sensible Cook meal, although it is mostly made up of the "good fats". You can easily reduce some of the fat by using less pesto, to taste. The portions are a bit smaller than typical too, so make a big side dish. Side dish suggestion: green salad & tomatoes

1 (9oz) pkg. cheese ravioli
1 container refrigerated pesto, room temperature
1 can (15 oz) quartered artichoke hearts in water, drained
½ cup black olives, sliced
1 Tbsp fresh basil, chopped

Cook pasta according to package directions. Drain and gently toss with remaining ingredients.

4 servings, each serving has 510 calories, 33g fat, 41g carbohydrate, 12g protein, 4g fiber

Basil is an amazing and versatile herb that is relatively easy to grow. You can keep fresh basil for up to 5 days in the refrigerator by wrapping in a damp paper towel and then in a plastic bag, or by standing them up with the stems in a glass of water (like flowers). When cooking with basil, add dried basil midway through cooking. Fresh basil will lose its flavor with prolonged simmering, so add it near the end of cooking.

New Orleans Red Beans

This vegetarian meal is super economical. You can serve it over rice, and get up to 12 servings out of this dish.

1 lb. dry red beans
8 cups water
1 large onion, chopped
4 bay leaves
1 large green pepper, chopped
3 Tbsp garlic, chopped
3 Tbsp parsley
2 tsp dried thyme, crushed
1- 1 ½ tsp salt (to taste)
1 tsp black pepper
2 tsp chicken bouillon granules
¼ tsp celery seed (optional)

Rinse beans and pre-soak according to package directions. Drain.

In a large pot combine beans, water, onion, and bay leaves. Bring to a boil; reduce heat. Cover and cook over low heat for about 1 ½ hours or until beans are tender. Stir, mashing the beans (about half of them) against side of pan. Add remaining ingredients. Simmer uncovered, over medium heat until creamy and thickened, about 30-60 minutes. Remove bay leaves.

8 servings, each serving has 110 calories, 0 g fat, 63g carbohydrate, 12 g protein, 27g fiber

Pasta with Roasted Vegetables
No side dish needed

16 oz penne pasta
1 lb. broccoli florets
1 small eggplant (optional), thinly sliced and quartered
1 can (15 oz) artichoke hearts (in water), quartered and drained
¼ cup pitted kalamata olives, sliced
4 garlic cloves, chopped
¼ cup olive oil
½ cup fresh basil, thinly sliced
¼ cup pine nuts, toasted
1 tsp salt
½ tsp pepper
Parmesan cheese (optional)

Cook pasta according to package directions. Meanwhile preheat oven to 450°. Place all of the vegetables in a large bowl and toss with olive oil. Turn into a cookie sheet. Sprinkle with salt and pepper and roast for 10- 15 minutes or until desired doneness, turning occasionally.

In a large bowl, toss roasted vegetables with pasta, basil and toasted pine nuts. Adjust olive oil, salt and pepper to your taste. Serve with Parmesan, if desired.

6 servings, each serving has 302 calories, 16g fat, 32g carbohydrate, 8g protein, 5g fiber

Caribbean Pasta
Omit the cayenne pepper if you don't like things spicy. No side dish needed.

5 large ripe tomatoes, coarsely chopped
1(15 oz) can black beans, rinsed & drained
2 Tbsp olive oil
5 cloves garlic, minced
¼ cup chopped cilantro
2 green onions, finely sliced
2 Tbsp lime juice
¾ tsp ground cumin
½ tsp pepper
½ tsp salt
¼ - ½ tsp cayenne pepper (optional, to taste)
8 oz thin spaghetti
½ cup Monterey Jack cheese (optional)

Place all ingredients, except pasta and cheese, in a bowl and stir to blend. Let stand, covered at room temperature for up to 1 hour to blend flavors.

Cook pasta according to package directions. Drain. Toss hot pasta with the tomato mixture. Sprinkle with cheese, if desired. Serve immediately.

4 servings, each serving without cheese has 265 calories, 8g fat, 39g carbohydrate, 10g protein, 7g fiber
4 servings, each serving with cheese has 320 calories, 13g fat, 39g carbohydrate, 13g protein, 7g fiber

Four Cheese Spaghetti

This recipe is higher in fat than the typical Sensible Cook recipe, but far better than the original version which contained 633 calories and 47 grams of fat per serving! With the adjustments that were made, it can become an occasional dish, and kids like it too. Side dish suggestion: Green Beans

8 oz spaghetti
2 Tbsp butter
¼ tsp salt
¼ tsp pepper
1 Tbsp flour
1 ½ cups fat free half & half
1 Tbsp dried parsley
¼ tsp garlic powder
1 cup shredded part-skim mozzarella cheese
4 oz fontina cheese, shredded
2 oz provolone cheese, shredded or diced
¼ cup shredded Parmesan cheese

Cook spaghetti according to package directions. Meanwhile, in a large saucepan, melt butter. Stir in the flour, salt and pepper until smooth. Gradually whisk in half & half. Bring to a boil. Add parsley and garlic powder. Cook and stir for 2 minutes or until slightly thickened. Remove from heat; stir in cheeses until melted. Drain spaghetti; toss with cheese sauce.

4 servings, each serving has 456 calories, 27g fat, 27g carbohydrate, 26g protein, 1g fiber

Linguine with Gorgonzola Sauce

Gorgonzola tastes like blue cheese, so if you like blue cheese, you'll probably like this pasta. The reverse is true as well. No side dish needed

12 ounces linguine
1 bunch fresh asparagus, trimmed and cut into 1 inch pieces
1 cup fat free half & half
4 oz Gorgonzola or other blue cheese
¼ tsp salt
¼ cup chopped walnuts

Cook linguine according to package directions, adding asparagus during the last 4 minutes of cooking. Meanwhile, in a medium saucepan, combine half & half, 3/4 cup of the Gorgonzola, and the salt. Bring to a boil. Reduce heat and simmer uncovered for 3 minutes, stirring often.

Pour sauce over drained linguine mixture. Toss gently to coat. Sprinkle servings with remaining Gorgonzola cheese and the walnuts.

4 servings, each serving has 495 calories, 15 g fat, 74 g carbohydrate, 21 g protein, 5 g fiber

Bean &Veggie Burritos

Make sure your rice is already cooked. Side dish suggestion: Green salad

1 cup cooked brown rice
1 tsp olive oil
1 large red bell pepper, cut into thin strips
1 large green bell pepper, cut into thin strips
1 medium onion, sliced
1 tsp salt
1 tsp Lime juice
4 large tortillas, warmed
1 can (16 oz) fat-free refried beans
½ avocado, sliced
3 cups fresh spinach, chopped
2 Tbsp cilantro, chopped
Salsa
Reduced fat cheddar cheese (optional)

Heat the oil in a large skillet over medium-high heat. Add the bell peppers, onions, and salt and cook, stirring frequently, for 5-7 minutes. Stir in the lime juice.

Meanwhile warm the refried beans. When ready to assemble the burritos, spread each tortilla with ⅓ cup refried beans and ¼ cup rice. Evenly divide the onion mixture, avocado, spinach, and cilantro among the tortillas. Tightly roll each burrito. Serve each burrito with salsa and cheese if desired.

4 servings, each serving has 379 calories, 10g fat, 61g carbohydrate, 12g protein, 12g fiber

When choosing fresh corn, choose corn with bright green, tight fitting husks. Peel back part of the husk and check for moist, light colored silk, which is a sign of freshness. Look for small, plump kernels, which indicates the corn is young and sweet. Once you get the corn home, leave the husk on until you are ready to cook it.

Pasta with Jalapeno Spinach Pesto

Side dish suggestion: Sliced tomatoes

3 garlic cloves, coarsely chopped
1 jalapeno pepper, stemmed and coarsely chopped (leave the seeds in for spicier pesto, seeds out otherwise)
2 cups shredded Parmesan cheese
1 tsp salt
1 tsp black pepper
1 cup chopped walnuts
5 oz baby spinach
¼ cup olive oil
1 lb. pasta, any kind

In a food processor, combine the garlic, jalapeno, cheese, salt, and pepper. Process until the mixture is smooth. Add the walnuts and pulse until the walnuts are finely chopped (but not pulverized). Remove from processor and put into a large bowl.

Add the spinach and olive oil to the food processor and process until blended. Stir into the walnut mixture.

Cook pasta according to package directions. Drain the pasta, reserving 1½ cups of the pasta water. Transfer the cooked pasta into the bowl with the pesto with 1 cup pasta water. Toss well. Gradually add more reserved pasta water, if needed.

8 servings, each serving has 367 calories, 24g fat, 21g carbohydrate, 17g protein, 2g fiber

"Cooking is an art and patience a virtue... Careful shopping, fresh ingredients and an unhurried approach are nearly all you need. There is one more thing – love. Love for food and love for those you invite to your table. With a combination of these things you can be an artist – not perhaps in the representational style of a Dutch master, but rather more like Gauguin, the naïve, or Van Gogh, the impressionist. Plates or pictures of sunshine taste of happiness and love."

~ Keith Floyd, in "A Feast of Floyd"

Soups, Salads, & Sandwiches

Cheesy Vegetable Soup
A favorite veggie soup... even kids like it!

1 cup diced potatoes
½ cup diced carrots
½ cup diced celery
½ cup chopped onion
1 tsp chicken bouillon granules
2 cups water
10 oz. Frozen mixed vegetables
10 oz. Frozen chopped broccoli
1 can cream of chicken soup
1½ cups water
4 oz. Light Velveeta cheese, cubed

Combine potatoes, carrots, celery, onion, and bouillon with 2 cups of water in a stockpot. Bring to a boil, and then reduce heat; simmer for 20 minutes. Add frozen mixed vegetables, frozen broccoli, chicken soup, and 1 ½ cups of water. Bring to a boil and stir in cheese.

6 servings, each serving has 159 calories, 5 g fat, 22 g carbohydrate, 8 g protein, 5g fiber

Lentil & Spinach Soup
Serve with warm, crusty bread

1 medium onion, chopped
⅓ cup pearl barley
4 garlic cloves, minced
7 ¼ cups water
2 Tbsp +1 tsp chicken bouillon granules
2 boneless skinless chicken breast halves
1 cup dried lentils, rinsed
2 cups picante sauce
1 can (15 oz) garbanzo beans or chickpeas, rinsed and drained
9-12 oz fresh spinach, chopped

Spray a large Dutch oven with cooking spray. Sauté the onion and garlic until almost tender. Stir in the barley and sauté for a minute longer. Add the water, bouillon, chicken, and lentils. Bring to a boil. Reduce heat and cover. Simmer for 20 minutes or until chicken is no longer pink. Remove chicken and set aside.

Stir in the picante sauce, and the garbanzo beans. Cover and simmer 20 minutes longer or until barley and lentils are tender. Shred chicken with two forks. Add the spinach and the chicken to the soup. Simmer uncovered for 3 to 5 minutes or until spinach is wilted.

Makes 12 cups, each cup has 163 calories, 1 g fat, 27 g carbohydrate, 12 g protein, 9 g fiber

Cauliflower Soup

Side dish suggestion: warm, crusty bread sticks

2 celery stalks, chopped
1 small onion, diced
1 carrot, chopped
2 Tbsp butter
1 large head cauliflower (2 pounds), cut into florets
6 cups water
2 Tbsp chicken bouillon granules
½ cup flour
2 cups skim milk
¾ cup fat-free half-and-half
1 Tbsp minced fresh parsley
1 tsp salt
1 tsp dill weed
¼ tsp pepper

The finer you dice vegetables in recipes, the easier it is to get kids to eat them.

In a Dutch oven, sauté the celery, onion, and carrot in butter for 3-5 minutes or until crisp-tender. Stir in cauliflower, water, and bouillon. Bring to a boil. Reduce heat; cover and simmer for 15-20 minutes or until tender. Cool slightly.

In a blender or food processor, process vegetable mixture in batches until smooth. Return to the pan. Heat over medium heat. In a small bowl, whisk flour and milk until smooth; stir into cauliflower mixture. Bring to a boil; cook and stir for 1-3 minutes or until thickened. Reduce heat; stir in the half-and-half, parsley, salt, dill, and pepper. Heat through.

8 servings, each serving has 127calories, 4g fat, 19 g carbohydrate, 6g protein, 3g fiber

Pumpkin Soup

If you're anything like me, you've been putting off even trying pumpkin soup, even though you've probably heard of it. With a little experimental cooking magic, I created this super easy pumpkin soup that nobody in my family thought they would like (including me), but actually found the unusual mixture quite appealing (and thus, ate it all).

1 (15oz) can pumpkin
1 (14 oz) can unsweetened coconut milk
1 (14 oz) can vegetable broth
1 tsp dried sage, crushed
½ tsp salt
¼ tsp pepper
1 (15 oz) can butter beans, drained

Whisk together all ingredients, except beans, and heat in a saucepan. Stir in beans and heat through.

5 servings, each serving has 277 calories, 15 g fat, 26 g carbohydrate, 7 g protein, 7g fiber

Chunky Tomato Soup

Side dish suggestion: Broiled cheesy bread

6 celery stalks, chopped
1 large onion, chopped
1 red pepper, chopped
2 Tbsp butter
3 cans (14½ oz each) diced tomatoes, un-drained
1 Tbsp ketchup
¾ cup fresh basil, chopped
3 tsp sugar
2 tsp salt
½ tsp pepper
¾ cup fat free half & half

In a large saucepan, sauté the celery, onion, and red pepper in butter for 5 minutes or until tender. Add tomatoes and ketchup. Bring to a boil. Reduce heat; cover and simmer for 40 minutes.

Remove from heat. Stir in the basil, sugar, salt, and pepper. Transfer ½ of the tomato mixture to a blender and puree until smooth. Pour the tomato puree back into the saucepan. Return to heat. Stir in the half & half and heat just until hot (do not boil).

4 servings, each serving has 190 calories, 7g fat, 31 g carbohydrate, 5g protein, 7g fiber

Broccoli Soup

1 large potato, peeled and cut into chunks
6 cups water
5 tsp chicken bouillon granules
4 cups frozen chopped broccoli, thawed
1 cup fat free half-and-half
¼ tsp ground nutmeg
½ tsp salt
½ tsp pepper
Shredded reduced fat cheddar cheese (optional)

In a medium saucepan, cook potato in water and bouillon until soft, about 20-30 minutes. Add broccoli and cook for another 5 minutes.

Pour soup mixture into a blender and puree. Return back to the sauce pan and stir in milk, nutmeg, salt, and pepper and heat until heated through. Serve as is, or sprinkle with cheddar cheese before serving.

6 servings, each serving has 93 calories, 1 g fat, 19 g carbohydrate, 4 g protein, 3g fiber

Tortellini Spinach & Tomato Soup

You can spread this out to make more servings simply by adding up to 2 more cups of water (you'll need to add more bouillon too). Side dish suggestion: bread sticks

½ cup chopped onion
1 garlic clove, minced
4 cups water
4 tsp chicken bouillon granules
1 (15oz) can diced tomatoes, un-drained
¼ tsp sea salt
¼ tsp pepper
¼ tsp onion powder
¼ tsp garlic powder
1 (9oz) pkg. fresh tortellini
10 oz frozen chopped spinach, defrosted and drained
¼ cup freshly shredded parmesan cheese (optional)

In a soup pot that has been sprayed with non-stick cooking spray, sauté the onion and garlic clove over medium high heat until onions are soft, about 5 minutes. Add water, bouillon, tomatoes, and seasonings. Bring to a boil. Reduce heat to a simmer and add the tortellini. Cook according to package time. 5 minutes before tortellini is done, add the spinach. Top each serving with a sprinkling of Parmesan cheese, if desired.

4 servings, each serving has 244 calories, 5g fat, 40g carbohydrate, 12g protein, 5g fiber

Cod Chowder

Side dish suggestion: warm, crunchy dinner rolls

6 slices turkey bacon, diced
3 cups loose frozen hash browns
1 cup water
1 can evaporated skim milk
1 can cream of shrimp (or potato) soup
¾ tsp dried dillweed
½ tsp pepper
½ tsp salt, or to taste
2 oz jar diced pimentos, un-drained
12 oz fresh cod, cut into bite-sized pieces

Cook bacon until crisp. Set aside.

Meanwhile, in a large saucepan, combine hash browns with water. Bring to a boil. Reduce heat, cover, and simmer for 5 minutes.

Stir in milk, soup, dillweed, pepper, and salt. Return to a simmer. Add fish, pimento, and bacon. Cover and simmer for 3-5 minutes or until fish easily flakes.

4 servings, each serving has 315 calories, 6g fat, 37g carbohydrate, 27g protein, 3g fiber

White Bean Chicken Soup *SLOW COOKER or STOVETOP*

You can cook this in a slow cooker or in a Dutch oven. Side dish suggestion: Cornbread

2 boneless, skinless chicken breast halves, cut into small pieces
¼ tsp salt
¼ tsp pepper
1 medium onion, chopped
5 garlic cloves, minced
1 jalapeno pepper, seeded and diced
2 cans (15 ounces *each*) white kidney beans, rinsed and drained
3 cups water, divided
2 tsp dried oregano
1 tsp ground cumin
1 Tbsp chicken bouillon granules
shredded cheddar cheese (optional)

Sprinkle chicken with salt and pepper. Spray a large skillet with cooking spray. Cook chicken over med-high heat for 2 minutes. Stir in the onion, garlic and jalapeno; cook 2 minutes longer, or until chicken is browned. Transfer to a slow cooker or Dutch oven.

In a small bowl or blender, mash 1 cup of beans with ½ cup of water. Add to the pot with 2 ½ cups more water and remaining ingredients (except cheese).

Cover and cook on low for 3-4 hours if using a slow cooker. If cooking on the stovetop, bring to a boil. Cover and reduce heat. Simmer for 20-30 minutes. Season with additional salt and sprinkle with cheese if desired.

4 servings, each serving has 256 calories, 1 g fat, 36g carbohydrate, 27g protein, 10g fiber

Tortellini Soup

Great with warm, crunchy bread!

5 cups water
5 tsp chicken bouillon granules
1 lb. Shredded carrots
1 yellow summer squash, chopped
4 cups torn spinach
1 pkg. (9 oz) refrigerated cheese tortellini

In a large saucepan, combine water, bouillon, carrots, and squash. Bring to a boil. Reduce heat and simmer for 3 minutes. Stir in spinach and tortellini. Cover and cook for 4-5 minutes or until tortellini is finished.

6 servings, each serving has 161 calories, 3g fat, 28g carbohydrate, 7g protein, 3g fiber

Corn &Potato Chowder

32 oz frozen corn kernels, thawed
3 cups water
8 slices Turkey bacon, finely chopped
1 onion, diced
2 large russet potatoes, peeled and cut into half-inch chunks
½ cup fat-free half & half
1/4 teaspoon ground thyme
3 teaspoons chicken bouillon granules
1/8 teaspoon cayenne pepper
1/8 teaspoon black pepper
1/4 teaspoon sea salt

Cook bacon in a large pot over medium-high heat until crisp. Remove from pan and set aside. Meanwhile, purée half the corn and 2 cups water in a blender or food processor until smooth. Set aside.

Sauté the onion and potatoes in the pot that cooked the bacon. Cook until onion is soft, about 5 minutes, spraying with cooking spray as needed. Stir in puréed corn mixture, ½ & ½, remaining 1 cup water, remaining corn, cayenne pepper, black pepper, salt, and chicken bouillon. Simmer until potatoes are tender, 15 to 25 minutes. Sprinkle with crisp bacon when ready to serve.

6 servings, each serving has 294 calories, 4 g fat, 59 g carbohydrate, 10 g protein, 6 g fiber

Hamburger Noodle Soup

1 ½ lbs. Lean ground beef
½ cup diced onion
2 stalks celery, sliced
2 carrots, sliced
7 cups water
2 Tbsp beef bouillon granules
1 envelope au jus mix
2 bay leaves
⅛ tsp pepper
2 cups small egg noodles

Cook hamburger, onion, carrots, and celery in a Dutch oven until hamburger is brown. Drain fat and return meat mixture to pan. Add remaining ingredients (except noodles) and bring to a boil. Add noodles and cook for 10-15 minutes or until noodles are tender. Discard bay leaves.

8 servings, each serving has 198 calories, 6g fat, 10g carbohydrate, 24g protein, 1g fiber

Minestrone Stew

This is actually a soup, but it's so hearty that it passes as a stew. No side dish needed, unless you want some warm crusty breadsticks to go along with it.

1 cup elbow macaroni
42 oz canned diced tomatoes
2 cups water
2 carrots, sliced
1 onion, chopped
1 zucchini, chopped
3 oz turkey pepperoni, diced
¾ tsp Garlic powder
2 tsp chicken bouillon granules
½ tsp basil
½ tsp oregano
2 cans (16 oz each) kidney beans, rinsed and drained
10 oz frozen spinach, thawed and squeezed dry
Parmesan cheese (optional)

Cook macaroni according to package directions. Meanwhile, in a large pot, add tomatoes, water, carrots, onion, and zucchini. Bring to a boil. Reduce heat and simmer 10 minutes or until carrots begin to soften. Add pasta and remaining ingredients, except for the cheese. Return to a gentle boil. Simmer for 5 minutes, or until heated through. Sprinkle serving with Parmesan cheese, if desired.

8 servings, each serving has 210 calories, 3 g fat, 36 g carbohydrate, 14 g protein, 9 g fiber

Tomato & Bean Salad

This salad is nearly identical to the Caribbean Pasta recipe. It showcases two versions of the same recipe. Omit the cayenne pepper if you don't like things spicy.

5 large ripe tomatoes, coarsely chopped
1(15 oz) can black beans, rinsed & drained
2 Tbsp olive oil
5 cloves garlic, minced
¼ cup chopped cilantro
2 green onions, finely sliced
2 Tbsp lime juice
¾ tsp ground cumin
½ tsp pepper
½ tsp salt
¼ - ½ tsp cayenne pepper (optional, to taste)

Place all ingredients in a bowl and stir to blend. Let stand, covered at room temperature for up to 1 hour to blend flavors.

8 servings, each serving has 88 calories, 4g fat, 11g carbohydrate, 3g protein, 3g fiber

Shrimp Slaw Salad

This is one of those unusual no-cook dishes that can work as a main dish or as a fresh side salad. Side dish suggestion: crackers

2 lbs. small cooked shrimp, peeled
14 oz package coleslaw mix (or 7 cups thinly sliced cabbage)
1 yellow or red pepper, sliced into bite-sized pieces
1 green pepper, sliced into bite-sized pieces
4 green onions, sliced thin
⅓ cup fresh chopped cilantro
¾ cup reduced fat mayonnaise
1 tsp finely shredded lime peel
½ tsp salt
¼ tsp cayenne pepper, to taste
2-4 Tbsp lime juice, to taste

In a very large bowl, mix together cold shrimp, coleslaw mix, peppers, green onions, and cilantro. In another bowl combine mayonnaise, lime peel, salt, cayenne pepper, and lime juice. Adjust lime juice and cayenne to taste. Pour dressing over the salad and toss to coat.

4 main-dish servings, each serving has 425 calories, 19g fat, 15g carbohydrate, 48g protein, 4g fiber
12 side dish servings, each serving has 142 calories, 6g fat, 5g carbohydrate, 16g protein, 1g fiber

Chicken & Brie Salad

Leave the papery-like skin on the cheese. No side dish needed

4 skinless, boneless chicken breast halves
3 Tbsp sugar
½ cup pecan halves
6 cups chopped Romaine lettuce
1 round of brie cheese (about 5 oz), sliced
½ cup light raspberry vinaigrette salad dressing

Trim all fat from breasts. Place chicken in a saucepan of boiling water until cooked through, about 15 minutes. Remove chicken and set aside to cool. Once cool, thinly slice.

Place sugar in a heavy skillet. Cook, without stirring, over medium-high heat until sugar begins to melt, shaking skillet as needed. Reduce heat and cook until sugar is melted. Using a wooden spoon, stir in pecans. Toss pecans with melted sugar to coat. Place pecans on a plate sprayed with cooking spray. Allow to cool completely, then break apart.

Line plates evenly with lettuce. Place chicken breast in the middle. Place pecans on one side, and line the brie slices on the other side. Serve with dressing.

4 servings, each serving has 382 calories, 20g fat, 17g carbohydrate, 34g protein, 2g fiber

Pork, Pear, & Cranberry Salad

No side dish needed

16 oz spinach leaves, coarsely chopped
1 pear, thinly sliced
1 Tbsp apple cider vinegar
1 tsp Dijon mustard
¾ tsp brown sugar
3 cloves garlic, minced & divided
1 ½ tsp dried thyme, divided
1 lb. lean pork tenderloin, trimmed and cut into thin ¼" slices
¾ tsp salt
¾ tsp pepper
2 Tbsp flour
3 Tbsp olive oil
4 green onions, chopped
¼ cup dried cranberries
¼ cup cranberry juice cocktail

In a large bowl, toss the spinach and pear. Set aside.

In a small bowl, combine vinegar, mustard, sugar, half of the garlic, and ¼ tsp thyme. Set aside.

In another bowl, combine pork, remaining garlic, 1 tsp thyme, salt, pepper, and flour. Toss well to coat

Heat 1 Tbsp oil in saucepan. Sauté green onions 2-3 minutes. Stir in cranberries and juice. Boil for 2 minutes, stirring often. Stir in vinegar mixture and bring to a gentle boil. Reduce heat to low. Cover & keep warm.

Heat 1 Tbsp of oil in a large non-stick skillet. Add the pork in a single layer (you may have to cook it in batches) and cook until browned on both sides and cooked through, about 5-6 minutes, adding additional 1 Tbsp oil if needed. Remove pork from skillet, toss pork with 1 Tbsp cranberry mixture. Pour remaining cranberry mixture over the spinach mixture and toss. Divide spinach mixture on to serving plates and top with pork.

4 servings, each serving has 294 calories, 13g fat, 19g carbohydrate, 27g protein, 4g fiber

> _"Age is just a number._
> _It's totally irrelevant unless, of course, you happen to be a bottle of wine. "_
> _Joan Collins_

Italian Salad

Great all by itself, but crunchy breadsticks go along nicely.

Dressing
3 cloves garlic, minced
2 green onions, diced
2 Tbsp Dijon Mustard
1½ tsp dried oregano
2 tsp dried parsley
½ tsp pepper
½ tsp sea salt
¼ cup red wine vinegar
1 cup olive oil
3 Tbsp grated Parmesan cheese

> *A Balanced life looks and feels different for everyone.*

Salad
10 oz iceberg lettuce, chopped into ¼ inch strips (about ½ head)
10 oz romaine lettuce, chopped into ¼ inch strips (about ½ head)
12 leaves basil, chopped
1 cup part-skim mozzarella cheese, shredded
1 cup garbanzo beans, rinsed and drained
5 Roma tomatoes, chopped
12 oz cooked turkey breast, diced
6 oz light salami, cut into thin strips
4 green onions, chopped

For dressing, whisk together ingredients in a small bowl and chill in refrigerator while preparing the salad. For salad, toss together the ingredients in a large bowl. Just before serving, toss salad with half of the dressing. Serve immediately. Save remaining salad dressing for up to a week in your refrigerator.

6 servings, each serving has 420 calories, 27g fat, 15g carbohydrate, 30g protein, 4g fiber

Southwest Salad

8 cups chopped romaine lettuce
2 cans (15oz) black beans, drained & rinsed
1 cup frozen corn, thawed
1 ½ cups salsa
1 cup reduced fat cheddar cheese, shredded
½ cup reduced fat ranch dressing
1 cup baked tortilla chips, broken

Put lettuce in a large serving bowl. Top with beans, corn, salsa, and cheese. Drizzle with dressing. Sprinkle with chips.

4 servings, each serving has 375 calories, 9g fat, 53g carbohydrate, 22 g protein, 11g fiber

Southwestern Steak Salad

Cooking a flank steak until well-done will make it tough. If you like well-done meat, you may want to consider a different cut of steak. No side dish needed

3 tsp olive oil, divided
1 lb. flank steak
1 cup fresh (or drained canned) corn kernels
2 tsp chipotle seasoning
1 (15 oz) can black beans, rinsed
1 pint cherry tomatoes, halved
1 avocado, diced
¼ onion, thinly sliced
Juice of ½ a lime

Heat ½ tsp oil over med-high heat in a large nonstick skillet. Add corn and cook for 1 minute. Remove corn, and place in a medium bowl.

Rub seasoning on both sides of the steak. Heat ½ tsp of oil in the skillet until hot. Add steak and cook 6-8 minutes on each side. Transfer to a cutting board and let stand for five minutes.

Meanwhile, add beans, tomatoes, avocado, onion, and 2 tsp olive oil into the bowl with corn. Toss to mix thoroughly. To serve: Spoon corn salad onto plates. Thinly slice steak across the grain. Place steak on top of the corn salad. Serve with balsamic vinegar.

4 servings, each serving has 418 calories, 18g fat, 31g carbohydrate, 35g protein, 9g fiber

Mediterranean Chicken Salad

Side dish suggestion: bread sticks

1 box (6oz) garlic couscous
1 can (15oz) chickpeas, rinsed and drained
2 cups cooked chicken breasts, diced
6 cups spinach, chopped
2 cucumbers, peeled and chopped
1 jar (6 oz) roasted red peppers, cut into thin strips
½ cup sliced green onions
4 oz reduced fat feta cheese
½ cup oil & vinegar dressing

Prepare couscous according to package directions (omitting butter). In a large bowl, toss couscous, chickpeas, chicken, spinach, cucumbers, red peppers, and green onions. Top with feta cheese. Serve salad dressing on the side.

4 servings, each serving has 511 calories, 14g fat, 57g carbohydrate, 40g protein, 10g fiber

Oyster & Spinach Salad

This warm salad can be used as a main dish or fancy pre-dinner course. The oysters are not the dominant flavor and are quite mild in the flavorful sauce. Good served with warm, crusty bread.

8 oz spinach, washed & chopped
1 red pepper
1 yellow pepper
1 small onion, thinly sliced
1 garlic clove, minced
10 oz shucked oysters in water
2 Tbsp soy sauce
2 Tbsp balsamic vinegar
2 Tbsp dry sherry
2 tsp Worcestershire sauce

Divide spinach leaves between 2 serving plates and set aside. Drain the oysters and reserve the juice. Pour the oyster juice into a bowl and stir in the soy sauce, vinegar, sherry, and Worcestershire sauce. Set aside.

Spray a large skillet with cooking spray and heat over med-high heat. Add peppers, onions and garlic and sauté until vegetables are crisp tender. Remove from pan and keep warm.

In the same skillet, cook oysters until lightly browned, 1-2 minutes on each side. Pour oyster sauce over the oysters in the skillet and bring to a rapid boil. Stir frequently until liquid begins to reduce, about 2-3 minutes.

To serve, top spinach leaves with pepper mixture. Arrange oysters on top and pour the hot oyster sauce over the salad. Serve immediately.

2 servings, each serving has 187 calories, 4g fat, 22g carbohydrate, 18g protein, 6g fiber

Tossed Shrimp Salad

Side dish suggestion: boiled egg halves and sourdough bread

16 oz small cooked shrimp, peeled
12 oz package salad or chopped lettuce
3 green onions, thinly sliced
⅓ cup fat-free zesty Italian salad dressing
⅓ cup slivered almonds

Spray a small skillet with cooking spray and heat to medium-high heat. Add almonds and cook, stirring constantly, until almonds begin to turn brown. Place toasted almonds in a large bowl. Add salad greens, green onions, shrimp, and salad dressing to the bowl and toss to coat. Season with pepper to taste.

4 servings, each serving has 189 calories, 6g fat, 8g carbohydrate, 26g protein, 2g fiber

Tuna & Spinach Salad

Start to finish: 15 minutes! Side dish suggestion: bread sticks

3 Tbsp lemon juice
1 ½ Tbsp olive oil
1 clove garlic, minced
¼ tsp sea salt
¼ tsp pepper
¼ tsp Dijon mustard
6 oz (about 1 cup) grape or cherry tomatoes, halved
1 small red onion, halved and thinly sliced
12 oz canned solid tuna (packed in water), drained
1 (15 oz) can cannellini (white kidney) beans, rinsed and drained
8 oz fresh spinach, chopped
¼ cup parmesan cheese, shaved

Whisk together the first 6 ingredients in a large bowl. Toss in remaining ingredients, except cheese. Mix gently, but well. Top with cheese.

4 servings, each serving has 288 calories, 7g fat, 26g carbohydrate, 34g protein, 8g fiber

Potato & Veggie Salad

This is a great alternative to a traditional picnic potato salad.

1 lb. red potatoes, cut into cubes
1 carrot, shredded
1 green pepper, diced
2 eggs, hardboiled and chopped
2 tsp basil
½ tsp salt
¼ cup reduced fat mayonnaise

Cook potatoes in boiling water until just tender. Drain, and cool completely. When potatoes are cool, mix all ingredients in a bowl. Cover and refrigerate until ready to serve.

6 servings, each serving has 140 calories, 5g fat, 19g carbohydrate, 4g protein, 2g fiber

Egg & Tomato Sandwich

1 tsp fat free mayonnaise
1 tsp basil pesto
2 slices whole wheat bread
1 hard-boiled egg, thinly sliced
1 small tomato, sliced

In a small bowl combine mayonnaise and pesto. Spread mixture on 1 slice of bread. Cover with egg, tomato and remaining bread.

1 serving, each sandwich has 250 calories, 10g fat, 28g carbohydrate, 12g protein, 3g fiber

Chicken & Slaw Sandwiches

The jalapeno gives the slaw just a little kick. Leave in the seeds if you like it spicier. You can serve these with the chicken either warm or cold. Side dish suggestion: baked chips

2 boneless, skinless chicken breast halves
1 clove garlic, minced
½ tsp salt
¼ cup rice wine vinegar
1 tsp sugar
2 medium carrots, peeled and grated
⅓ cup minced onion
1 jalapeno pepper, seeded and diced (optional)
1 loaf ciabatta bread or other hearty bread
4 tsp fat free mayonnaise
1 Tbsp lime juice
½ tsp Five Spice Powder
½ cup cilantro, chopped

Cook the chicken breasts by either grilling or boiling, until no longer pink and the juices run clear. Slice the chicken in half horizontally to make 4 thin pieces.

Meanwhile, mash together garlic and salt into a paste. Transfer to a mixing bowl and add vinegar and sugar, stirring to dissolve. Add carrots, onions and jalapeno, and mix. Slice the bread horizontally to make a top and bottom piece. Spread the mayonnaise on the bottom piece.

Arrange the chicken on the bottom half. Sprinkle with lime juice and five spice powder. Top with the carrot slaw and cilantro. Cover with bread top and slice into sandwich size pieces.

4 servings, each serving has 418 calories, 5 g fat, 66 g carbohydrate, 24 g protein, 3 g fiber

Pepperoni &Cheese Sandwiches

Side dish suggestion: tomato soup sprinkled with basil

For EACH sandwich you will need:
2 slices bread
1 oz part-skim mozzarella cheese, sliced
8 slices Turkey pepperoni, chopped
1 tsp light margarine

Lightly spread the margarine onto one side each piece of bread. Place one slice of bread, buttered side down in a skillet over medium heat. Top with cheese, and chopped pepperoni. Top with remaining slice of bread, margarine side up. Turn as needed to gently brown both sides and to melt the cheese.

1 sandwich, each sandwich has 299 calories, 13g fat, 26g carbohydrate, 18g protein, 1g fiber

Cilantro Lime Chicken Salad Wraps

Side dish suggestion: baked chips

1 (12 oz) can chunk white chicken, drained
⅓ cup chopped cilantro
½ lime, juice of
½ cucumber, chopped
1 tomato, seeded & chopped
2 cloves garlic, minced
½ tsp oregano
¼ tsp pepper
1 tsp olive oil
4 (10 inch) tortillas

Combine all ingredients in a medium bowl, except tortillas. Spoon mixture into tortillas. Wrap & eat.

4 servings, each serving has 275 calories, 7g fat, 26g carbohydrate, 28g protein, 4g fiber

Shrimp & Avocado Sandwiches

Most of the fat in these sandwiches comes from the avocados which are "good fats", so don't let it discourage you from trying this yummy & different sandwich combination. Side dish suggestion: carrot sticks

1 lb. cooked shrimp, peeled
2 large avocados, peeled and chopped
1 carrot, shredded
⅓ cup bottled coleslaw salad dressing
4 hoagie buns

In a large bowl, combine shrimp, avocados, carrot, and salad dressing, Spoon onto buns and serve.

4 servings, each serving has 587 calories, 30g fat, 51g carbohydrate, 33g protein, 9g fiber

> Save money by buying a head of lettuce, rather than the bagged kind, which can cost over twice as much. If you do buy bagged lettuce, make sure you wash it (even if it claims to be pre-washed).

Side Dishes

Roasted Vegetables

2 rutabagas, peeled and cubed
3 large red potatoes, cubed
1 onion, cut into wedges
2 carrots, sliced
2 parsnips, peeled and sliced
1 ½ tsp olive oil
¼ tsp dried thyme
¼ tsp dried oregano
¼ tsp dried rosemary, crushed
¼ tsp pepper
¼ tsp salt

Preheat oven to 425°. In a large bowl, combine all ingredients and toss to coat. Transfer to a large baking pan that has been coated with cooking spray. Bake uncovered for 30 to 45 minutes or until vegetables are tender, stirring occasionally.

6 servings, each serving has 174 calories, 2 g fat, 37 g carbohydrate, 4 g protein, 7 g fiber

Grilled Parmesan Corn on the Cob

2-8 ears of corn, husked and silk removed.
¼ cup butter, melted
2 Tbsp grated Parmesan cheese
1 tsp parsley

Wrap each piece of corn in foil. Grill corn over medium high heat for 15-20 minutes, or until corn is tender. Meanwhile, mix the remaining ingredients in a bowl. Brush cooked corn with butter mixture before serving.

2-8 servings, each serving has 142 calories, 6g fat, 22 carbohydrate, 4g protein, 2g fiber

Spinach with Feta

4 garlic cloves, minced
1 Tbsp olive oil
10 oz bagged spinach
½ cup reduced fat feta cheese

Heat olive oil in a large skillet over medium heat. Add garlic and spinach and cook until spinach is wilted through. Remove from heat. Stir in feta cheese. Serve immediately.

4 servings, each serving has 75 calories, 5 g fat, 3 g carbohydrate, 5 g protein, 2 g fiber

Green Beans with Almonds

16 oz frozen French style green beans
2 Tbsp butter
¼ cup slivered almonds
¼ tsp dried savory
1 tsp lemon juice
½ tsp salt
⅛ tsp cayenne pepper

Cook green beans according to package directions. Drain and set aside. Meanwhile, in a large skillet, sauté almonds in butter until toasted. Turn heat to low and stir in savory, lemon juice, salt, and cayenne pepper. Add drained beans to the pan and toss gently to coat.

4 servings, each serving has 125 calories, 9 g fat, 9 g carbohydrate, 4 g protein, 5 g fiber

Mashed Cauliflower & Potatoes

1 large potato, peeled and cut into cubes
1 head cauliflower, cut into florets
3 Tbsp fat free half & half
1 Tbsp light margarine
1 clove garlic, minced
½ tsp salt
1/8 tsp pepper

Bring a large pot of water to a boil. Add potato and cauliflower and boil until soft (about 20 minutes). Drain.

Put hot, drained veggies into a bowl with remaining ingredients. Mix with a mixer (or squash with a masher) until mashed. Stir & serve.

6 servings, each serving has 68 calories, 1 g fat, 13g carbohydrate, 3 g protein, 3 g fiber

Parmesan Mashed Potatoes

2 lbs. potatoes, peeled and cut into cubes
2 tsp chicken bouillon granules
4 oz reduced fat cream cheese
½ cup fat free sour cream
3 Tbsp grated Parmesan Cheese

Place potatoes in saucepan and cover with water ½ inch past the top of the potatoes. Add bouillon and bring to a boil. Cook 15 minutes, or until potatoes are very soft. Drain potatoes and put into a large bowl. Add remaining ingredients and blend with a mixer until well blended and mashed.

8 servings, each serving has 138 calories, 3g fat, 23g carbohydrate, 5g protein, 3g fiber

Ultimate Mashed Potatoes

4 cups water
4 tsp chicken bouillon granules
4 large potatoes, peeled and cut into ½" pieces
½ cup fat free half & half
½ cup fat free sour cream
¼ cup chopped fresh chives
2 Tbsp butter
3 slices turkey bacon, cooked and crumbled
¼ tsp black pepper

Heat the water, bouillon, and potatoes in a large saucepan to boiling. Cook for 15-20 minutes or until the potatoes are tender. Reserve ½ cup of broth, then drain.
Mash the potatoes with the remaining ingredients. Add the additional broth, if needed, until desired consistency.

8 servings, each serving has 191 calories, 4g fat, 35g carbohydrate, 5g protein, 3g fiber

Cheese & Veggie Macaroni

This makes a hearty side dish, or can even be used as a main dish.

8 oz macaroni or bow tie pasta
2 cups chopped broccoli
1 red bell pepper, chopped
4 oz mushrooms, sliced
1 tsp dried basil
¼ tsp paprika
1 Tbsp dried parsley
¼ tsp pepper
1 Tbsp Butter Buds
½ tsp chicken bouillon granules
½ cup water
¾ cup skim milk
1 Tbsp flour
½ cup sharp cheddar cheese, shredded
½ cup parmesan cheese, shredded

Cook pasta according to pasta directions. Meanwhile, spray a non-stick skillet with cooking spray. Sauté vegetables until tender-crisp, about 5 minutes. Turn heat to low and keep warm.

In medium saucepan, mix the spices, Butter Buds, bouillon, and water. Heat to boiling. Reduce heat to simmer. Meanwhile, in a small bowl, whisk the milk and the flour. Stir into the simmering saucepan, stirring constantly, and let mixture thicken slightly. Stir in cheeses. Continue stirring until cheese is melted.

Toss hot, drained noodles with vegetables and cheese sauce.

4 servings, each serving has 250 calories, 9g fat, 27g carbohydrate, 16 protein, 4g fiber

Mashed Potatoes Florentine

This is a yummy version of mashed potatoes that requires no gravy and adds spinach to pump up the vitamins & minerals!

2 large potatoes, peeled and cut into cubes
½ cup onion, chopped
1 ½ Tbsp butter
2 cloves garlic, minced
10 oz pkg. chopped spinach, cooked and squeezed dry
6 oz fat free plain yogurt
½ tsp salt
2 Tbsp milk

Boil potatoes in a saucepan of water until soft, about 15-20 minutes. A few minutes before the potatoes are done cooking, put the onion, butter, and garlic in a bowl. Microwave for 1-2 minutes or until onion is soft. Put onion mixture into a bigger bowl and add remaining ingredients. Add hot, drained potatoes. Mix with a mixer on med-high speed until potatoes are mashed, adding additional milk if needed. The mixture will not be smooth, but potatoes should be thoroughly blended.

6 servings, each serving has 149 calories, 3 g fat, 26 g carbohydrate, 6 g protein, 3 g fiber

Tomato Stacks

This is a simple and attractive side dish.

2 large tomatoes, each cut into 6 slices
6 oz part-skim mozzarella cheese, cut into 6 slices
12 Tbsp Fat free Zesty Italian salad dressing
6 thin slices red onion
1 cucumber, peeled and sliced thin
6 fresh basil leaves

Place 6 slices of tomato on 6 small individual salad plates. Drizzle each with 1 Tbsp dressing. Top each with one slice of cheese, onion, cucumber. Top with 2nd tomato slice. Drizzle with another 1 Tbsp dressing and top each with a basil leaf.

6 servings, each serving has 105 calories, 5 g fat, 9 g carbohydrate, 8 g protein, 1 g fiber

Cheesy Broccoli &Corn Bake

1 can (16 oz) cream-style corn
1 egg or ¼ cup egg substitute
2 tsp dried onion flakes
⅓ cup shredded reduced-fat cheddar cheese
3 cups frozen chopped broccoli, thawed
10 Ritz Reduced Fat Crackers, made into crumbs

Preheat oven to 350°. Spray an 8 X 8 inch baking dish with cooking spray. In a large bowl, combine corn, egg, onion flakes, and cheese. Stir in broccoli. Pour mixture into prepared baking dish. Evenly sprinkle cracker crumbs over top. Bake 35-40 minutes. Let rest for 5 minutes.

6 servings, each serving has 116 calories, 2g fat, 21g carbohydrate, 6g protein, 2g fiber

Appetizers

Bell Pepper Skins

These make fresh tasting appetizers or snacks.

2 large green peppers
7 slices turkey bacon
1 cup shredded reduced fat cheddar cheese
2 green onions, thinly sliced
3 Tbsp fat free sour cream

Preheat the oven to 350°. Dice the bacon and cook in a skillet over med-high heat until crispy. Remove from heat, drain if needed, and set aside.

Meanwhile, cut peppers in half and discard the insides. Slice each half into quarters (or smaller if the peppers are very big). Bake peppers, skin side down, on a cookie sheet that has been sprayed with cooking spray for 20 minutes. Remove from oven and blot any moisture away with a paper towel. Top pepper shells with cheese, bacon, and green onions. Turn oven up to broil. Cook peppers until cheese melts and bubbles. Watch them carefully, so they don't burn. Top each with ¼ tsp sour cream. Serve immediately.

4 servings, each serving has 92 calories, 3g fat, 6g carbohydrate, 9g protein, 2g fiber

Buffalo Chicken Dip

This is a great football watching dip! Serve with crackers.

8 oz reduced fat cream cheese
1 cup fat free sour cream
½ cup Louisiana-style hot sauce
3 cups shredded cooked chicken breast

Preheat oven to 350°. In a large bowl, beat the cream cheese, sour cream, and hot sauce together until smooth. Stir in chicken. Transfer to a 8x8 inch baking dish that has been sprayed with cooking spray. Bake for 20 minutes or until heated through. Serve warm.

10 servings, serving size: ¼ cup, each serving has 108 calories, 4 g fat, 5 g carbohydrate, 11 g protein, 0 g fiber

"Though we travel the world over to find beautiful, we must carry it with us, or we find it not."

Ralph Waldo Emerson

Buffalo Chicken "Wings" with Blue Cheese Dip

These make a good appetizer (serve with napkins). You can turn this into a fun dinner with a side of macaroni & cheese, celery & carrot sticks.

Dip
¾ cup fat free mayonnaise
¾ tsp onion powder
½ cup fat free sour cream
1 tsp lemon juice
1 tsp white vinegar
½ cup crumbled blue cheese
2 cloves garlic, minced

"Wings"
4-8 boneless, skinless chicken breast halves, cut into ¾" strips
2 Tbsp butter
2 tsp vinegar
⅔ cup hot pepper sauce (like Louisiana Hot sauce)
Cayenne pepper (optional)

Mix all dip ingredients and chill 2 hour and up to overnight.

Preheat oven to 450°. Spread chicken pieces out on a cookie sheet or broiling pan that has been sprayed with cooking spray. Mix melted butter, vinegar, and hot pepper sauce. Brush butter mixture onto chicken. Bake 20-30 minutes, or until wings are cooked through, turning and basting once during cooking. Sprinkle with cayenne (optional) during the last 5 minutes of cooking if you want them spicier. Serve hot with dip.

4-8 servings, each serving with approx 4 Tbsp Dip has 216 calories, 7g fat, 6g carbohydrate, 30g protein, 0g fiber

Easy Black Bean Salsa Dip

Serve with baked tortilla chips

1 can black beans, rinsed and drained
2 garlic cloves, minced
1 cup salsa

Pour beans into a bowl and lightly mashed. Add garlic and salsa. Stir together. Eat.

8 servings, each serving has 50 calories, 0 g fat, 9g carbohydrate, 3g protein, 3g fiber

Pesto Crostini

This is a super simple & delicious appetizer.

Pesto Sauce
reduced fat cream cheese
1 thin baguette loaf

For each appetizer desired, slice a ¼ " thick piece of baguette bread. Toast carefully under the broiler until lightly toasted. Spread with 1 tsp cream cheese and place ¼ tsp of pesto in the center.

Each appetizer has 35 calories, 1g fat, 4g carbohydrate, 1g protein, 0g fiber

Stuffed Mushrooms

1 package (6 oz.) Chicken flavor stuffing mix
24 large mushrooms
¼ cup butter or margarine
¼ cup red pepper, finely diced
¼ cup green pepper, finely diced
Butter spray *(I Can't Believe it's Not Butter)*

Prepare stuffing mix as directed on package, omitting butter. Remove stems from mushrooms; chop stems. Melt ¼ cup butter in skillet. Add mushroom caps; cook and stir until lightly browned. Arrange in a shallow baking dish. Cook and stir chopped mushroom stems and the peppers in the skillet until tender; stir into prepared stuffing. Spoon stuffing mixture into mushroom caps; spray with butter spray. Place under broiler for about 5 minutes. Serve warm.

Each stuffed mushroom has 91 calories, 4g fat, 5g carbohydrate, 1g protein, 0 g fiber

Pub Fondue

This is a appetizer, but can also double as a unique, light summer dinner by dipping chunks of bread, crackers, salami, and veggies in this easy to make fondue sauce.

1 (11 oz) can cheddar cheese soup, undiluted
¾ cup beer (light or non-alcoholic)
2 cups shredded cheddar cheese
2 tsp mustard
1 tsp Worcestershire sauce

Add the soup and beer to a saucepan; bring mixture to a boil, stirring constantly. Gradually add shredded cheese, mustard, and Worcestershire sauce; stir continuously until cheese melts.

6 servings, each serving contains 194 calories, 14g fat, 6g carbohydrate, 10g protein, 0g fiber

Tuna Pate Dip

No one will ever guess that this quick & tasty dip is made with tuna fish. Serve with vegetables or spread on crackers.

4 oz reduced fat cream cheese
1 can (6 oz) water-packed tuna, drained and flaked
1 tsp dried parsley
½ tsp onion powder
¼ cup jarred roasted red peppers

In a blender or food processor blend all ingredients until smooth.

8 servings, each serving has 58 calories, 3 g fat, 1 g carbohydrate, 7 g protein, 0 g fiber

Basil Boats

16 large fresh basil leaves
2 Roma tomatoes, finely chopped
1 carrot, finely diced
3 oz cojita cheese, crumbled
2 Tbsp fat free Italian salad dressing
2 tsp grated Parmesan cheese

Place basil leaves upside-down on a serving plate. In a bowl, combine tomatoes, carrot, cojita cheese, and salad dressing. Spoon mixture into the center of the leaves. Sprinkle with Parmesan.

Makes 16 appetizers. Each one has 20 calories, 1g fat, 1g carbohydrate, 1g protein, 0g fiber

Australian researchers put two groups on diets; one low-carb, one low fat. Both groups lost the same amount of weight but the low–carb group was depressed, angry, and confused. Why? The brain uses carbs for fuel! Plus carbs stimulate serotonin which greatly helps our mood. So eat the good carbs already! Around 30 grams or so of healthy carbs per meal is just about perfect for most people.

What are "good" carbs? Rice, whole grains, pasta, peas, potatoes, squash... those kinds.

What are the trouble making carbs? Sugar and the derivatives of it. Go easy on these.

Breakfast

Hashbrown Casserole

This is a versatile and easy recipe that works for breakfast, brunch, or dinner! Simply serving toast as a side dish works great for early in the day eating, while canned green beans make a nice side dish for evening. It also nice because you can cook it right after you assemble it, or you can make it ahead of time, cover it, and keep in your fridge until you are ready to bake it!

30 oz frozen hash browns, thawed
1 can cream of mushroom soup
1 can cream of chicken soup
½ cup skim milk
¼ tsp pepper
8 oz shredded reduced-fat sharp cheddar cheese, divided

Preheat oven to 350°. In a large bowl mix all of the ingredients, but only mixing in half of the cheese. Spray a 8X8 square baking dish with cooking spray and fill it with the hashbrown mixture. Press it evenly into the pan. Top with remaining cheese. Bake uncovered for 50-60 minutes or until bubbly on cheese is melted.

6 servings, each serving has 270 calories, 8g fat, 35g carbohydrate, 15g protein, 4g fiber

Egg in a Nest

You can use cookie cutters to make this fun and simple breakfast.

1 slice whole wheat bread (for each serving)
Butter
1 egg or ¼ cup egg substitute (for each serving)

Very lightly spread the butter or margarine on both sides of the bread. Take the cookie cutter and cut a hole in the center of the bread. Remove the cut section and set aside.

Place bread on a pre-heated skillet. Put the cut section to the side of the bread. Carefully crack (or pour) the egg into the hole in the bread slice. Cook until the bottom of the bread is lightly browned. Carefully turn over the bread slice and bread. Place bread slice to a serving plate, and top with the bread cut out.

1 serving using a whole egg contains 189 calories, 12g fat, 12g carbohydrate, 9g protein, 1g fiber
1 serving using egg substitute contains 146 calories, 7g fat, 13g carbohydrate, 8g protein, 1g fiber

Tofu Smoothie

¾ cup water
3 Tbsp frozen orange juice concentrate
1 ice cube
½ cup silken tofu
1 banana

Put everything into a blender until smooth.

1 serving, each serving contains 262 calories, 5g fat, 49g carbohydrate, 11g protein, 4g fiber

Breakfast Queso

This dish won't win any beauty contests but it tastes really good. Plus it's easy to make! Serve it over scrambled eggs with toast or warm tortillas.

1 lb. lean ground breakfast sausage
8 oz reduced fat cream cheese
1 (10 oz) can diced tomatoes and green chilies

Brown the sausage, breaking it up into small pieces as it cooks. Drain if needed. Mash in the cream cheese and pour in the tomatoes. Cook and stir until cheese is melted and mixture is bubbly and well-mixed. Serve over warm scrambled eggs.

6 servings, each serving has 224 calories, 15g fat, 5g carbohydrate, 17g protein, 0g fiber

Date & Nut Topping

This is a great topping for toasted English muffins or bagels

1 cup fat free ricotta cheese
½ cup whipped cream cheese
⅓ cup chopped walnuts
8 pitted dates, chopped
½ tsp ground cinnamon
1 packet Equal or Stevia powder

Stir everything together until thoroughly blended.

12 servings, each serving has 81 calories, 5 g fat, 7g carbohydrate, 3g protein, 1g fiber

Peanut Butter Pancakes

You don't have to use the cottage cheese, but the addition makes the pancakes very moist.

2 cups flour
2 packets stevia powder
1 Tbsp baking powder
2 eggs
⅔ cup reduced fat crunchy peanut butter
2 cups skim milk
1 cup fat free cottage cheese (optional)

Stir together flour, sugar and baking powder in large bowl.

Beat egg with peanut butter in small bowl until blended. Stir in milk and oil. Add all at once to the dry ingredients, beating until blended.

Heat skillet over medium heat or griddle to 375°F. Spray with no-stick cooking spray. Pour by using a ¼ cup measuring cup of batter for each pancake onto skillet. Cook until bubbles break the surface. Turn and brown the other side. Serve with syrup, fresh fruit or powdered sugar.

Makes 18 pancakes.
Each pancake (without cottage cheese) has 119 calories, 4g fat, 16g carbohydrate, 5g protein, 1g fiber
Each pancake (with cottage cheese) has 126 calories, 4g fat, 16g carbohydrate, 7g protein, 1g fiber

Pumpkin Bread

2 cups canned pumpkin
1 ½ cups sugar
1 cup water
1 cup apple sauce
4 eggs
2 tsp baking soda
2 tsp cinnamon
1 tsp salt
1 tsp baking powder
½ tsp nutmeg
¾ tsp ground cloves
3 ½ cups flour

Preheat oven to 350. In a large mixing bowl, combine all ingredients except flour. Beat until well mixed. Slowly add the flour, beating until smooth.

Spray two 9 x 5 inch loaf pans with cooking spray and dust with flour. Evenly divide the batter between the two pans. Bake for 60-70 minutes or until a toothpick inserted in center comes out clean. Cool for 10-15 minutes, then remove from pans.

16 servings, each serving has 207 calories, 2 g fat, 44 g carbohydrate, 5 g protein, 2 g fiber

Desserts

Apple Strudel

1 sheet frozen puff pastry, thawed
1 egg
1 Tbsp water
2 Tbsp granulated sugar substitute
1 Tbsp flour
¼ tsp ground cinnamon
3 medium red apples, peeled, cored and sliced
2 Tbsp raisins

Heat the oven to 375°F. Beat the egg and water in a small bowl with a fork and set aside. Stir the sugar, flour and cinnamon in a medium bowl. Add the apples and raisins and toss to coat.

Unfold the pastry sheet on a lightly floured surface. Roll the pastry sheet into a 16 x 12-inch rectangle. Spoon the apple mixture onto the bottom half of the pastry sheet to within 1 inch of the edge. Roll up like a jelly roll. Place seam-side down onto a baking sheet that has been sprayed with cooking spray. Tuck the ends under or pinch the ends to seal. Brush the pastry with the egg mixture. Cut several slits in the top of the pastry.

Bake for 35 minutes or until golden brown. Let cool on the baking sheet on a wire rack for 20 minutes.

6 servings, each serving has 208 calories, 11 g fat, 24 g carbohydrate, 3 g protein, 1 g fiber

Tropical Cupcakes

2 cups packaged yellow cake mix
20 oz can crushed pineapple, divided
Coconut extract
1 egg white
1 packaged sugar free vanilla pudding snack (3.5 oz cup)
2 oz reduced fat cream cheese, room temperature

Preheat oven to 350°. Drain pineapple, but reserve the juice.

For the frosting, blend together cream cheese, 1/8 tsp coconut extract, and pudding. Fold in ½ cup drained pineapple. Refrigerate until ready to use.

In a large mixing bowl, blend together the cake mix, ½ tsp coconut extract, egg white, remaining pineapple and reserved juice until completely blended. Divide evenly among 12 muffin tins that have been sprayed with cooking spray or lined with baking cups. Bake for 20-25 minutes or until a toothpick inserted in the center comes out clean. Let cupcakes completely cool, then frost. Keep cupcakes refrigerated until ready to eat.

Makes 12 cupcakes, each cupcake has 122 calories, 2 g fat, 23 g carbohydrate, 2 g protein, 1 g fiber

S'More Snack Cake

2 ½ cups reduced-fat graham cracker crumbs (about 15 whole crackers)
⅔ cup flour
2 tsp baking powder
¼ tsp salt
3 egg whites
1 cup skim milk
¼ cup + 2 Tbsp unsweetened applesauce
2 Tbsp olive oil
2 ½ cups miniature marshmallows
¾ cup semisweet chocolate chips

Preheat oven to 350°. In a large bowl, blend the graham cracker crumbs, flour, baking powder, and salt. Stir in the egg whites, milk, applesauce, and olive oil, just until blended. Transfer to a 13 x 9 baking pan coated with cooking spray.

Bake for 12-15 minutes or until a toothpick inserted near the center comes out clean. Sprinkle with marshmallows. Bake 4-6 minutes longer or until marshmallows are softened and lightly toasted. Cool on a wire rack for 10 minutes.

In a microwave, melt chocolate chips; stir until smooth. Drizzle over cake. Cool.

12 servings, each serving has 175 calories, 4 g fat, 31g carbohydrate, 4g protein, 1g fiber

Layered Strawberry Trifle

This is beautiful served in a trifle bowl (a glass bowl), but it tastes just as good layered into a regular bowl, if you don't have one.

1 lb. strawberries, sliced
1 Tbsp sugar
8 oz fat free cream cheese
8 oz reduced fat cream cheese
1 ½ cups skim milk
1 small box fat-free sugar-free instant vanilla pudding mix
8 oz fat free whipped topping, thawed
1 frozen pound cake, thawed and cut into 1 inch cubes
2 Tbsp fat free chocolate syrup

Combine berries and sugar. Stir and set aside.

Beat cream cheese until creamy. Gradually beat in milk. Beat in pudding mix and blend well. Fold in half of the whipped topping. Spoon half of this mixture into the bottom of the bowl. Top with cake, strawberries, and remaining cream cheese mixture. Top with remaining whipped topping and drizzle chocolate over the top.

10 servings, each serving has 297 calories, 14g fat, 42g carbohydrate, 10g protein, 2g fiber

No-Bake Peanut Butter Balls

½ cup reduced-fat creamy peanut butter
2 Tbsp apple juice
1 tsp vanilla extract
⅛ ground cinnamon
½ cup raisins or chopped dried cherries
1 whole low-fat graham cracker (the 4 little squares), crushed
½ cup cornflakes (not crushed)
1 Tbsp powdered sugar (optional)

In a large bowl, mix all ingredients except powdered sugar. Roll into 12 balls and place uncovered in the refrigerator for 1 hour. After they have chilled, roll each ball in powdered sugar to coat, if desired. Store in tightly covered container in refrigerator.

Makes 12 treats. Each one has 80 calories, 3 g fat, 11g carbohydrate, 2g protein, 1g fiber

Eggnog Bread Pudding

2 cups light eggnog
½ cup sugar (or granular sugar substitute)
4 egg whites
1 tsp. Nutmeg
1 tsp. Vanilla
8 slices raisin bread, cubed

Preheat oven to 350°.Mix all ingredients except bread in a large bowl. Fold in bread cubes. Spray a 2 quart baking dish with non-stick cooking spray and pour mixture into prepared pan. Bake for 40-45 minutes or until a knife inserted in the middle comes out clean. Serve warm.

Topping ideas: go topless, syrup, milk, whipped topping, or ice cream.

8 servings, each serving has 190 calories, 3 g fat, 36 g carbohydrate, 6 g protein, 1 g fiber

Strawberry Rhubarb Cream

½ cup chopped fresh rhubarb
2 Tbsp sugar
3 Tbsp water
1 lb sliced fresh strawberries
8 oz fat free whipped topping

In a small saucepan, combine the rhubarb, sugar, and water. Bring to a boil. Reduce heat. Simmer, uncovered, for 10 minutes or until tender. Transfer to a small bowl; cool to room temperature.

Place strawberries and rhubarb mixture into a food processor; cover and process until finely chopped. Fold in whipped cream. Spoon into four dessert dishes. Refrigerate until chilled.

4 servings, each serving has 158 calories, 0g fat, 35g carbohydrate, 1g protein, 2g fiber

Caramel Apple Pudding

4 apples, cut into cubes, skin on
1 pkg fat free, sugar free butterscotch pudding mix
1 (14oz) can of pineapple tidbits, un-drained
1 (8oz) container of fat free whipped topping

Cut apples and place in a mixing bowl. Sprinkle pudding mix over apples. Add pineapple and stir. Fold in whipped topping. Refrigerate for at least 15 minutes.

6 servings, each serving has 167 calories, 0g fat, 40g carbohydrate, 1g protein, 3g fiber

Irish Cream Bundt Cake

This recipe contains alcohol, all of which will not cook off. Therefore, you may want to reserve this cake for adults only or substitute a non-alcoholic version of the liqueur.

Cake
½ cup chopped pecans
1 box yellow cake mix
1 box sugar-free instant vanilla pudding
8 egg whites
¼ cup water
½ cup apple sauce
¾ cup Irish cream liqueur

Glaze
¼ cup butter
½ cup sugar
2 Tbsp water
2 Tbsp Irish cream liqueur

Preheat oven to 325°. Grease and flour a 10 inch Bundt pan. Sprinkle nuts evenly over bottom of pan.

In a large bowl, combine cake mix and pudding mix. Mix in eggs, ¼ cup water, applesauce, and ¾ cup Irish cream liqueur. Beat for 3-5 minutes at high speed. Pour batter 2/3 full in the pan (you may have some extra batter, depending on your pan). Bake for 50- 60 minutes, or until a toothpick inserted into the cake comes out clean.

Cool for 10 minutes in the pan, then invert onto the serving dish. Prick top and sides of cake with a toothpick or fork.

To make the glaze: In a saucepan, combine butter, 2 Tbsp water and sugar. Bring to a boil, reduce heat, and simmer for 3-5 minutes, stirring constantly, until sugar is dissolved. Remove from heat and stir in 2 Tbsp Irish cream. Brush glaze over top and onto sides of cake. Allow to absorb glaze and repeat if desired.

12 servings, each serving has 325 calories, 13g fat, 46g carbohydrate, 4g protein, 1 g fiber

172

Cream of Coconut Cake

1 box yellow cake mix
1¼ cups water
⅓ cup apple sauce
6 egg whites
8 oz container fat free whipped topping
1 cup fat free sour cream
2 ½ cups sweetened flaked coconut
½ cup lite coconut milk

Preheat oven to 350° for shiny metal or glass pans or 325° for dark or non stick pans. Spray two round cake pans with cooking spray and set aside.

Beat cake mix, water, applesauce, and egg whites in a large bowl on low speed for 30 seconds, then on medium speed for 2 minutes, scraping the bowl occasionally. Pour batter evenly into pans.

Bake 8" layers 29- 4 minutes or 9" layers 24-29 minutes or until toothpick inserted in center comes out clean. Cool for 10 minutes before removing from pans, then place on rack to cool completely before frosting.

While cake cools, make frosting by combining the whipped topping, sour cream, and 2 cups coconut.

Toast remaining coconut in the oven (you can use the broiler, but watch it close), until lightly browned. Remove from oven and allow to cool.

Place first layer on serving dish before starting to frost cake. Punch a lot of holes in the cake layer with a toothpick or fork. Drizzle half the coconut milk over this layer. Let sit for a few minutes to absorb. Frost this layer and top with second layer. Punch holes in this top layer as with first layer and drizzle with remaining coconut milk. Frost top and sides. then sprinkle with reserved toasted coconut.

Cake can be served immediately, but seems to get even better when it sits in the refrigerator for a day or two.

12 servings, each serving has 271 calories, 8g fat, 46g carbohydrate, 4g protein, 2g fiber

True generosity doesn't leave you with less; it leaves you with more.

Easiest Fudge Ever

Make no mistake… this is not exactly "healthy" fudge. But the recipe was so easy, I thought I'd share it anyway.

1 can chocolate frosting
12 oz semisweet chocolate chips
½ cups chopped walnuts (or other nuts)
½ cup miniature marshmallows

Line a 9 inch square baking pan with foil and spray with cooking spray. Set aside.

In a microwave, melt frosting and chocolate chips. Stir until smooth. Stir in nuts and let cool for 10 minutes. Stir in marshmallows. Put mixture into prepared dish. Cover and refrigerate until firm.

Using the foil, lift fudge out of the pan. Cut into 1 inch squares. Store in an airtight container in the fridge.

Makes 24 pieces. Each piece has 166 calories, 9 g fat, 22 g carbohydrate, 1g protein, 0 g fiber

Peanut Butter Cream Pie

3 whole low fat graham crackers, crumbled
1 package (8 oz) reduced-fat cream cheese
½ cup reduced-fat creamy peanut butter
1 can (14 ounces) fat-free sweetened condensed milk *(or use my condensed milk recipe to save calories)*
1 tsp vanilla extract
1 carton (8 oz) frozen fat-free whipped topping, thawed
¼ cup sugar-free chocolate syrup
⅓ cup chopped unsalted peanuts

Spray a pie pan lightly with non-stick cooking spray. Evenly spread the graham cracker crumbles in the bottom of the pan. Drizzle with 2 Tablespoons of chocolate syrup. Set aside.

In a large bowl, beat cream cheese, peanut butter, condensed milk, and vanilla until blended. Fold in peanuts & whipped topping. Pour over graham crackers. Drizzle the top with remaining chocolate syrup. Refrigerate for 3-4 hours or until well chilled.

8 servings, each serving using store bought condensed milk contains 358 calories, 14g fat, 46g carbohydrate, 13g protein, 2g fiber
Each serving using home-made sugar-free condensed milk contains 258 calories, 14g fat, 21g carbohydrate, 13g protein, 2g fiber

Pumpkin Pie Pudding   CROCKPOT

1 (15 oz) can pumpkin
1 can evaporated skim milk
½ cup sugar
½ cup baking mix
2 eggs, beaten
1 Tbsp Butter Buds
2 tsp pumpkin pie spice
1 teaspoon vanilla or almond extract
Fat free whipped topping

In a large bowl mix together the first eight ingredients. Transfer to crock pot coated with cooking spray. Cover and cook on low 5-6 hours. Serve in bowls with topped with whipped topping.

6 servings, each serving has 211 calories, 2g fat, 39g carbohydrate, 7g protein, 2g fiber

Coconut Pistachio Ice Cream

2 Cans (15 oz each) unsweetened lite coconut milk
½ cup fructose
¼ tsp coconut extract
1 cup unsweetened coconut shreds or flakes
¼ cup chopped pistachios

Combine coconut milk and fructose, stirring to dissolve the fructose. Stir in remaining ingredients. Chill in freezer, stirring occasionally until hardened, or prepare in an ice cream maker according to the manufacturer's directions.

6 servings, each serving has 243 calories, 16g fat, 21g carbohydrate, 1g protein, 2g fiber

No-Bake Protein Bars

Nonstick cooking spray
1½ cup dry oatmeal
2 scoops chocolate whey protein powder
2 Tbsp. flaxseeds
1 cup nonfat dry powdered milk
¼ cup peanut butter
½ cup water (more or less, depending on the protein powder)
1 tsp vanilla extract
½ cup raisins (other dried fruit may be substituted)

Spray an 8 x 8 inch square baking pan with nonstick cooking spray, set the pan aside.

In a large bowl, combine all ingredients. Press into pan. Put in the fridge for a couple of hours to fir. Cut into 9 bars. Individually wrap and store in fridge.

Makes 9 bars. Each bar has 188 calories, 4g fat, 27g carbohydrate, 13g protein, 2g fiber

Jello Cookies

These colorful and fun little cookies are easy to make.

⅔ cup butter, softened
⅓ cup sugar
½ tsp baking powder
1 pkg (.3oz) sugar free raspberry gelatin mix (or other flavor)
1 egg white
½ tsp vanilla
1¾ cups flour

Preheat oven to 400°. In medium mixing bowl, beat butter and sugar with a mixer until well blended. Mix in baking powder, gelatin, egg white, and vanilla. Gradually mix in flour until blended.

Shape dough into 2 inch balls. Place on ungreased cookie sheet. Flatten slightly with the bottom of a glass.

Bake for 10-12 minutes. Remove from cookie sheet to cooling racks to cool.

16 cookies, each cookie has 134 calories, 8g fat, 15g carbohydrate, 2g protein, 0g fiber

Rhubarb Pie

Pie dough, for double-crust 9-inch pie
1 ½ cups sugar
2 ½ Tbsp cornstarch
¼ tsp ground nutmeg
½ tsp orange extract
¼ cup lemon-lime soda
2 Tbsp butter
4-5 cups rhubarb, sliced

Roll half of pastry to 1/8-inch thickness on a lightly floured surface. Place in a 9-inch pie plate; trim off excess pastry along edges.

Combine sugar, cornstarch and nutmeg in a heavy saucepan, stirring to blend cornstarch well. Stir in orange extract, soda, and butter. Cook over medium-high heat, stirring constantly, until thickened and bubbly. Remove from heat and stir in rhubarb.

Spoon rhubarb mixture into prepared pie shell. Roll remaining pastry to 1/4-inch thickness; cut into 1/2-inch strips. Arrange strips, lattice fashioned, across top of pie. Trim strips even with edges; fold edges under. Place on a cookie sheet lined with foil and bake at 350° for 40 minutes or until crust is brown.

8 servings, each serving has 368 calories, 14g fat, 61g carbohydrate, 1g protein, 1g fiber

Sugar-Free Apple Bread Pudding *SLOW COOKER*

8 slices raisin bread, cubed
2 apples, peeled and sliced
1 cup chopped pecans
4 pkg. stevia powder
1 tsp cinnamon
½ tsp nutmeg
6 egg whites
2 cups fat-free half & half
¼ cup apple juice
1 Tbsp Butter Buds

Spray your slow cooker with cooking spray. Place bread, apples and pecans inside.

In a bowl, combine all remaining ingredients until thoroughly mixed. Pour over bread mixture. Cover and cook on low for 3-4 hours or until a knife inserted near the center comes outs clean.

6 servings, each serving has 320 calories, 16g fat, 36g carbohydrate, 10g protein, 3g fiber

Monster Cookies

2 cups oats
1 large apple, finely diced
¾ cup raisins or currants
1 cup of reduced fat peanut butter
24 whole pecans
¼ cup light butter, melted
½ cup chocolate or carob chips
4 egg whites
1 cup water
15 drops liquid *stevia
*stevia is a calorie free sweetener found in the health food section

Preheat oven to 350°. Combine oats, eggs, water, & butter in a large bowl. Stir in remaining ingredients expect pecans. Using ¼ cup scoop, place onto a cookie sheet that has been sprayed with cooking spray, and form it into a ball (the best you can, the batter is sticky…. Or you can use a ⅓ cup measuring cup to scoop out the batter). Place a pecan on top of each ball. Bake for 10-12 minutes

Makes 24 cookies, serving size: 1 cookie, 176 calories per serving, 9 fat grams per serving

> *"Food, like a loving touch or a glimpse of divine power, has that ability to comfort."*
>
> *~ Norman Kolpas*

Fruit & Nut Pinwheels

These are easy to make little dessert pastries.

1 pre-made rollout pie crust
½ cup raisins
2 oz sliced almonds
⅓ cup reduced sugar orange marmalade
⅛ tsp allspice

Preheat oven to 425°. Make sure pie crust is at room temperature. Roll out pie crust. Spread with orange marmalade to within a ½ inch of the edges. Sprinkle evenly with remaining ingredients. Starting on one end, roll up jelly roll like fashion. Cut off about ½ inch from each end of the role and discard. Slice the remaining roll into 12 equal pieces. Spray a nonstick baking sheet with cooking spray and place slices cut side down on baking sheet. Bake for 20 to 22 minutes or until golden. Remove and let cool.

Make 12 pinwheels. Each pinwheels has 136 calories, 7g fat, 17g carbohydrate, 2g protein, 1g fiber

Apricot Almond Balls

You can save a lot of calories by using the Sugar-Free Sweetened Condensed Milk recipe that can be found in this book instead of using store-bought canned. Just be sure to make it in advance.

2 cups chopped dried apricots
2 cups flaked coconut
1 cup chopped almonds
1 can sweetened condensed milk

In a large bowl, combine all ingredients. Shape into 1" balls. Store covered in the fridge.

Makes 24, serving size: 2
***Using canned sweetened condensed milk** each serving has 243 calories, 9 g fat, 39g carbohydrate, 5 g protein, 3 g fiber*
***Using home-made sugar-free sweetened condensed milk** each serving has 189 calories, 9 g fat, 25g carbohydrate, 6 g protein, 3 g fiber*

"Happiness resides not in possessions and not in gold;
the feeling of happiness dwells in the soul."
~ Democritus

Apple, Pear or Asian Pear Pie

There's no added sugar in this pie, but no one will know! Make your own crust or buy pre-made pie crust in the dairy section (Pillsbury works well).

4 cups peeled cored and sliced pears or apples
½ tsp apple pie spice
2 Tbsp minute tapioca
2 Tbsp olive oil
½ cup Apple juice concentrate
pie crust (2) for bottom and top crust

Preheat oven to 350°. In a large bowl stir together fruit, pie spice, tapioca, olive oil, and concentrate. Let mixture sit for 10 minutes. Pour mixture into the pie shell and top with pie crust. Vent top crust. Bake 60 to 75 minutes or until top crust is golden brown. Remove pie from oven and place on a wire rack to cool. Serve warm or cold.

8 servings, each serving has 321 calories, 18 g fat, 42 g carbohydrate, 1 g protein, 2 g fiber

Mocha Mousse

4 oz. Reduced fat cream cheese
¼ cup granulated sugar substitute
¼ cup unsweetened baking cocoa
1 Tbsp instant coffee granules
⅓ cup skim milk
1 tsp vanilla extract
8 oz fat free whipped topping, thawed

In a large mixing bowl, beat everything but the whipped topping until fairly smooth. Fold in the whipped topping. Divide into 4 serving dishes. Refrigerate for 30 minutes or freeze for a frozen treat (if frozen, let sit on the counter for 10 minutes before serving).

4 servings, each serving has 180 calories, 6 g fat, 25 g carbohydrate, 3 g protein, 2 g fiber

Cherry Cream Pie

1 frozen pie crust
1 can (20 oz) lite cherry pie filling
8 oz reduced fat cream cheese
10 drops liquid stevia
⅛ tsp allspice

Preheat oven to 350°. In a bowl, mix the cream cheese, stevia, allspice, and 1 Tbsp of the cherry pie filling (without cherries) together until well blended. Spread the cream cheese mixture into the bottom of the frozen pie crust. Top with cherry pie filling. Bake for 1 hour or until crust is browned. Cool completely. Store in refrigerator.

8 servings, each serving has 216 calories, 12g fat, 22g carbohydrate, 4g protein, 0g fiber

Misc.

(random recipes to good to leave out)

Tortillas

There are some great low-fat tortillas in the market these days. Still, if you're in the mood for a thick, fluffy, home-made tortilla, there's no substitute. These are a treat at my house, and are often popular all by themselves. Silicon mats & rolling pins make rolling things out a breeze.

4 cups flour
2 tsp salt
2 Tbsp baking powder
5 Tbsp olive oil
1½ cups lukewarm water

Mix dry ingredients in a large bowl. Cut in olive oil using a pastry blender or a fork until mixture is crumbly. Add water and mix well. Dough should be slightly sticky. Divide dough and form into 16 balls. Set on plate. Cover with wax paper and let stand for 20-30 minutes.

Press flat, and roll into a circle with a rolling pin, using flour to keep from sticking if needed. Cook on a med-high heated griddle, turning once. Place on a plate and cover with a clean kitchen towel while continuing to cook the others. Repeat process with remaining tortillas.

Make 16 tortillas. Each tortilla has 151 calories, 5g fat, 24g carbohydrate, 3g protein, 1g fiber

Pesto Sauce

This basic recipe has plenty of room to modify for your personal taste buds. Adjust any ingredient amount to taste. Pesto is great on many things, but is especially good on pasta. I usually make several batches of this because it freezes well.

3 cloves garlic
2 cups basil (densely packed)
¼ tsp salt
¼ cup olive oil
2 Tbsp pine nuts

Put garlic and basil in a food processor and mix until well chopped. Add remaining ingredients and blend again with food processor. Adjust to taste.

Serving sizes vary according to use. The entire recipe has 565 calories, 61g fat, 3g carbohydrate, 4g protein, 2g fiber

Sugar–Free Sweetened Condensed Milk

Use this for recipes that call for sweetened condensed milk. It replaces one regular can.

1 ⅓ cup nonfat powdered milk
½ cup water
½ cup granulated sugar substitute

Combine powdered milk and water in a small bowl. Microwave until hot but not boiling. Stir in sugar replacement. Cover and refrigerate at least 4 hours. Can keep in the fridge for up to 2 weeks.

The entire recipe has 316 calories, ½ g fat, 46 g carbohydrate, 31g protein, 0 g fiber

Turkey Brine

This is a soaking liquid for a turkey, like a marinade of sorts. It helps make a great, moist turkey.

1 gallon of water
2 pkg. Dry onion soup mix
1 Tbsp sage leaves
1 Tbsp Rosemary
1 Tbsp Thyme
¾ tsp ground savory
1 cup sea salt
Ice water

Bring all ingredients, except ice water, to a simmer, until salt dissolves. Remove from heat and add enough ice cubes to cool it down. Pour into a container big enough to submerge your turkey into. Add the turkey to the container, breast side down, making sure that the cavity gets full of brine. Add enough ice water to cover the turkey. Cover and keep chilled until ready to cook the turkey.

When it's time to roast the turkey, remove it from the brine and rinse the turkey off. Season with poultry seasoning, if desired. Cook turkey in a turkey baking bag, if desired. Bake according to cooking instructions (brined turkey usually cooks about 20-30 minutes faster). Alternatively, start baking at 300° for 1 hour, increase temperature to 325° for 30 minutes, then increase temperature to 350° for the duration of the cooking time. Using a pop-up timer is recommended.

Soaking a turkey in a brine mixture can produce a deliciously moist turkey. Give it a try the next time you bake a turkey. It works for baked chicken too.

Got leftover turkey? Dice cooked turkey. Freeze 1 cup portions in freezer bags. Use for recipes that call for cooked chicken or turkey.

Reduced Fat Cooking Substitutions

Simple substitutions can make a big difference in calories per serving. Unless you tell, most people won't even realize that it's a low or no fat version. Note: The recipes in this cookbook have already been modified to produce the best taste with the lowest fat.

Instead of:	Choose:
Whole milk	Skim milk
Evaporated milk, cream, or ½ & ½	Evaporated skim milk or fat free ½ & ½
Mayonnaise	Low fat or fat-free mayonnaise
Sour cream	Fat free sour cream or plain non-fat yogurt
Hamburger	Cook beef, then rinse with hot water in a salad colander before seasoning.
Other meat	Remove skin & trim fat before cooking
Cheese	Reduced fat or use part-skin mozzarella or with a touch or dry mustard or Worcestershire sauce
1 egg	2 egg whites or ¼ cup egg substitute
Butter	Use half
Sour cream	Fat free sour cream or plain non-fat yogurt
Cream cheese	Reduced fat or non-fat cream cheese
Sugar	Most recipes will be fine by simply reducing sugar to half of the "requirement", or substitute part or with stevia or other sugar substitute
1 oz Baker's chocolate	3 Tbsp cocoa powder + 1 Tbsp olive oil
Oil in baked goods	Equivalent amount of applesauce or other pureed fruit

Emergency Substitutions

If you don't have:	Use:
1 Tbsp cornstarch	2 Tbsp flour
1 cup sugar	1 cup packed brown sugar
1 cup honey	1 ¼ cups sugar + ¼ cup liquid
1 cup milk	½ cup evaporated milk + ½ cup water
2 cups tomato sauce	¾ cup tomato paste + 1 cup water
1 cup tomato juice	½ cup tomato sauce + ½ cup water
1 clove garlic	⅛ tsp garlic powder
1 small onion	1 tsp onion powder or 1 Tbsp minced dried onion
1 Tbsp fresh herbs	1 tsp dried herbs
1 tsp dry mustard	1 Tbsp prepared mustard
1 tsp lemon or orange peel	½ tsp lemon or orange extract
2 tsp sea salt	1 tsp table salt
1 tsp baking powder	½ Tbsp cream or tarter plus ¼ tsp baking soda
¼ cup fine dry bread crumbs	¾ cup soft bread crumbs or ¼ cup cracker crumbs

Weights, Measures, & Abbreviations

Tsp or t. = teaspoon
Tbsp or T. = tablespoon
C. = cup
oz = ounce
lb = pound
3 tsp = 1 Tbsp
4 Tbsp = ¼ cup
5 ⅓ Tbsp = ⅓ cup

1 Tbsp = ½ fluid oz
1 cup = 8 fluid oz or ½ pint
2 cups = 1 pint
4 cups or 2 pints = 1 quart
4 quarts = 1 gallon

The Grocery Lists

How to Use the Grocery Lists

Keep in mind that the side dish suggestions and/or accompaniments are not listed, since these items are optional. You may want to peek at the recipe itself ahead of time and see if you want to add these items to your list.

Remember to check your cupboards for what you might already have on hand, and scratch those items off of your list before you go to the store.

It's easy to modify your list. If there is a meal listed that you do not to make. Simply scratch those ingredients off of your shopping list. The name of the recipe is in (quotations) beside the ingredient, so you can easily tell which ingredients to cross off of your list.

Other Tips

Make a photocopy of your grocery list (yes, you have permission), grab a pen, & put in on a clipboard, along with any coupons you might have. You can also just tear the grocery lists right out of the book if you want. Heck, you're about to save so much money on your grocery bill, you'll be able to afford another book!   ☺
If are opposed to tearing out pages of a perfectly good book, you can always print out copies of these grocery lists which are located at The Sensible Cook website on-line at http://www.thesensiblecook.com/Grocery_Lists.html

Keep a little list on your fridge for incidentals as you run out of them. Then when you are ready to go to the store, simply transfer the mini-list to your master list.

Enjoy!

~~~~~~

Dear Copyright People,

These grocery lists may be reproduced to be used by the owner of this book for their grocery shopping bliss.

Sincerely,

Kaylan (Okay, so that's not my real signature, but it's still OK)

Spring Grocery List #1 (does not include side dish suggestions)

*Chicken Bonne Femme * "Fried" Scallops * Marinated London Broil II*
*Ham with Fruit Sauce * Meatballs & Gravy*

Produce
3 medium onions *(Chicken Bonne Femme, Marinated London Broil II, Meatballs & Gravy)*
16 oz sliced mushrooms *(Chicken Bonne Femme, Marinated London Broil II)*
2 medium potatoes *(Chicken Bonne Femme)*
1 red pepper, sliced *(Marinated London Broil II)*
garlic *(Marinated London Broil III)*

Meat, Poultry, & Fish
4 boneless chicken breast halves *(Chicken Bonne Femme)*
1 lb. Sea scallops *("Fried" Scallops)*
1 lb. London broil or sirloin steaks *(Marinated London Broil II)*
1 fully cooked smoked ham slice, 3/4"thick *(Ham with Fruit Sauce)*
1 lb. ground lean turkey or beef *(Meatballs & Gravy)*

Dairy
2 oz buttermilk *("Fried" Scallops)*
2 oz skim milk *(Meatballs & Gravy)*
orange juice (or from frozen section) *(Ham with Fruit Sauce)*
fat-free sour cream *(Meatballs & Gravy)*

Pasta, Rice, & Legumes
12 oz wide egg noodles *(Meatballs & Gravy)*

Baking Aisle
flour *(Chicken Bonne Femme)*
olive oil *(Chicken Bonne Femme, Marinated London Broil II)*
seasoned dry bread crumbs *("Fried" Scallops)*
plain dry bread crumbs *(Meatballs & Gravy)*
Butter flavored non-stick cooking spray *("Fried" Scallops)*
cornstarch *(Marinated London Broil II, Ham with Fruit Sauce)*
red currant jelly *(Ham with Fruit Sauce)*
¼ cup golden or dark raisins (or from bin section) *(Ham with Fruit Sauce)*

Canned
1 (15oz) can quartered artichoke hearts in water (not marinade) *(Marinated London Broil II)*
1 (8oz) can peaches *(Ham with Fruit Sauce)*
1 jar (2.5 oz) sliced mushrooms *(Meatballs & Gravy)*
1 can (15 oz) beef gravy *(Meatballs & Gravy)*

Soups and Packaged Mixes
chicken bouillon granules *(Chicken Bonne Femme, Marinated London Broil II)*

Spices and seasonings
salt
pepper
tarragon *(Chicken Bonne Femme)*
ground thyme *("Fried" Scallops)*
basil *(Marinated London Broil)*
dried parsley *(Meatballs & Gravy)*
dried minced garlic *(Meatballs & Gravy)*

Condiments
red wine vinegar *(Marinated London Broil II)*

Non-Food Items
white wine *(Chicken Bonne Femme)*
red wine *(Marinated London Broil II)*

Spring Grocery List #2 (does not include side dish suggestions)

*Chicken & Cheesy Potatoes * Balsamic Pork Chops * Kielbasa Lime Chili*
*French Dip Roast * Shrimp Linguine*

Produce
lemon juice *(Shrimp Linguine)*
lime juice *(Kielbasa Lime Chili, Shrimp Linguine)*
1 bunch green onions, sliced (optional) *(Kielbasa Lime Chili)*
4 oz fresh snow peas *(Shrimp Linguine)*
1 bunch green onions *(Shrimp Linguine)*
parsley *(Shrimp Linguine)*
garlic *(Shrimp Linguine)*

Meat, Poultry, & Fish
3 boneless chicken breast halves *(Chicken & Cheesy Potatoes)*
4 cooked, smoked pork chops *(Balsamic Pork Chops)*
12 oz turkey kielbasa *(Kielbasa Lime Chili)*
1 rump roast *(French Dip Roast)*
1 lb medium shrimp, shelled and deveined *(Shrimp Linguine)*

Dairy
4 oz reduced fat sharp cheddar cheese *(Chicken & Cheesy Potatoes)*
6 oz skim milk *(Chicken & Cheesy Potatoes)*

Pasta, Rice, & Legumes
8 oz linguine *(Shrimp Linguine)*

Breads and Tortillas
Hoagie rolls (optional) *(French Dip Roast)*

Frozen
1 (16oz) pkg frozen French cut green beans *(Balsamic Pork Chops)*

Canned
2 (15oz) cans chili beans in sauce *(Kielbasa Lime Chili)*

Soups and Packaged Mixes
1 pkg. Julienne potatoes mix *(Chicken & Cheesy Potatoes)*
beef bouillon granules *(French Dip Roast)*

Spices and seasonings
pepper
dried parsley *(Chicken & Cheesy Potatoes)*
ground sage *(Balsamic Pork Chops)*
thyme leaves *(French Dip Roast)*
bay leaves *(French Dip Roast, Shrimp Linguine)*
peppercorns *(French Dip Roast)*
garlic powder *(French Dip Roast)*
basil *(Shrimp Linguine)*
Lemon pepper *(Shrimp Linguine)*

Condiments
balsamic vinegar *(Balsamic Pork Chops)*

Asian
soy sauce *(French Dip Roast)*

Mexican
12 oz salsa *(Kielbasa Lime Chili)*

Non-Food Items
dry white wine *(Shrimp Linguine)*

Spring Grocery List #3 (does not include side dish suggestions)

*Spanish Chicken & Rice * Corned Beef & Cabbage * Costa Rican Beans ** *Gorgonzola and Vegetable Pasta * Spicy Baked Fish*

Produce
4 medium potatoes *(Corned Beef & Cabbage)*
4 medium carrots *(Corned Beef & Cabbage)*
9 small onions *(Corned Beef & Cabbage, Costa Rican Beans)*
3 medium parsnips *(Corned Beef & Cabbage)*
2 medium rutabagas *(Corned Beef & Cabbage)*
1 small cabbage *(Corned Beef & Cabbage)*
1 green pepper *(Costa Rican Beans)*
1 mild chili pepper *(Costa Rican Beans)*
3 large tomatoes *(Costa Rican Beans, Gorgonzola and Vegetable Pasta)*
8 oz spinach *(Gorgonzola and Vegetable Pasta)*
lemon juice *(Gorgonzola and Vegetable Pasta, Spicy Baked Fish)*

Meat, Poultry, & Fish
3 boneless chicken breast halves *(Spanish Chicken & Rice)*
1 (3-4lb) corned beef brisket *(Corned Beef & Cabbage)*
3 oz cooked ham *(deli ham is fine) (Costa Rican Beans)*
1 lb firm boneless whitefish fillets *(Spicy Baked Fish)*

Dairy
Sharp reduced fat cheddar cheese (optional) *(Spanish Chicken & Rice)*
Fat free sour cream (optional) *(Spanish Chicken & Rice)*
4 oz crumbled Gorgonzola cheese *(Gorgonzola and Vegetable Pasta)*
Butter *(Spicy Baked Fish)*

Pasta, Rice, & Legumes
1 pkg. Spanish rice mix *(Spanish Chicken & Rice)*
Rice *(Costa Rican Beans)*
16 oz rotini noodles *(Gorgonzola and Vegetable Pasta)*

Baking Aisle
olive oil *(Gorgonzola and Vegetable Pasta)*
½ cup pine nuts *(these may be cheaper in the bin section) (Gorgonzola and Vegetable Pasta)*

Canned
2 (15oz) cans black beans *(Spanish Chicken & Rice, Costa Rican Beans)*
1 (15oz) can diced tomatoes *(Spanish Chicken & Rice)*

Spices and seasonings
Salt
pepper
rosemary *(Spicy Baked Fish)*
basil *(Spicy Baked Fish)*
cayenne pepper *(Spicy Baked Fish)*
garlic powder *(Spicy Baked Fish)*

Mexican
Salsa (optional) *(Spanish Chicken & Rice)*

Spring Grocery List #4 (does not include side dish suggestions)

*Chicken Cordon Bleu * Stuffed Flank Steak * Sesame Flounder *
Bean and Veggie Burritos * French Onion Meatloaf*

Produce
1 bunch green onions *(Stuffed Flank Steak)*
lemon juice *(Sesame Flounder)*
Lime juice *(Bean and Veggie Burritos)*
1 large red bell pepper *(Bean and Veggie Burritos)*
1 large green bell pepper *(Bean and Veggie Burritos)*
1 medium onion *(Bean and Veggie Burritos)*
1 avocado, sliced *(Bean and Veggie Burritos)*
spinach *(Bean and Veggie Burritos)*
cilantro *(Bean and Veggie Burritos)*

Meat, Poultry, & Fish
4 thin chicken (or turkey) cutlets *(Chicken Cordon Bleu)*
4 slices deli style ham *(Chicken Cordon Bleu)*
1 (1½ -2 lbs) flank steak *(Stuffed Flank Steak)*
4 flounder fillets *(Sesame Flounder)*
1 lb lean ground beef *(French Onion Meatloaf)*

Dairy
4 slices reduced fat Swiss cheese *(Chicken Cordon Bleu)*
Reduced fat cheddar cheese (optional) *(Bean and Veggie Burritos)*
Smallest container low fat buttermilk *(Sesame Flounder)*
skim milk *(French Onion Meatloaf)*

Pasta, Rice, & Legumes
brown rice *(Bean and Veggie Burritos)*

Breads and Tortillas
4 large tortillas *(Bean and Veggie Burritos)*
bread *(French Onion Meatloaf)*

Baking Aisle
honey *(Chicken Cordon Bleu)*
plain dry bread crumbs *(Chicken Cordon Bleu, Sesame Flounder)*
Cooking spray *(Chicken Cordon Bleu)*
olive oil

Canned
1 can (4oz) mushrooms *(Stuffed Flank Steak)*

Soups and Packaged Mixes
1 package (6oz) stuffing mix, any flavor *(Stuffed Flank Steak)*
1 envelope dry brown gravy mix *(Stuffed Flank Steak)*
beef bouillon granules *(Stuffed Flank Steak)*
chicken bouillon granules *(Chicken & Mushroom Pasta)*
Dry French onion soup mix *(French Onion Meatloaf)*

Spices and seasonings
salt
pepper
sesame seeds *(Sesame Flounder)*

Condiments
Dijon mustard *(Chicken Cordon Bleu)*
Ketchup (optional) *(French Onion Meatloaf)*

Asian
soy sauce *(Sesame Flounder)*
sesame oil *(Sesame Flounder)*

Mexican
1 can (16 oz) fat-free refried beans *(Bean and Veggie Burritos)*
Salsa (optional) *(Bean and Veggie Burritos)*

Non-Food Items
Toothpicks *(Chicken Cordon Bleu)*

Spring Grocery List #5 (does not include side dish suggestions)

Garlic Shrimp Pasta Southwestern Steak Salad * Hashbrown Casserole*
*Tortellini Spinach & Tomato Soup * Sour Cream Enchiladas*

Produce

1 bunch green onions *(Sour Cream Enchiladas)*

3 onions *(Garlic Shrimp Pasta, Southwestern Steak Salad, Tortellini Spinach & Tomato Soup)*

garlic *(Garlic Shrimp Pasta, Tortellini Spinach & Tomato Soup)*

2 ears corn (unless getting canned) *(Southwestern Steak Salad)*

1 pint cherry tomatoes *(Southwestern Steak Salad)*

1 avocado *(Southwestern Steak Salad)*

1 lime *(Southwestern Steak Salad)*

Meat, Poultry, & Fish

1½ lbs shrimp *(Garlic Shrimp Pasta)*

1 lb. flank steak *(Southwestern Steak Salad)*

1 lb. Lean ground beef *(Sour Cream Enchiladas)*

Dairy

butter *(Garlic Shrimp Pasta)*

3 oz part-skim mozzarella cheese *(Garlic Shrimp Pasta)*

12 oz reduced-fat sharp cheddar cheese *(Hashbrown Casserole, Sour Cream Enchiladas)*

4 oz Parmesan cheese *(Garlic Shrimp Pasta, Tortellini Spinach & Tomato Soup)*

12 oz skim milk *(Hashbrown Casserole, Sour Cream Enchiladas)*

1 (9oz) pkg. fresh tortellini *(Tortellini Spinach & Tomato Soup)*

8 oz sour cream *(Sour Cream Enchiladas)*

Breads & Tortillas

8 tortillas (8") *(Sour Cream Enchiladas)*

Pasta, Rice, & Legumes

1 lb spaghetti *(Garlic Shrimp Pasta)*

Baking Aisle

olive oil

flour *(Sour Cream Enchiladas)*

Frozen

30 oz frozen hash browns *(Hashbrown Casserole)*

10 oz frozen chopped spinach *(Tortellini Spinach & Tomato Soup)*

Canned

1 (15oz) can diced tomatoes *(Tortellini Spinach & Tomato Soup)*

Soups and Packaged Mixes

1 can cream of mushroom soup *(Hashbrown Casserole)*

1 can cream of chicken soup *(Hashbrown Casserole)*

chicken bouillon granules *(Tortellini Spinach & Tomato Soup, Sour Cream Enchiladas)*

Spices and seasonings

black pepper

salt

sea salt *(Tortellini Spinach & Tomato Soup)*

chili powder *(Sour Cream Enchiladas)*

ground cumin *(Sour Cream Enchiladas)*

onion powder *(Tortellini Spinach & Tomato Soup)*

garlic powder *(Tortellini Spinach & Tomato Soup)*

garlic seasoned salt *(Garlic Shrimp Pasta)*

lemon pepper seasoning *(Garlic Shrimp Pasta)*

paprika *(Garlic Shrimp Pasta)*

Italian seasoning *(Garlic Shrimp Pasta)*

garlic salt *(Garlic Shrimp Pasta)*

chipotle seasoning *(Southwestern Steak Salad)*

Mexican

1 (7oz) can diced green chilies *(Sour Cream Enchiladas)*

Spring Grocery List #6 (does not include side dish suggestions)

*Caraway Chicken * Sweet & Sour Meatballs * Four Cheese Spaghetti*
*Boiled Ham & Veggies * Beef or Chicken Fajitas*

Produce

4 onions *(Caraway Chicken, Sweet & Sour Meatballs, Boiled Ham & Veggies, Beef or Chicken Fajitas)*

fresh dill *(Caraway Chicken)*

6 carrots *(Boiled Ham & Veggies)*

2 large potatoes *(Boiled Ham & Veggies)*

1 small head cabbage *(Boiled Ham & Veggies)*

lemon juice *(Beef or Chicken Fajitas)*

1 green pepper *(Beef or Chicken Fajitas)*

1 red pepper *(Beef or Chicken Fajitas)*

1 Avocado (optional) *(Beef or Chicken Fajitas)*

Meat, Poultry, & Fish

4 thin chicken cutlets *(Caraway Chicken)*

3 oz diced smoked deli ham *(Caraway Chicken)*

1½ lb. lean ground beef *(Sweet & Sour Meatballs)*

16 oz lean ham pieces *(Boiled Ham & Veggies)*

1 ½ lb. lean beef or chicken breasts *(Beef or Chicken Fajitas)*

Dairy

6 oz plain low-fat yogurt *(Caraway Chicken)*

2 oz skim milk *(Sweet & Sour Meatballs)*

eggs *(Sweet & Sour Meatballs)*

butter *(Four Cheese Spaghetti)*

12 oz fat free half & half *(Four Cheese Spaghetti)*

4 oz part-skim mozzarella cheese *(Four Cheese Spaghetti)*

4 oz fontina cheese *(Four Cheese Spaghetti)*

2 oz provolone cheese *(Four Cheese Spaghetti)*

1 oz Parmesan cheese *(Four Cheese Spaghetti)*

Shredded cheddar cheese (optional) *(Beef or Chicken Fajitas)*

Fat free sour cream (optional) *(Beef or Chicken Fajitas)*

Pasta, Rice, & Legumes

8 oz spaghetti *(Four Cheese Spaghetti)*

Breads and Tortillas

Reduced fat saltine crackers *(Sweet & Sour Meatballs)*

8 flour tortillas *(Beef or Chicken Fajitas)*

Baking Aisle

Cooking spray

flour *(Caraway Chicken, Four Cheese Spaghetti)*

rye flour *(Caraway Chicken)*

olive oil

cornstarch *(Sweet & Sour Meatballs)*

brown sugar *(Sweet & Sour Meatballs)*

Canned

1 small can pineapple tidbits (or chunks) *(Sweet & Sour Meatballs)*

1 (15oz) can garbanzo beans (optional) *(Boiled Ham & Veggies)*

Soups and Packaged Mixes

chicken bouillon granules *(Caraway Chicken)*

Spices and seasonings

Salt

Pepper

Zesty seasoned salt *(Boiled Ham & Veggies, Beef or Chicken Fajitas)*

ground cumin *(Beef or Chicken Fajitas)*

caraway seed *(Caraway Chicken)*

ground ginger *(Sweet & Sour Meatballs)*

parsley *(Four Cheese Spaghetti)*

garlic powder *(Four Cheese Spaghetti, Cuban Pork Sandwiches, Beef or Chicken Fajitas)*

chili powder *(Beef or Chicken Fajitas)*

crushed red pepper flakes *(Beef or Chicken Fajitas)*

Condiments

Dijon mustard *(Caraway Chicken)*

vinegar *(Sweet & Sour Meatballs)*

Asian

soy sauce *(Sweet & Sour Meatballs)*

Mexican

Salsa (optional) *(Beef or Chicken Fajitas)*

Spring Grocery List #7 (does not include side dish suggestions)

*White Bean Chicken Soup * Mexican Stuffed Pasta * Chicken Fried Steak * Seared Scallops
* Chinese Pork Chops*

Produce

2 medium onions *(White Bean Chicken Soup, Chinese Pork Chops)*
garlic *(White Bean Chicken Soup, Chinese Pork Chops)*
1 jalapeno pepper *(White Bean Chicken Soup)*
10 oz fresh spinach *(Seared Scallops)*

Meat, Poultry, & Fish

2 boneless chicken breast halves *(White Bean Chicken Soup)*
1 lb lean ground beef *(Mexican Stuffed Pasta)*
1 ½ lb thin lean round steak or cube steak *(Chicken Fried Steak)*
6 boneless pork loin chops (4 oz each) *(Chinese Pork Chops)*
1 lb Sea scallops *(Seared Scallops)*
turkey bacon *(Seared Scallops)*

Dairy

8 oz reduced-fat cheddar cheese *(Mexican Stuffed Pasta, White Bean Chicken Soup)*
Eggs *(Chicken Fried Steak)*
skim milk *(Chicken Fried Steak)*

Pasta, Rice, & Legumes

12 extra-jumbo pasta shells (8 oz) or manicotti shells *(Mexican Stuffed Pasta)*

Breads and Tortillas

saltine crackers *(Chicken Fried Steak)*

Baking Aisle

olive oil *(Chicken Fried Steak, Seared Scallops)*
flour *(Seared Scallops)*
brown sugar *(Chinese Pork Chops)*

Canned

2 cans (15oz *each*) white kidney beans *(White Bean Chicken Soup)*
1 (8oz) can tomato sauce *(Mexican Stuffed Pasta)*

Soups and Packaged Mixes

chicken bouillon granules *(White Bean Chicken Soup)*

Spices and seasonings

salt
pepper
oregano *(White Bean Chicken Soup)*
cumin *(White Bean Chicken Soup)*
ground ginger *(Chinese Pork Chops)*
blackened steak seasoning *(Seared Scallops)*

Condiments

ketchup *(Chinese Pork Chops)*
balsamic vinegar *(Seared Scallops)*

Asian

soy sauce *(Chinese Pork Chops)*

Mexican

8 oz medium salsa *(Mexican Stuffed Pasta)*
1 (4oz) can chopped green chilies *(Mexican Stuffed Pasta)*

Spring Grocery List #8 *(does not include side dish suggestions)*

*Tuna Casserole II * Black Beans & Rice * Pot Au Feu * Herb-Marinated Steak * Baked Beefy Bread*

Produce

4 onions *(Tuna Casserole II, Pot Au Feu, Herb-Marinated Steak, Baked Beefy Bread)*

1 green bell pepper *(Tuna Casserole II)*

2 stalks celery *(Pot Au Feu)*

parsley *(Pot Au Feu, Herb-Marinated Steak, Baked Beefy Bread)*

garlic *(Pot Au Feu, Herb-Marinated Steak)*

4 carrots *(Pot Au Feu)*

4 parsnips *(Pot Au Feu)*

8 oz sliced mushrooms *(Pot Au Feu)*

8 oz fresh spinach *(Pot Au Feu)*

Meat, Poultry, & Fish

1 cut up chicken OR 6 chicken breast halves *(Pot Au Feu)*

1 lb boneless beef chuck shoulder steak, 1" thick *(Herb-Marinated Steak)*

1 lb lean hamburger *(Baked Beefy Bread)*

Dairy

8 oz skim milk *(Tuna Casserole II, Baked Beefy Bread)*

3 oz reduced-fat cheddar cheese *(Tuna Casserole II)*

1 oz Parmesan cheese *(Baked Beefy Bread)*

2 oz Reduced Fat Swiss cheese *(Baked Beefy Bread)*

Eggs *(Baked Beefy Bread)*

Pasta, Rice, & Legumes

elbow macaroni *(Tuna Casserole II)*

rice *(Black Beans & Rice)*

Baking Aisle

reduced fat baking mix (like Bisquick) *(Baked Beefy Bread)*

olive oil

Canned

4 oz can sliced mushrooms *(Tuna Casserole II)*

Small jar chopped pimiento *(Tuna Casserole II)*

1 (6 oz) can white tuna, packed in water *(Tuna Casserole II)*

2 cans (15 oz each) black beans *(Black Beans & Rice)*

Soups and Packaged Mixes

1 can Cream of Celery or Mushroom Soup *(Tuna Casserole II)*

chicken bouillon granules *(Pot Au Feu)*

Spices and seasonings

salt

garlic salt *(Black Beans & Rice)*

1 bay leaf *(Pot Au Feu)*

rosemary *(Pot Au Feu)*

whole cloves *(Pot Au Feu)*

dried thyme leaves *(Herb-Marinated Steak)*

Condiments

hot pepper sauce *(Pot Au Feu, Baked Beefy Bread)*

fat free mayonnaise *(Baked Beefy Bread)*

vinegar *(Herb-Marinated Steak)*

Dijon mustard *(Herb-Marinated Steak)*

Mexican

1 can (4 oz) diced green chilies *(Black Beans & Rice)*

4 oz salsa *(Black Beans & Rice)*

Spring Grocery List #9 (does not include side dish suggestions)

*Snapper Veracruz * Beef Mushroom Dips * Fettuccine with Mushrooms * Spinach Burgers * Chicken Carne Asada Tacos*

Produce
Large Portobello mushrooms (1 for each person) *(Beef Mushroom Dips)*
1 lb fresh white mushrooms *(Fettuccine with Mushrooms)*
green onions *(Fettuccine with Mushrooms)*
2 medium red onions *(Spinach Burgers, Chicken Carne Asada Tacos)*
garlic *(Fettuccine with Mushrooms, Spinach Burgers)*
2 medium tomatoes *(Fettuccine with Mushrooms)*
basil (or use dried) *(Fettuccine with Mushrooms)*
1 avocado *(Chicken Carne Asada Tacos)*
lime juice *(Chicken Carne Asada Tacos)*

Meat, Poultry, & Fish
4 snapper fillets (or other firm white fish) *(Snapper Veracruz)*
Beef Round Roast- any size (each 1 ½ lbs. will serve 4) *(Beef Mushroom Dips)*
20 oz ground turkey *(Spinach Burgers)*
3 boneless chicken breast halves *(Chicken Carne Asada Tacos)*

Dairy
reduced fat ricotta cheese *(Fettuccine with Mushrooms)*
reduced fat feta cheese *(Fettuccine with Mushrooms, Spinach Burgers)*
2 oz orange juice *(Chicken Carne Asada Tacos)*
2 oz Cotija cheese *(Chicken Carne Asada Tacos)*

Pasta, Rice, & Legumes
1 (8-10 oz) pkg. seasoned yellow rice mix *(Snapper Veracruz)*
8 oz fettuccine *(Fettuccine with Mushrooms)*

Breads and Tortillas
Hoagie buns (1 per serving) *(Beef Mushroom Dips)*

Baking Aisle
Non-stick cooking spray
olive oil
sugar *(Chicken Carne Asada Tacos)*

Frozen
10 oz frozen chopped spinach *(Spinach Burgers)*

Canned
1 (14½ oz) can Mexican style diced tomatoes *(Snapper Veracruz)*

Soups and Packaged Mixes
1 box dry mushroom onion soup mix *(Beef Mushroom Dips)*

Spices and seasonings
Salt
pepper
oregano *(Spinach Burgers, Chicken Carne Asada Tacos)*
Steak seasoning (I use Montreal Spicy Steak Seasoning) *(Spinach Burgers)*
ground cumin *(Chicken Carne Asada Tacos)*

Condiments
1 (4 oz) can sliced olives *(Snapper Veracruz)*
hot pepper sauce (optional) *(Snapper Veracruz)*

Mexican
8 corn tortillas *(Chicken Carne Asada Tacos)*

Spring Grocery List #10 (does not include side dish suggestions)

*Hungarian Goulash * Smothered Chicken II * Italian Salad*
*Shrimp & Scallop Teriyaki * Stuffed Taco Burgers*

Produce

2 medium onions *(Hungarian Goulash, Smothered Chicken II)*
16 oz sliced mushrooms *(Smothered Chicken II, Shrimp and Scallop Teriyaki)*
5 Roma tomatoes *(Italian Salad)*
1 large tomato *(Stuffed Taco Burgers)*
1 head iceberg lettuce *(Italian Salad, Stuffed Taco Burgers)*
10 oz romaine lettuce *(Italian Salad)*
12 leaves fresh basil *(Italian Salad)*
garlic *(Italian Salad, Shrimp and Scallop Teriyaki)*
2 bunches green onions *(Italian Salad, Shrimp and Scallop Teriyaki)*
6 oz snow pea pods *(Shrimp and Scallop Teriyaki)*

Meat, Poultry, & Fish

1½ lbs beef top round steak *(Hungarian Goulash)*
4 boneless chicken breast halves *(Smothered Chicken II)*
12 oz turkey breast *(Italian Salad)*
6 oz light salami *(Italian Salad)*
8 oz scallops *(Shrimp and Scallop Teriyaki)*
8 oz medium shrimp *(Shrimp and Scallop Teriyaki)*
1 ½ lbs lean ground beef *(Stuffed Taco Burgers)*

Dairy

fat free sour cream *(Hungarian Goulash)*
6 oz shredded part-skim mozzarella cheese *(Smothered Chicken II, Kitchen Sink Salad)*
4 oz shredded reduced fat sharp cheddar cheese *(Smothered Chicken II, Stuffed Taco Burgers)*
grated Parmesan cheese *(Italian Salad)*

Pasta, Rice, & Legumes

16 oz wide egg noodles *(Hungarian Goulash)*

Breads and Tortillas

6 hamburger buns *(Stuffed Taco Burgers)*

Baking Aisle

flour *(Hungarian Goulash)*
olive oil
cornstarch *(Shrimp and Scallop Teriyaki)*

Canned

1 can (15 oz) diced tomatoes *(Hungarian Goulash)*
1 can (8oz) garbanzo beans *(Italian Salad)*

Soups and Packaged Mixes

1 pkg. taco seasoning mix *(Stuffed Taco Burgers)*

Spices and seasonings

Pepper
Salt
sea salt *(Italian Salad)*
oregano *(Smothered Chicken II, Italian Salad)*
garlic powder *(Smothered Chicken II)*
cayenne pepper *(Smothered Chicken II)*
paprika *(Hungarian Goulash)*
garlic salt *(Hungarian Goulash)*
1 bay leaf *(Hungarian Goulash)*
dried parsley *(Italian Salad)*
ginger *(Shrimp and Scallop Teriyaki)*

Condiments

Dijon Mustard *(Italian Salad)*
red wine vinegar *(Italian Salad)*
dry sherry *(Shrimp and Scallop Teriyaki)*
fat free mayonnaise *(Stuffed Taco Burgers)*

Asian

teriyaki sauce *(Shrimp and Scallop Teriyaki)*

Mexican

salsa *(Stuffed Taco Burgers)*

Spring Grocery List #11 (does not include side dish suggestions)

*Pasta with Spinach & Sausage * Oriental Orange Chicken * Shredded Beef for Tacos*
*Pork, Pear, & Cranberry Salad * Honey Glazed Salmon & Asparagus*

Produce

30 oz spinach *(Pasta with Spinach & Sausage, Pork, Pear, & Cranberry Salad)*

2 onions *(Pasta with Spinach & Sausage, Shredded Beef for Tacos)*

1 bunch green onions *(Oriental Orange Chicken, Pork, Pear, & Cranberry Salad)*

garlic *(Oriental Orange Chicken, Shredded Beef for Tacos, Pork, Pear, & Cranberry Salad)*

2 serrano chilies *(Shredded Beef for Tacos)*

1 pear *(Pork, Pear, & Cranberry Salad)*

1 lb fresh asparagus spears *(Honey Glazed Salmon & Asparagus)*

Meat, Poultry, & Fish

1 lb. Italian sausages *(Pasta with Spinach & Sausage)*

4 boneless chicken breast halves *(Oriental Orange Chicken)*

2-3 lb. Round roast *(Shredded Beef for Tacos)*

1 lb. lean pork tenderloin *(Pork, Pear, & Cranberry Salad)*

4 (4oz) salmon fillets *(Honey Glazed Salmon & Asparagus)*

Dairy

Fat-free half & half *(Pasta with Spinach & Sausage)*

Parmesan cheese (optional) *(Pasta with Spinach & Sausage)*

eggs *(Oriental Orange Chicken)*

Pasta, Rice, & Legumes

16 oz. rotini or other pasta *(Pasta with Spinach & Sausage)*

Juices

cranberry juice cocktail *(Pork, Pear, & Cranberry Salad)*

Condiments

rice wine vinegar *(Oriental Orange Chicken)*

white vinegar *(Oriental Orange Chicken)*

apple cider vinegar *(Pork, Pear, & Cranberry Salad)*

Dijon mustard *(Pork, Pear, & Cranberry Salad, Honey Glazed Salmon & Asparagus)*

Worcestershire sauce *(Honey Glazed Salmon & Asparagus)*

Baking Aisle

cornstarch *(Oriental Orange Chicken)*

flour *(Oriental Orange Chicken, Pork, Pear, & Cranberry Salad)*

Olive oil

sugar *(Oriental Orange Chicken)*

brown sugar *(Pork, Pear, & Cranberry Salad)*

¼ cup dried cranberries *(or check the bin section) (Pork, Pear, & Cranberry Salad)*

½ cup chopped walnuts *(or check the bin section) (Honey Glazed Salmon & Asparagus)*

honey *(Honey Glazed Salmon & Asparagus)*

Soups and Packaged Mixes

chicken bouillon granules *(Pasta with Spinach & Sausage)*

Spices and seasonings

Salt

Pepper

Butter Buds *(Honey Glazed Salmon & Asparagus)*

ground nutmeg *(Pasta with Spinach & Sausage)*

dried minced orange peel *(Oriental Orange Chicken)*

ground ginger *(Oriental Orange Chicken)*

crushed red pepper *(Oriental Orange Chicken)*

dried thyme *(Pork, Pear, & Cranberry Salad)*

Asian

soy sauce *(Oriental Orange Chicken)*

Spring Grocery List #12 (does not include side dish suggestions)

*Cheesy Spaghetti * Southwestern Stir-Fry * Mediterranean Chicken Salad*
*Beef & Cabbage Wraps * Pasta with Broccoli & Tomatoes*

Produce

2 onions *(Southwestern Stir-Fry, Beef & Cabbage Wraps)*

1 green bell pepper *(Southwestern Stir-Fry)*

12 cherry or grape tomatoes *(Southwestern Stir-Fry)*

6 cups spinach *(Mediterranean Chicken Salad)*

2 cucumbers *(Mediterranean Chicken Salad)*

1 bunch green onions *(Mediterranean Chicken Salad)*

1 package shredded cabbage with carrots (coleslaw mix) *(Beef & Cabbage Wraps)*

3 ½ cups broccoli florets *(Pasta with Broccoli & Tomatoes)*

garlic *(Pasta with Broccoli & Tomatoes)*

Meat, Poultry, & Fish

2 boneless chicken breast halves *(Cheesy Spaghetti)*

2 cups cooked chicken breasts *(Mediterranean Chicken Salad)*

1 lb pork tenderloin *(Southwestern Stir-Fry)*

1 lb. lean ground beef *(Beef & Cabbage Wraps)*

Dairy

4 oz light Velteeta Cheese (or similar) *(Cheesy Spaghetti)*

grated Parmesan Cheese *(Cheesy Spaghetti, Pasta with Broccoli & Tomatoes)*

4 oz reduced fat feta cheese *(Mediterranean Chicken Salad)*

Pasta, Rice, & Legumes

12 oz spaghetti *(Cheesy Spaghetti)*

12 oz penne pasta *(Pasta with Broccoli & Tomatoes)*

1 box (6oz) garlic couscous *(Mediterranean Chicken Salad)*

Breads and Tortillas

8 (8 inch) flour tortillas *(Beef & Cabbage Wraps)*

Baking Aisle

cornstarch *(Southwestern Stir-Fry)*

olive oil

sugar *(Pasta with Broccoli & Tomatoes)*

Frozen

10 oz box frozen whole kernel corn *(Beef & Cabbage Wraps)*

Canned

16 oz spaghetti sauce *(Cheesy Spaghetti)*

1 (28 oz) Can crushed tomatoes *(Pasta with Broccoli & Tomatoes)*

1 can (15oz) chickpeas *(Mediterranean Chicken Salad)*

1 jar (6 oz) roasted red peppers *(Mediterranean Chicken Salad)*

Spices and seasonings

Salt

Ground cumin *(Southwestern Stir-Fry)*

garlic powder *(Southwestern Stir-Fry)*

Seasoned salt *(Southwestern Stir-Fry)*

basil *(Pasta with Broccoli & Tomatoes)*

Condiments

dry sherry *(Southwestern Stir-Fry)*

oil & vinegar dressing *(Mediterranean Chicken Salad)*

barbecue or hoisin sauce *(Beef & Cabbage Wraps)*

Asian

sesame oil *(Beef & Cabbage Wraps)*

Non-Food Items

2 oz red wine *(Pasta with Broccoli & Tomatoes)*

Spring Grocery List #13 (does not include side dish suggestions)

*Maple Pecan Pork Chops * Braised Cornish Game Hens * Chicken & Mushroom Pasta*
*Pot Roast & Gravy * Moo Shu Joes*

Produce

1 bunch celery *(Braised Cornish Game Hens)*
2 onions *(Braised Cornish Game Hens, Moo Shu Joes)*
1 lb. Baby carrots *(Braised Cornish Game Hens)*
8 oz sliced mushrooms *(Chicken & Mushroom Pasta)*
garlic *(Chicken & Mushroom Pasta)*
Small piece gingerroot *(Moo Shu Joes)*
1 red pepper *(Moo Shu Joes)*
1 pkg coleslaw mix *(Moo Shu Joes)*

Meat, Poultry, & Fish

4 boneless pork loin chops *(Maple Pecan Pork Chops)*
2 chicken breast halves *(Chicken & Mushroom Pasta)*
Lean Beef Roast (cut of your choice, up to 5 lbs) *(Pot Roast & Gravy)*
1 lb lean ground beef *(Moo Shu Joes)*

Dairy

butter or Smart Squeeze Butter Spread *(Maple Pecan Pork Chops)*
2 oz shredded Parmesan cheese *(Chicken & Mushroom Pasta)*

Pasta, Rice, & Legumes

12 oz fettuccine *(Chicken & Mushroom Pasta)*

Breads and Tortillas

8 small flour tortillas *(Moo Shu Joes)*

Frozen

2 Cornish games hens *(Braised Cornish Game Hens)*

Baking Aisle

⅓ cup chopped pecans (or find in bin section of store) *(Maple Pecan Pork Chops)*
sugar free maple pancake syrup *(Maple Pecan Pork Chops)*
flour *(Braised Cornish Game Hens, Chicken & Mushroom Pasta)*
olive oil
small can evaporated skim milk *(Chicken & Mushroom Pasta)*
cornstarch *(Moo Shu Joes*

Soups and Packaged Mixes

chicken bouillon granules *(Braised Cornish Game Hens)*
1 can Cream of Mushroom Soup *(Pot Roast & Gravy)*
1 package dry onion soup mix *(Pot Roast & Gravy)*

Spices and seasonings

thyme leaves *(Braised Cornish Game Hens)*
garlic powder *(Moo Shu Joes)*

Condiments

cooking sherry *(Braised Cornish Game Hens)*
barbeque sauce *(Moo Shu Joes)*

Asian

hoisin sauce *(Moo Shu Joes)*
soy sauce *(Moo Shu Joes)*

Summer Grocery List #14 (does not include side dish suggestions)

*Spaghetti with Vegetable * Beef & Spicy Rice * Scallops & Spinach*
*Latin Chicken * Grilled Steak Salad*

Produce
2 zucchini *(Spaghetti with Vegetables)*
4 carrots *(Spaghetti with Vegetables)*
Garlic *(Spaghetti with Vegetables)*
1 lemon *(Spaghetti with Vegetables)*
10 oz fresh spinach *(Scallops & Spinach)*
lime juice *(Latin Chicken)*
lemon juice *(Grilled Steak Salad)*
fresh chives *(Grilled Steak Salad)*
6 cups spinach or arugula *(Grilled Steak Salad)*

Spices and seasonings
salt
pepper
chili powder *(Beef & Spicy Rice)*
garlic powder *(Beef & Spicy Rice)*
blackened steak seasoning or Cajun seasoning *(Scallops & Spinach)*
thyme *(Grilled Steak Salad)*

Meat, Poultry, & Fish
1 lb lean ground beef or turkey *(Beef & Spicy Rice)*
1 lb. sea or bay scallops *(Scallops & Spinach)*
turkey bacon *(Scallops & Spinach)*
2 - 8 boneless chicken breast halves *(1 per serving desired) (Latin Chicken)*
1 lb. flank steak *(Grilled Steak Salad)*

Dairy
butter *(Spaghetti with Vegetables)*
Parmesan cheese *(Spaghetti with Vegetables, Grilled Steak Salad)*

Pasta, Rice, & Legumes
16 oz spaghetti *(Spaghetti with Vegetables)*
white rice *(Beef & Spicy Rice)*

Baking Aisle
Olive oil
flour *(Scallops & Spinach)*
honey *(Latin Chicken)*

Canned
1 (8 oz) can tomato sauce *(Beef & Spicy Rice)*

Condiments
balsamic vinegar *(Scallops & Spinach)*
Dijon mustard *(Grilled Steak Salad)*

Asian
soy sauce *(Latin Chicken)*

Mexican
1 (16 oz) jar Salsa *(Beef & Spicy Rice)*
small can chipotle chilies in a adobe sauce *(Latin Chicken)*

Summer Grocery List #15 (does not include side dish suggestions)

*Thai Rice * Ravioli in Garlic Oil * Cream Cheese & Horseradish Burgers1*
*Shrimp Tacos * Tuscan Chicken*

Produce

3 bell peppers (preferably different colors) *(Thai Rice)*
8 oz sliced fresh mushrooms *(Thai Rice)*
4 carrots *(Thai Rice)*
1 bunch green onions *(Thai Rice)*
cilantro *(Thai Rice, Shrimp Tacos)*
lime juice *(Thai Rice)*
parsley *(Ravioli in Garlic Oil)*
garlic *(Ravioli in Garlic Oil)*
bagged coleslaw mix *(Shrimp Tacos)*
1 large avocado *(Shrimp Tacos)*
Optional: lettuce, tomato *(Cream Cheese & Horseradish Burgers)*

Meat, Poultry, & Fish

1 lb. lean ground turkey *(Thai Rice)*
2 lbs. lean ground beef *(Cream Cheese & Horseradish Burgers)*
1 lb. large or extra-large shrimp *(Shrimp Tacos)*
4 boneless chicken breasts *(Tuscan Chicken)*

Dairy

20 oz cheese ravioli *(Ravioli in Garlic Oil)*
3 oz reduced fat cream cheese *(Cream Cheese & Horseradish Burgers)*

Pasta, Rice, & Legumes

white rice (not quick-cooking) *(Thai Rice)*

Breads and Tortillas

8 hamburger buns *(Cream Cheese & Horseradish Burgers)*
4 large flour tortillas *(Shrimp Tacos)*

Baking Aisle

peanut or olive oil *(Thai Rice)*
olive oil

Soups and Packaged Mixes

Chicken bouillon granules *(Thai Rice)*

Spices and seasonings

salt
pepper
crushed red pepper flakes *(Ravioli in Garlic Oil)*
onion powder *(Ravioli in Garlic Oil)*
seasoned salt *(Cream Cheese & Horseradish Burgers)*
chili powder *(Shrimp Tacos)*
Italian seasoning *(Tuscan Chicken)*

Condiments

A-1 type steak sauce *(Cream Cheese & Horseradish Burgers)*
mustard *(Cream Cheese & Horseradish Burgers)*
horseradish *(Cream Cheese & Horseradish Burgers)*
light ranch dressing *(Shrimp Tacos)*
pitted Kalamata olives *(Tuscan Chicken)*

Asian

soy sauce *(Thai Rice)*

Non-Food Items

white wine (or chicken broth) *(Tuscan Chicken)*

Summer Grocery List #16 (does not include side dish suggestions)

*Chicken Chili * BBQ Ground Beef Sandwiches * Grilled Marinated Pork*
*Summer Vegetable Stew * Smoked Salmon Pizza*

Produce

1 green pepper *(Chicken Chili)*

2 onions *(Chicken Chili, Summer Vegetable Stew)*

1 small eggplant *(Summer Vegetable Stew)*

1 zucchini *(Summer Vegetable Stew)*

1 red bell pepper *(Summer Vegetable Stew)*

1 cup fresh basil leaves *(Summer Vegetable Stew)*

lemon juice *(Grilled Marinated Pork)*

garlic *(Summer Vegetable Stew)*

2 Roma tomatoes *(Smoked Salmon Pizza)*

Meat, Poultry, & Fish

8 oz ground chicken or turkey *(Chicken Chili)*

1 lb. lean ground beef *(BBQ Ground Beef Sandwiches)*

4 pork chops or pork steaks *(Grilled Marinated Pork)*

1 package (3 oz) smoked cooked salmon *(Smoked Salmon Pizza)*

Dairy

2 oz crumbled reduced-fat feta cheese *(Smoked Salmon Pizza)*

4 slices provolone cheese *(Smoked Salmon Pizza)*

Breads and Tortillas

4 hamburger buns *(BBQ Ground Beef Sandwiches)*

1 pre-baked Italian bread shell pizza crust (like Boboli Bread) *(Smoked Salmon Pizza)*

Baking Aisle

olive oil

Canned

1 (4 oz) can mushrooms *(Chicken Chili)*

1 small can tomato paste *(Chicken Chili)*

2 (15 oz) cans diced tomatoes *(Chicken Chili, Summer Vegetable Stew)*

1 (15 oz) can red kidney beans *(Chicken Chili)*

1 small can V-8 juice *(Grilled Marinated Pork)*

Spices and seasonings

Pepper

salt

sea salt *(Chicken Chili)*

chili powder *(Chicken Chili)*

oregano *(Chicken Chili)*

basil *(Chicken Chili, Grilled Marinated Pork)*

dried minced onion *(Grilled Marinated Pork)*

dried parsley *(Grilled Marinated Pork)*

garlic powder *(Grilled Marinated Pork)*

marjoram *(Grilled Marinated Pork)*

thyme *(Grilled Marinated Pork, Summer Vegetable Stew)*

rosemary *(Grilled Marinated Pork)*

Condiments

BBQ sauce *(BBQ Ground Beef Sandwiches)*

ketchup *(BBQ Ground Beef Sandwiches)*

hot pepper sauce *(Grilled Marinated Pork)*

white vinegar *(Grilled Marinated Pork)*

reduced-fat ranch salad dressing *(Smoked Salmon Pizza)*

Non-Food Items

1 large resealable plastic bag *(Grilled Marinated Pork)*

Summer Grocery List #17 (does not include side dish suggestions)

*Rosemary Turkey Burgers * Pasta with Jalapeno Spinach Pesto*
*Greek Shrimp & Beans * BBQ Fajitas * Southwestern Pork Chops*

Produce

8 oz grape tomatoes *(Greek Shrimp & Beans)*

8 oz fresh green beans *(Greek Shrimp & Beans)*

1 jalapeno pepper *(Pasta w/Jalapeno Spinach Pesto)*

2 green peppers *(BBQ Fajitas, Southwestern Pork Chops)*

1 red pepper *(BBQ Fajitas)*

2 onions *(BBQ Fajitas, Southwestern Pork Chops)*

9 oz baby spinach *(Rosemary Turkey Burgers, Pasta w/Jalapeno Spinach Pesto)*

garlic *(Rosemary Turkey Burgers, Greek Shrimp & Beans, Pasta w/Jalapeno Spinach Pesto)*

Pasta, Rice, & Legumes

1 lb. pasta, any kind *(Pasta w/Jalapeno Spinach Pesto)*

rice *(Southwestern Pork Chops)*

Meat, Poultry, & Fish

1 ½ lb ground turkey *(Rosemary Turkey Burgers)*

1 lb shrimp *(Greek Shrimp & Beans)*

2 boneless chicken breast halves *(BBQ Fajitas)*

4 pork chops, ¾ -1" thick *(Southwestern Pork Chops)*

Dairy

1 oz reduced fat feta cheese *(Greek Shrimp & Beans)*

8 oz shredded Parmesan cheese *(Pasta w/Jalapeno Spinach Pesto)*

4 oz cojita cheese *(BBQ Fajitas)*

Fat free sour cream *(BBQ Fajitas, Southwestern Pork Chops)*

Breads and Tortillas

6 burger buns *(Rosemary Turkey Burgers)*

8 (8 inch) flour tortillas *(BBQ Fajitas)*

Baking Aisle

Cooking spray

olive oil

1 cup chopped walnuts *(Pasta w/Jalapeno Spinach Pesto)*

Canned

1 can (15 oz) cannellini beans *(Greek Shrimp & Beans)*

1 can (14 oz) stewed tomatoes *(Southwestern Pork Chops)*

Soups and Packaged Mixes

dry enchilada mix *(Southwestern Pork Chops)*

Spices and seasonings

Salt

Pepper

dried rosemary leaves *(Rosemary Turkey Burgers)*

oregano *(Greek Shrimp & Beans)*

dried lemon peel *(Greek Shrimp & Beans)*

Condiments

light mayonnaise *(Rosemary Turkey Burgers)*

¼ cup Kalamata olives *(Greek Shrimp & Beans)*

BBQ sauce (spicy is good, but any will work) *(BBQ Fajitas)*

1 can (4 oz) sliced black olives *(Southwestern Pork Chops)*

Mexican

1 can (4 oz) green chilies, chopped *(Southwestern Pork Chops)*

Non-Food Items

Aluminum foil *(Greek Shrimp & Beans)*

9x13 disposable foil pan *(BBQ Fajitas)*

Summer Grocery List #18 (does not include side dish suggestions)

*Mexi Mac * Shrimp Pasta Primavera * Kielbasa & Roasted Vegetables*
*Smothered Chicken * Grilled Polenta & Steak*

Produce

1 green pepper *(Mexi Mac)*
1 red pepper *(Shrimp Pasta Primavera)*
2 onions *(Kielbasa & Roasted Vegetables, Shrimp Pasta Primavera)*
8 carrots *(Kielbasa & Roasted Vegetables, Shrimp Pasta Primavera)*
4 potatoes *(Kielbasa & Roasted Vegetables)*
Garlic *(Shrimp Pasta Primavera)*
½ cup snow peas *(Shrimp Pasta Primavera)*
lemon juice *(Shrimp Pasta Primavera)*
10 oz fresh spinach *(Smothered Chicken)*
8 oz sliced fresh mushrooms *(Smothered Chicken)*
1 bunch green onions *(Smothered Chicken)*
1 large ripe avocado *(Grilled Polenta & Steak)*
cilantro *(Grilled Polenta & Steak)*

Meat, Poultry, & Fish

1 lb. lean ground beef *(Mexi Mac)*
12 oz shrimp *(Shrimp Pasta Primavera)*
1 (14oz) turkey kielbasa *(Kielbasa & Roasted Vegetables)*
4 boneless skinless chicken breast halves *(Smothered Chicken)*
1 lb. flank steak *(Grilled Polenta & Steak)*

Dairy

4 oz fat free sour cream *(Kielbasa & Roasted Vegetables)*
2 slices reduced-fat provolone cheese *(Smothered Chicken)*
2 oz cotija cheese *(look for it by the salsa)* *(Grilled Polenta & Steak)*

Pasta, Rice, & Legumes

8 oz medium shell pasta (or other) *(Shrimp Pasta Primavera)*

Grains

1 tube plain polenta *(Grilled Polenta & Steak)*

Baking Aisle

olive oil
cornstarch *(Shrimp Pasta Primavera)*
2 Tbsp chopped pecans *(Smothered Chicken)*

Frozen

10 oz frozen corn *(Mexi Mac)*

Soups and Boxed Mixes

1 box (14 oz) Deluxe macaroni & cheese dinner *(Mexi Mac)*
chicken bouillon granules *(Shrimp Pasta Primavera)*

Spices and seasonings

salt
pepper
sea salt *(Grilled Polenta & Steak)*
garlic salt *(Shrimp Pasta Primavera)*
dried basil *(Shrimp Pasta Primavera)*
crushed red pepper *(Shrimp Pasta Primavera)*
rotisserie chicken seasoning *(Smothered Chicken)*
ground cumin *(Grilled Polenta & Steak)*
chipotle chili powder *(Grilled Polenta & Steak)*

Condiments

Dijon mustard *(Kielbasa & Roasted Vegetables)*

Mexican

8 oz salsa *(Mexi Mac, Grilled Polenta & Steak)*

Summer Grocery List #19 (does not include side dish suggestions)

*Italian Pork Chops * Steak & Lime Pasta * Tuna & Spinach Salad*
*Turkey Pecan Enchiladas * Chicken & Vegetable Stir-Fry*

Produce

garlic

2 green peppers *(Italian Pork Chops, Steak & Lime Pasta)*

lime juice *(Steak & Lime Pasta)*

lemon juice *(Tuna & Spinach Salad)*

6 oz grape or cherry tomatoes *(Tuna & Spinach Salad)*

1 small red onion *(Tuna & Spinach Salad)*

1 medium onion *(Turkey Pecan Enchiladas)*

8 oz fresh spinach *(Tuna & Spinach Salad)*

1 bunch green onions *(Steak & Lime Pasta, Chicken & Vegetable Stir-Fry)*

cilantro leaves *(Steak & Lime Pasta)*

4 cups broccoli *(Chicken & Vegetable Stir-Fry)*

4 oz mushrooms *(Chicken & Vegetable Stir-Fry)*

4 carrots *(Chicken & Vegetable Stir-Fry)*

4 stalks celery *(Chicken & Vegetable Stir-Fry)*

Meat, Poultry, & Fish

6 pork chops, ½ " thick *(Italian Pork Chops)*

1½ lbs boneless beef top sirloin steak *(Steak & Lime Pasta)*

4 cups cubed cooked turkey breast *(Turkey Pecan Enchiladas)*

2 boneless chicken breast halves *(Chicken & Vegetable Stir-Fry)*

Dairy

6 slices part-skim mozzarella cheese *(Italian Pork Chops)*

Parmesan cheese *(Italian Pork Chop, Tuna & Spinach Salad)*

3 oz reduced-fat cheddar cheese *(Turkey Pecan Enchiladas)*

8 oz fat free sour cream *(Turkey Pecan Enchiladas)*

8 oz skim milk *(Turkey Pecan Enchiladas)*

8 oz reduced-fat cream cheese *(Turkey Pecan Enchiladas)*

Pasta, Rice, & Legumes

rice *(Italian Pork Chops)*

16 oz Rotini or other medium pasta *(Steak & Lime Pasta)*

Breads and Tortillas

8 (8 inch) flour tortillas *(Turkey Pecan Enchiladas)*

Baking Aisle

1 oz chopped pecans *(Turkey Pecan Enchiladas)*

cornstarch *(Chicken & Vegetable Stir-Fry)*

Frozen

10 oz frozen corn *(Steak & Lime Pasta)*

Canned

1 (15oz) can tomato sauce *(Italian Pork Chops)*

1 (15oz) can diced tomatoes w/green chilies *(Steak & Lime Pasta)*

1 (15oz) can black beans *(Steak & Lime Pasta)*

1 (15oz) can cannellini beans *(Tuna & Spinach Salad)*

12 oz can solid tuna (packed in water) *(Tuna & Spinach Salad)*

Soups and Packaged Mixes

1 can (14 oz) Vegetable broth *(Chicken & Vegetable Stir-Fry)*

1 can cream of chicken soup *(Turkey Pecan Enchiladas)*

Spices and seasonings

pepper

sea salt *(Tuna & Spinach Salad)*

basil *(Italian Pork Chops)*

ground cumin *(Steak & Lime Pasta, Turkey Pecan Enchiladas)*

ground ginger *(Chicken & Vegetable Stir-Fry)*

Condiments

Dijon mustard *(Tuna & Spinach Salad)*

Asian

soy sauce *(Chicken & Vegetable Stir-Fry)*

Mexican

4 oz can chopped green chilies *(Turkey Pecan Enchiladas)*

Summer Grocery List #20 (does not include side dish suggestions)

*Pierogies & Cabbage * Creamy Mushroom Steaks * Cream Cheese Chipotle Burgers*
*Scallops Bonne Femme * Pepperoni & Cheese Sandwiches*

Produce
1 small head of cabbage *(Pierogies & Cabbage)*
lettuce *(Cream Cheese Chipotle Burgers)*
1 tomato *(Cream Cheese Chipotle Burgers)*
8 oz fresh mushrooms *(Creamy Mushroom Steaks, Scallops Bonne Femme)*
1 onion *(Creamy Mushroom Steaks, Scallops Bonne Femme)*
1 Tbsp lemon juice *(Scallops Bonne Femme)*
parsley *(Scallops Bonne Femme)*

Meat, Poultry, & Fish
4 small beef top sirloin steaks *(Creamy Mushroom Steaks)*
1 lb. lean ground beef *(Cream Cheese Chipotle Burgers)*
1 lb sea scallops (or bay scallops) *(Scallops Bonne Femme)*
1 package Turkey pepperoni *(Pepperoni & Cheese Sandwiches)*

Dairy
butter or margarine *(Creamy Mushroom Steaks, Scallops Bonne Femme)*
light margarine *(Pepperoni & Cheese Sandwiches)*
20 oz fat free half & half *(Creamy Mushroom Steaks, Scallops Bonne Femme)*
4 oz reduced fat cream cheese *(Cream Cheese Chipotle Burgers)*
Parmesan Cheese (optional) *(Scallops Bonne Femme)*
Block part-skim mozzarella cheese *(Pepperoni & Cheese Sandwiches)*

Breads and Tortillas
4 hamburger buns *(Cream Cheese Chipotle Burgers)*
sandwich bread *(Pepperoni & Cheese Sandwiches)*

Baking Aisle
flour *(Creamy Mushroom Steaks, Scallops Bonne Femme)*

Frozen
32 oz Potato & Cheddar Pierogies *(Pierogies & Cabbage)*

Canned
1 can (15oz) diced tomatoes *(Pierogies & Cabbage)*

Spices and seasonings
Pepper
salt
garlic salt *(Cream Cheese Chipotle Burgers)*
chipolte chili powder *(Cream Cheese Chipotle Burgers)*

Asian
soy sauce *(Creamy Mushroom Steaks)*

Mexican
Small can chipolte chili peppers in adobe sauce *(Cream Cheese Chipotle Burgers)*

Non-Food Items
dry white wine *(Scallops Bonne Femme)*

Summer Grocery List #21 (does not include side dish suggestions)

*Enchilada Bake * Pasta with No-Cook Sauce * Turkey Chili * Tai Pot Rice * Salmon w/Lime Butter*

Produce

2 onions *(Enchilada Bake, Turkey Chili)*

garlic *(Enchilada Bake, Turkey Chili, Thai Pot Rice)*

5-6 mushrooms *(Enchilada Bake)*

2 green peppers *(Enchilada Bake, Thai Pot Rice)*

1 red pepper *(Turkey Chili)*

1 cup celery *(Pasta with No-Cook Sauce)*

7 large Roma tomatoes *(Pasta with No-Cook Sauce)*

fresh basil *(Pasta with No-Cook Sauce)*

lemon juice *(Pasta with No-Cook Sauce)*

lime juice *(Salmon with Lime Butter)*

1 bunch green onions *(Thai Pot Rice)*

Meat, Poultry, & Fish

1 lb. Ground turkey *(Turkey Chili)*

1 lb. shrimp **or** 1 lb. boneless chicken breasts *(Thai Pot Rice)*

1 ½ lbs salmon fillet *(Salmon with Lime Butter)*

Dairy

5 oz part-skim Mozzarella cheese *(Enchilada Bake, Pasta with No-Cook Sauce)*

4 oz fat free ricotta cheese *(Enchilada Bake)*

6 oz fat free plain yogurt *(Enchilada Bake)*

butter *(Salmon with Lime Butter)*

Pasta, Rice, & Legumes

16 oz elbow macaroni or other medium pasta *(Pasta with No-Cook Sauce)*

rice *(Thai Pot Rice)*

Breads and Tortillas

8 (8 inch) wheat flour tortillas *(Enchilada Bake)*

Baking Aisle

olive oil

⅓ cup peanuts *(Thai Pot Rice)*

Frozen

1 box frozen peas *(Thai Pot Rice)*

Canned

1 (15oz) can beans (pinto or kidney beans) *(Enchilada Bake)*

1 (15 oz) can red kidney beans *(Turkey Chili)*

1 (15 oz) can black beans *(Turkey Chili)*

1 (15oz) can stewed tomatoes *(Enchilada Bake)*

1 (15 oz) can tomato sauce *(Turkey Chili)*

1 can (15oz) artichoke hearts packed in water *(Pasta with No-Cook Sauce)*

1 can (20 oz) pineapple chunks *(Thai Pot Rice)*

Soups and Packaged Mixes

chicken bouillon granules *(Turkey Chili)*

Spices and seasonings

salt

pepper

ground ginger *(Thai Pot Rice)*

Sea salt *(Turkey Chili, Salmon with Lime Butter)*

Red chili flakes *(Turkey Chili)*

chili powder *(Enchilada Bake, Turkey Chili)*

Cumin *(Enchilada Bake, Turkey Chili)*

oregano *(Turkey Chili)*

Condiments

1 can (2 oz) sliced black olives *(Enchilada Bake)*

Dijon mustard *(Pasta with No-Cook Sauce)*

Asian

soy sauce *(Thai Pot Rice)*

Non-Food Items

dry red wine *(Enchilada Bake)*

Summer Grocery List #22 (does not include side dish suggestions)

*Tomato & Cheese Spaghetti * Chicken & Corn Quesadillas * Sesame Beef * Crab Enchiladas * Grilled Ham*

Produce
6 med tomatoes *(Tomato & Cheese Spaghetti)*
basil *(Tomato & Cheese Spaghetti)*
garlic *(Tomato & Cheese Spaghetti, Chicken & Corn Quesadillas, Sesame Beef)*
cilantro *(Chicken & Corn Quesadillas, Crab Enchiladas)*
lime juice *(Chicken & Corn Quesadillas)*
1 bunch green onions *(Sesame Beef)*
1 onion *(Crab Enchiladas)*

Meat, Poultry, & Fish
4 boneless chicken breast halves *(Chicken & Corn Quesadillas)*
1 lb. boneless sirloin steak *(Sesame Beef)*
8 oz real or imitation crab meat *(Crab Enchiladas)*
1 fully cooked ham (choose the size according to how many servings you want) *(Grilled Ham)*

Dairy
12 oz part-skim mozzarella cheese *(Tomato & Cheese Spaghetti)*
2 oz queso fresco cheese *(Chicken & Corn Quesadillas)*
4 oz Monterey Jack cheese *(Crab Enchiladas)*
8 oz skim milk *(Crab Enchiladas)*

Pasta, Rice, & Legumes
16 oz spaghetti *(Tomato & Cheese Spaghetti)*

Breads and Tortillas
4 (10 inch) flour tortillas *(Chicken & Corn Quesadillas)*
8 small flour tortillas *(Crab Enchiladas)*

Baking Aisle
olive oil
sugar *(Sesame Beef)*

Frozen
fresh or frozen corn kernels *(Chicken & Corn Quesadillas)*
1 (10 oz) pkg. chopped spinach *(Crab Enchiladas)*

Soups and Packaged Mixes
1 (10¾ oz) can cream of mushroom soup *(Crab Enchiladas)*

Spices and seasonings
salt
pepper
chili powder *(Chicken & Corn Quesadillas)*
ground cumin *(Chicken & Corn Quesadillas)*
sesame seeds *(Sesame Beef)*
ground nutmeg *(Crab Enchiladas)*

Condiments
1 can (2 oz) sliced black olives *(Tomato & Cheese Spaghetti)*
balsamic vinegar *(Tomato & Cheese Spaghetti)*
hot pepper sauce (like Tabasco) *(Crab Enchiladas)*

Asian
soy sauce *(Sesame Beef)*
sweet chili sauce *(Grilled Ham)*

Mexican
8 oz salsa *(Chicken & Corn Quesadillas)*

Side Dish Suggestions
garlic bread *(Tomato & Cheese Spaghetti)*
green salad *(Chicken & Corn Quesadillas)*
brown rice *(Sesame Beef)*
yellow rice *(Crab Enchiladas)*
Yams *(Grilled Ham)*

Summer Grocery List #23 (does not include side dish suggestions)

*Pepperoni Pizza Potatoes * Carne Asada Tacos * Eggplant Pasta*
*Tuscan Chicken II * Balsamic Glazed Salmon*

Produce
4 medium baking potatoes *(Pepperoni Pizza Potatoes)*
lime juice *(Carne Asada Tacos)*
4 Roma tomatoes *(Carne Asada Tacos)*
4 tomatoes *(Eggplant Pasta)*
1 jalapeno pepper *(Carne Asada Tacos)*
garlic *(Carne Asada Tacos, Eggplant Pasta, Tuscan Chicken II, Balsamic Glazed Salmon)*
1 bunch green onions *(Carne Asada Tacos)*
cilantro *(Carne Asada Tacos)*
Shredded lettuce *(Carne Asada Tacos)*
2 small onions *(Eggplant Pasta, Tuscan Chicken II)*
1 red pepper *(Eggplant Pasta)*
1 eggplant *(Eggplant Pasta)*
chives *(Balsamic Glazed Salmon)*

Meat, Poultry, & Fish
15 slices turkey pepperoni *(Pepperoni Pizza Potatoes)*
2 lbs. flank steak or thin round steaks *(Carne Asada Tacos)*
4 boneless chicken breast halves *(Tuscan Chicken II)*
1-3 lb. salmon fillet *(4 oz = 1 serving) (Balsamic Glazed Salmon)*

Dairy
fat free ricotta cheese *(Pepperoni Pizza Potatoes)*
2 oz part-skim mozzarella cheese, divided *(Pepperoni Pizza Potatoes)*

Pasta, Rice, & Legumes
16 oz spaghetti *(Eggplant Pasta)*

Breads and Tortillas
Corn or flour tortillas *(Carne Asada Tacos)*

Baking Aisle
olive oil

Canned
1 can (16 oz) tomato sauce *(Pepperoni Pizza Potatoes)*
1 (15 oz) can diced tomatoes *(Tuscan Chicken II)*

Soups and Packaged Mixes
chicken bouillon granules *(Eggplant Pasta)*

Spices and seasonings
Salt
Pepper
sea salt *(Balsamic Glazed Salmon)*
garlic powder *(Pepperoni Pizza Potatoes, Carne Asada Tacos)*
oregano *(Pepperoni Pizza Potatoes, Carne Asada Tacos, Tuscan Chicken II)*
red pepper flakes *(Carne Asada Tacos)*
parsley *(Tuscan Chicken II)*

Condiments
capers *(Eggplant Pasta)*
balsamic vinegar *(Eggplant Pasta, Balsamic Glazed Salmon)*
¼ cup pitted kalamata olives *(Tuscan Chicken II)*
Dijon mustard *(Balsamic Glazed Salmon)*

Non-Food Items
white wine *(Tuscan Chicken II)*

Summer Grocery List #24 (does not include side dish suggestions)

*Pasta with Tomatoes & Asparagus * BBQ Salisbury Steak * Greek Shrimp*
*Mexican Chicken & Beans * Marinated Pork Chops*

Produce
1 bunch asparagus *(Pasta with Tomatoes & Asparagus)*
garlic *(Pasta with Tomatoes & Asparagus, Greek Shrimp, Marinated Pork Chops)*
1 pint cherry or grape tomatoes *(Pasta with Tomatoes & Asparagus)*
lemon juice *(Pasta with Tomatoes & Asparagus)*
lime juice *(Marinated Pork Chops)*
15 fresh basil leaves *(Pasta with Tomatoes & Asparagus)*
1 small onion *(BBQ Salisbury Steak)*
8 oz mushrooms *(BBQ Salisbury Steak)*

Meat, Poultry, & Fish
1 ½ lb. lean ground beef *(BBQ Salisbury Steak)*
1 lb. shrimp *(Greek Shrimp)*
3 boneless chicken breast halves *(Mexican Chicken & Beans)*
6 boneless pork loin chops or steaks *(Marinated Pork Chops)*

Dairy
4 oz smoked Gouda cheese (or Swiss cheese) *(Pasta with Tomatoes & Asparagus)*
reduced-fat feta cheese *(Greek Shrimp)*
4 oz reduced fat cream cheese (optional) *(Mexican Chicken & Beans)*

Pasta, Rice, & Legumes
16 oz penne pasta *(Pasta with Tomatoes & Asparagus)*

Baking Aisle
olive oil
¼ cup pine nuts *(Greek Shrimp)*
sugar *(Marinated Pork Chops)*

Canned
2 (15 oz) cans diced tomatoes *(Greek Shrimp, Mexican Chicken & Beans)*
2 (15 oz) cans black beans *(Mexican Chicken & Beans)*
1 (15 oz) can corn *(Mexican Chicken & Beans)*

Soups and Packaged Mixes
1 (6 oz) pkg. stuffing mix for chicken *(BBQ Salisbury Steak)*

Spices and seasonings
Salt
pepper
oregano *(Greek Shrimp)*
ground cumin *(Mexican Chicken & Beans)*
chili powder *(Mexican Chicken & Beans)*
garlic salt *(Mexican Chicken & Beans)*
paprika *(Marinated Pork Chops)*

Condiments
BBQ sauce *(BBQ Salisbury Steak)*
Worcestershire sauce *(Marinated Pork Chops)*
balsamic vinegar *(Marinated Pork Chops)*

Mexican
1 (16 oz) jar salsa Verde *(Mexican Chicken & Beans)*

Summer Grocery List #25 (does not include side dish suggestions)

Basil Shrimp * Crock Pot Roast * Pasta with Roasted Vegetables
Breaded Pork with Dill Sauce * Chicken & Slaw Sandwiches

Produce
garlic *(Basil Shrimp, Pasta with Roasted Vegetables, Chicken & Slaw Sandwiches)*
fresh basil *(Basil Shrimp, Pasta with Roasted Vegetables)*
lemon juice *(Basil Shrimp)*
lime juice *(Chicken & Slaw Sandwiches)*
5 carrots *(more or less, one for each person)* *(Crock Pot Roast)*
2 carrots *(Chicken & Slaw Sandwiches)*
1 lb. broccoli florets *(Pasta with Roasted Vegetables)*
1 small eggplant (optional) *(Pasta with Roasted Vegetables)*
cilantro *(Chicken & Slaw Sandwiches)*
1 onion *(Chicken & Slaw Sandwiches)*
1 jalapeno pepper (optional) *(Chicken & Slaw Sandwiches)*

Meat, Poultry, & Fish
1 ½ lbs. shrimp *(Basil Shrimp)*
1 beef roast, any type *(Crock Pot Roast)*
8 thin pork loin chops or tenderloins *(Breaded Pork with Dill Sauce)*
2 boneless chicken breast halves *(Chicken & Slaw Sandwiches)*

Dairy
butter *(Basil Shrimp)*
Parmesan cheese (optional) *(Pasta with Roasted Vegetables)*
fat free sour cream *(Breaded Pork with Dill Sauce)*
egg substitute or eggs *(Breaded Pork with Dill Sauce)*
skim milk *(Breaded Pork with Dill Sauce)*

Pasta, Rice, & Legumes
16 oz penne pasta *(Pasta with Roasted Vegetables)*

Breads and Tortillas
1 loaf ciabatta bread or other hearty bread *(Chicken & Slaw Sandwiches)*

Baking Aisle
olive oil
¼ cup pine nuts *(Pasta with Roasted Vegetables)*
flour *(Breaded Pork with Dill Sauce)*
fine dry bread crumbs *(Breaded Pork with Dill Sauce)*
sugar *(Chicken & Slaw Sandwiches)*

Canned
1 can (15 oz) artichoke hearts (in water), quartered *(Pasta with Roasted Vegetables)*

Soups and Packaged Mixes
1 package dry brown gravy mix *(Crock Pot Roast)*
chicken bouillon granules *(Breaded Pork with Dill Sauce)*

Spices and seasonings
salt
pepper
seasoned salt *(Breaded Pork with Dill Sauce)*
paprika *(Breaded Pork with Dill Sauce)*
dried dill weed *(Breaded Pork with Dill Sauce)*

Condiments
Dijon mustard *(Basil Shrimp)*
1 package dry Italian salad dressing mix *(Crock Pot Roast)*
1 package dry ranch dressing mix *(Crock Pot Roast)*
¼ cup pitted kalamata olives *(Pasta with Roasted Vegetables)*
rice wine vinegar *(Chicken & Slaw Sandwiches)*
fat free mayonnaise *(Chicken & Slaw Sandwiches)*

Asian
Five Spice Powder *(Chicken & Slaw Sandwiches)*

Fall Grocery List #26 (does not include side dish suggestions)

*Shrimp Slaw Salad * "Fried" Chicken & Buttermilk Gravy * Stuffed Taco Burgers II*
*Honey Spiced Pork Tenderloin * Steak Verde*

Produce

14 oz package coleslaw mix (or small head of cabbage) *(Shrimp Slaw Salad)*
1 yellow or red pepper *(Shrimp Slaw Salad)*
1 green pepper *(Shrimp Slaw Salad)*
1 bunch green onions *(Shrimp Slaw Salad)*
cilantro *(Shrimp Slaw Salad)*
1 lime *(Shrimp Slaw Salad)*
lime juice *(Shrimp Slaw Salad)*
1 avocado *(Stuffed Taco Burgers II)*
1 tomato *(Stuffed Taco Burgers II)*

Meat, Poultry, & Fish

2 lbs. small cooked shrimp *(Shrimp Slaw Salad)*
4 boneless chicken breast halves *("Fried" Chicken & Buttermilk Gravy)*
1 lb lean ground beef *(Stuffed Taco Burgers II)*
1 lb. pork tenderloin *(Honey Spiced Pork Tenderloin)*
4 sirloin steaks *(Steak Verde)*

Dairy

grated Parmesan cheese *("Fried" Chicken & Buttermilk Gravy)*
8 oz reduced fat buttermilk *("Fried" Chicken & Buttermilk Gravy)*
1 container chive & onion cream cheese *(Stuffed Taco Burgers)*
1 oz slice cheddar cheese *(Stuffed Taco Burgers II)*
4 slices Havarti cheese *(Steak Verde)*

Breads and Tortillas

4 hamburger buns *(Stuffed Taco Burgers II)*

Baking Aisle

dry plain bread crumbs *("Fried" Chicken & Buttermilk Gravy)*
honey *(Honey Spiced Pork Tenderloin)*

Soups and Packaged Mixes

1 envelope dry chicken gravy mix *("Fried" Chicken & Buttermilk Gravy)*
1 pkg. taco seasoning mix *(Stuffed Taco Burgers II)*

Spices and seasonings

salt
pepper
cayenne pepper *(Shrimp Slaw Salad, Steak Verde)*
paprika *("Fried" Chicken & Buttermilk Gravy, Honey Spiced Pork Tenderloin, Steak Verde)*
dried sage *("Fried" Chicken & Buttermilk Gravy)*
chili powder *(Honey Spiced Pork Tenderloin)*
garlic powder *(Honey Spiced Pork Tenderloin)*
dry mustard *(Honey Spiced Pork Tenderloin)*
ground thyme *(Honey Spiced Pork Tenderloin)*
ground cumin *(Steak Verde)*

Condiments

reduced fat mayonnaise *(Shrimp Slaw Salad)*
fat free Catalina salad dressing *(Honey Spiced Pork Tenderloin)*

Mexican

salsa *(Stuffed Taco Burgers II)*
green chili salsa *(Steak Verde)*

Fall Grocery List #27 (does not include side dish suggestions)

*Mediterranean Pork * Cheesy Spaghetti & Smoky Meatballs * Blackened Salmon*
*Turkey Cordon Bleu * Beef Caesar Kabobs*

Produce

lemon juice *(Mediterranean Pork)*
1 large tomato *(Mediterranean Pork)*
1 yellow squash *(Mediterranean Pork)*
2 zucchinis *(Mediterranean Pork, Beef Caesar Kabobs)*
8 basil leaves *(Mediterranean Pork)*
2 small onions *(Cheesy Spaghetti & Smoky Meatballs)*
parsley *(Cheesy Spaghetti & Smoky Meatballs)*
garlic *(Cheesy Spaghetti & Smoky Meatballs)*
16 cherry tomatoes *(Beef Caesar Kabobs)*
8 small mushrooms *(Beef Caesar Kabobs)*
1 large green pepper *(Beef Caesar Kabobs)*

Meat, Poultry, & Fish

4 thin, boneless pork chops *(Mediterranean Pork)*
1 lb lean ground beef *(Cheesy Spaghetti & Smoky Meatballs)*
4-8 serving size salmon filets *(Blackened Salmon)*
4 ham slices (deli style) *(Turkey Cordon Bleu)*
4 turkey cutlets *(Turkey Cordon Bleu)*
1 lb. beef steak *(Beef Caesar Kabobs)*

Dairy

eggs *(Cheesy Spaghetti & Smoky Meatballs)*
2 oz smoked (or use regular) mozzarella cheese *(Cheesy Spaghetti & Smoky Meatballs)*
2 oz Romano cheese *(Cheesy Spaghetti & Smoky Meatballs)*
2 oz Parmesan cheese *(Cheesy Spaghetti & Smoky Meatballs)*
4 provolone cheese slices *(Turkey Cordon Bleu)*

Pasta, Rice, & Legumes

12 oz spaghetti *(Cheesy Spaghetti & Smoky Meatballs)*

Baking Aisle

olive oil
seasoned dried bread crumbs *(Cheesy Spaghetti & Smoky Meatballs)*

Canned

1 can (15 oz) quartered artichoke hearts (packed in water) *(Mediterranean Pork)*
1 (15 oz) can crushed or diced tomatoes *(Cheesy Spaghetti & Smoky Meatballs)*

Spices and seasonings

Salt
sea salt (or table salt) *(Blackened Salmon)*
pepper
dried rosemary *(Mediterranean Pork)*
crushed red pepper flakes *(Cheesy Spaghetti & Smoky Meatballs)*
garlic powder *(Blackened Salmon)*
dried parsley flakes *(Blackened Salmon)*
dried basil *(Blackened Salmon)*
thyme *(Blackened Salmon)*
cayenne pepper *(Blackened Salmon)*
oregano *(Turkey Cordon Bleu)*

Condiments

capers *(Mediterranean Pork)*
ketchup *(Cheesy Spaghetti & Smoky Meatballs)*
light Caesar salad dressing *(Beef Caesar Kabobs)*

Non-Food Items

Foil *(Mediterranean Pork)*

Fall Grocery List #28 (does not include side dish suggestions)

*Caribbean Pasta * Sausage & Potato Tacos * Southwest Creamy Chicken*
*Italian Pepper Steak * Shrimp & Avocado Sandwiches*

Produce

7 large ripe tomatoes *(Caribbean Pasta, Sausage & Potato Tacos)*

garlic *(Caribbean Pasta)*

cilantro *(Caribbean Pasta, Sausage & Potato Tacos)*

1 bunch green onions *(Caribbean Pasta, Sausage & Potato Tacos)*

lime juice *(Caribbean Pasta)*

1 jalapeno *(Sausage & Potato Tacos)*

2 medium red potatoes *(Sausage & Potato Tacos)*

1 yellow squash or zucchini *(Sausage & Potato Tacos)*

1 green pepper *(Italian Pepper Steak)*

1 red pepper *(Italian Pepper Steak)*

1 small onion *(Italian Pepper Steak)*

2 large avocados *(Shrimp & Avocado Sandwiches)*

1 carrot *(Shrimp & Avocado Sandwiches)*

Meat, Poultry, & Fish

1 lb. lean ground sausage (mild or spicy, depending on your preference) *(Sausage & Potato Tacos)*

4 frozen boneless chicken breasts *(Southwest Creamy Chicken)*

1 lb. lean beef sirloin *(Italian Pepper Steak)*

1 lb. cooked shrimp *(Shrimp & Avocado Sandwiches)*

Dairy

2 oz Monterey Jack cheese (optional) *(Caribbean Pasta)*

6 oz queso fresco cheese *(Sausage & Potato Tacos)*

1 (8 oz) reduced fat cream cheese *(Southwest Creamy Chicken)*

9 oz fresh refrigerated fettuccini *(Italian Pepper Steak)*

Pasta, Rice, & Legumes

8 oz thin spaghetti *(Caribbean Pasta)*

Breads and Tortillas

12 corn tortillas *(Sausage & Potato Tacos)*

4 hoagie buns *(Shrimp & Avocado Sandwiches)*

Baking Aisle

olive oil

Canned

2 (15 oz) cans black beans *(Caribbean Pasta, Southwest Creamy Chicken)*

1 (15 oz) can corn *(Southwest Creamy Chicken)*

1 (15oz) can Italian diced tomatoes *(Italian Pepper Steak)*

Spices and seasonings

ground cumin *(Caribbean Pasta)*

pepper

salt

cayenne pepper (optional) *(Caribbean Pasta)*

crushed red pepper *(Italian Pepper Steak)*

Condiments

balsamic vinegar *(Italian Pepper Steak)*

coleslaw salad dressing *(Shrimp & Avocado Sandwiches)*

Mexican

16 oz salsa *(Southwest Creamy Chicken)*

Fall Grocery List #29 (does not include side dish suggestions)

*Japanese Noodles * Cilantro Lime Chicken Salad Wraps * Steak Tampiquena*
*Honey Garlic Pork Chops * Tomato Baguette Pizza*

Produce

1 red bell pepper *(Japanese Noodles)*
3 carrots *(Japanese Noodles)*
2 small onions *(Japanese Noodles, Steak Tampiquena)*
1 medium onion *(Tomato Baguette Pizza)*
garlic
1 bunch green onions *(Japanese Noodles)*
cilantro *(Cilantro Lime Chicken Salad Wraps)*
1 lime *(Cilantro Lime Chicken Salad Wraps)*
1 cucumber *(Cilantro Lime Chicken Salad Wraps)*
4 tomatoes *(Cilantro Lime Chicken Salad Wraps, Tomato Baguette Pizza)*
2 Roma tomatoes *(Steak Tampiquena)*
8 oz sliced fresh mushrooms *(Tomato Baguette Pizza)*
fresh basil leaves *(Tomato Baguette Pizza)*

Meat, Poultry, & Fish

2 boneless chicken breast halves *(Japanese Noodles)*
2 quality cuts of steak (1 lb. each), about ½" - ¾ " thick *(Steak Tampiquena)*
6 boneless pork chops *(Honey Garlic Pork Chops)*

Dairy

4 oz Monterey Jack cheese *(Steak Tampiquena)*
6 oz part-skim mozzarella cheese *(Tomato Baguette Pizza)*

Breads and Tortillas

4 (10 inch) tortillas *(Cilantro Lime Chicken Salad Wraps)*
1 French bread baguette (10-12 oz) *(Tomato Baguette Pizza)*

Baking Aisle

olive oil
honey *(Honey Garlic Pork Chops)*

Canned

1 (12 oz) can chunk white chicken *(Cilantro Lime Chicken Salad Wraps)*

Spices and seasonings

Pepper
red pepper flakes *(Japanese Noodles)*
sesame seeds *(Japanese Noodles)*
oregano *(Cilantro Lime Chicken Salad Wraps)*
Seasoning salt *(Steak Tampiquena)*
Italian seasoning *(Tomato Baguette Pizza)*
garlic salt *(Tomato Baguette Pizza)*

Asian

12 oz Japanese noodles (or chow mein or spaghetti noodles) *(Japanese Noodles)*
soy sauce *(Japanese Noodles, Honey Garlic Pork Chops)*
teriyaki sauce *(Japanese Noodles)*

Mexican

1 (7oz) can whole roasted green chilies *(Steak Tampiquena)*

Fall Grocery List #30 (does not include side dish suggestions)

*Stuffed Sole * Potato & Ham Skillet * Chicken in Wine Sauce*
*Mexican Stewed Beef * Hamburger Noodle Soup*

Produce

Lemon Juice *(Stuffed Sole)*

6 medium red potatoes *(Potato & Ham Skillet)*

garlic *(Chicken in Wine Sauce, Mexican Stewed Beef)*

green onions *(Chicken in Wine Sauce)*

2 onions *(Mexican Stewed Beef, Hamburger Noodle Soup)*

2-3 jalapeno peppers *(Mexican Stewed Beef)*

2 stalks celery *(Hamburger Noodle Soup)*

2 carrots *(Hamburger Noodle Soup)*

Meat, Poultry, & Fish

6 thin sole fillets *(Stuffed Sole)*

1 fully cooked ham steak *(Potato & Ham Skillet)*

4 chicken breast halves *(Chicken in Wine Sauce)*

4 thin slices deli ham *(Chicken in Wine Sauce)*

2 ½ lbs round roast *(Mexican Stewed Beef)*

1 ½ lbs. Lean ground beef *(Hamburger Noodle Soup)*

Dairy

butter *(Stuffed Sole, Chicken in Wine Sauce)*

Pasta, Rice, & Legumes

small egg noodles *(Hamburger Noodle Soup)*

Baking Aisle

dry bread crumbs *(Stuffed Sole)*

olive oil

flour *(Mexican Stewed Beef)*

Frozen

1 pkg.(16 oz) frozen broccoli florets *(Potato & Ham Skillet)*

Canned

1 can crab meat *(Stuffed Sole)*

1 can tomato paste *(Mexican Stewed Beef)*

Soups and Packaged Mixes

1 envelope dry mushroom and onion soup mix *(Potato & Ham Skillet)*

beef bouillon granules *(Mexican Stewed Beef, Hamburger Noodle Soup)*

1 envelope au jus mix *(Hamburger Noodle Soup)*

Spices and seasonings

Salt

Pepper

onion powder *(Stuffed Sole)*

celery salt *(Stuffed Sole)*

parsley *(Stuffed Sole)*

Cayenne Pepper *(Stuffed Sole)*

paprika *(Stuffed Sole)*

dried sage leaves *(Chicken in Wine Sauce)*

cumin *(Mexican Stewed Beef)*

chili powder *(Mexican Stewed Beef)*

bay leaves *(Hamburger Noodle Soup)*

Non-Food Items

white wine (or chicken broth) *(Chicken in Wine Sauce)*

Fall Grocery List #31 (does not include side dish suggestions)

Chinese BBQ Chicken Legs * Tossed Shrimp Salad * Moroccan stew
Chicken with Rosemary & Onion Sauce * Super Joes

Produce

garlic *(Chinese BBQ Chicken Legs, Moroccan Stew, Chicken with Rosemary & Onion Sauce)*

12 oz package salad or head of lettuce *(Tossed Shrimp Salad)*

green onions *(Tossed Shrimp Salad)*

3 medium onions *(Moroccan Stew, Chicken with Rosemary & Onion Sauce, Super Joes)*

cilantro *(Moroccan Stew)*

3 large carrots *(Moroccan Stew, Super Joes)*

1 zucchini *(Moroccan Stew)*

1 red bell pepper *(Super Joes)*

Meat, Poultry, & Fish

18 chicken legs *(Chinese BBQ Chicken Legs)*

4 boneless chicken breast halves *(Chicken with Rosemary & Onion Sauce)*

16 oz small cooked shrimp *(Tossed Shrimp Salad)*

1 lb. ground turkey or ground beef *(Super Joes)*

Dairy

4 oz fat-free milk *(Chicken with Rosemary & Onion Sauce)*

Breads and Tortillas

8 whole wheat buns *(Super Joes)*

Baking Aisle

cornstarch *(Chinese BBQ Chicken Legs, Slow Cooked Pork Roast)*

brown sugar *(Chinese BBQ Chicken Legs, Super Joes)*

flour *(Chicken with Rosemary & Onion Sauce)*

Canned

1 can (8oz) tomato sauce *(Chinese BBQ Chicken Legs)*

1 can (15 oz.) tomato sauce *(Super Joes)*

1 can (15 oz) stewed tomatoes *(Moroccan Stew)*

1 can (15 oz) garbanzo beans *(Moroccan Stew)*

Soups and Packaged Mixes

chicken bouillon granules *(Moroccan Stew, Chicken with Rosemary & Onion Sauce)*

Spices and seasonings

salt

pepper

rosemary *(Chicken with Rosemary & Onion Sauce)*

onion powder *(Slow Cooked Pork Roast)*

dry mustard *(Slow Cooked Pork Roast)*

curry powder *(Moroccan Stew)*

ground cumin *(Moroccan Stew)*

Condiments

fat-free zesty Italian salad dressing *(Tossed Shrimp Salad)*

Worcestershire sauce *(Super Joes)*

ketchup *(Super Joes)*

Asian

soy sauce *(Chinese BBQ Chicken Legs)*

Bin Foods

1/3 cup slivered almonds *(Tossed Shrimp Salad)*

1/3 cup Golden raisins *(Moroccan Stew)*

Fall Grocery List #32 (does not include side dish suggestions)

*Polenta & Chili Bake * Crab Stir-Fry * Chicken & Artichoke Pasta * Balsamic Glazed Pork Chops * Beef, Broccoli & Rice Skillet*

Produce

2 carrots *(Crab Stir-Fry)*
1 cup snow peas *(Crab Stir-Fry)*
1 red pepper *(Crab Stir-Fry)*
Small piece ginger root *(Crab Stir-Fry)*
garlic *(Crab Stir-Fry ,Balsamic Glazed Pork Chops)*
8 oz fresh mushrooms *(Chicken & Artichoke Pasta)*
1 bunch green onions *(Chicken & Artichoke Pasta)*
1 small onion *(Balsamic Glazed Pork Chops)*
1 head broccoli *(Beef, Broccoli & Rice Skillet)*

Meat, Poultry, & Fish

1 lb. imitation crab *(Crab Stir-Fry)*
2 boneless chicken breast halves *(Chicken & Artichoke Pasta)*
4 lean pork chops *(Balsamic Glazed Pork Chops)*
1 ½ lbs lean ground beef *(Beef, Broccoli & Rice Skillet)*

Dairy

12 oz reduced fat cheddar cheese *(Polenta & Chili Bake, Beef, Broccoli & Rice Skillet)*
2 oz Parmesan cheese *(Chicken & Artichoke Pasta)*
butter *(Balsamic Glazed Pork Chops)*

Pasta, Rice, & Legumes

12 oz bowtie pasta *(Chicken & Artichoke Pasta)*
Instant rice *(Beef, Broccoli & Rice Skillet)*

Baking Aisle

Non-stick cooking spray
yellow cornmeal *(Polenta & Chili Bake)*
cornstarch *(Crab Stir-Fry, Chicken & Artichoke Pasta)*
olive oil *(Balsamic Glazed Pork Chops)*
honey *(Balsamic Glazed Pork Chops)*

Frozen

1 package (16 oz) frozen mixed vegetables *(Polenta & Chili Bake)*

Canned

3 cans (15 oz each) fat-free vegetarian chili *(Polenta & Chili Bake)*
1 can (15 oz) diced tomatoes *(Chicken & Artichoke Pasta)*
1 can (14 oz) water packed, quartered artichoke hearts *(Chicken & Artichoke Pasta)*

Soups and Packaged Mixes

chicken bouillon granules *(Crab Stir-Fry, Balsamic Glazed Pork Chops)*

Spices and seasonings

Salt
pepper
thyme *(Balsamic Glazed Pork Chops)*
rosemary *(Balsamic Glazed Pork Chops)*
garlic powder *(Chicken & Artichoke Pasta)*
basil *(Chicken & Artichoke Pasta)*
oregano *(Beef, Broccoli & Rice Skillet)*

Condiments

balsamic vinegar *(Balsamic Glazed Pork Chops)*
fat free zesty Italian dressing *(Beef, Broccoli & Rice Skillet)*

Asian

soy sauce *(Crab Stir-Fry)*

Non-Food Items

white wine or chicken broth *(Chicken & Artichoke Pasta)*

Fall Grocery List #33 (does not include side dish suggestions)

*Tortellini Soup * Shrimp Newburg * Stuffed Chicken Breasts*
*Turkey Cutlets * Honeyed Ham Steak*

Produce
1 lb. carrots *(Tortellini Soup)*
1 yellow summer squash *(Tortellini Soup)*
spinach *(Tortellini Soup)*
1 bunch asparagus *(Shrimp Newberg)*
1 bunch green onions *(Shrimp Newberg)*
½ cup chopped onion *(Stuffed Chicken Breasts)*
1 bunch or pkg spinach *(Stuffed Chicken Breasts)*
garlic *(Stuffed Chicken Breasts)*
1 lemon *(Stuffed Chicken Breasts)*

Meat, Poultry, & Fish
1 lb shrimp *(Shrimp Newberg)*
4 boneless chicken breast halves *(Stuffed Chicken Breasts)*
4 thin turkey (or chicken) breast cutlets *(Turkey Cutlets)*
1 fully cooked smoked ham, center slice, ½" thick *(Honeyod Ham Steak)*

Dairy
1 pkg. (9 oz) refrigerated cheese tortellini *(Tortellini Soup)*
1 oz reduced fat feta cheese *(Stuffed Chicken Breasts)*
Butter or margarine *(Honeyed Ham Steak)*

Pasta, Sauces, Rice, & Legumes
16 oz bowtie (farfalle) pasta *(Shrimp Newberg)*
15 oz bottled Alfredo sauce *(Shrimp Newberg)*

Baking Aisle
Non-stick cooking spray
cornstarch *(Turkey Cutlets)*
olive oil
Honey *(Honeyed Ham Steak)*

Frozen
apple juice concentrate *(Turkey Cutlets)*

Canned
1 can (14 ½ oz) diced tomatoes *(Shrimp Newberg)*

Soups and Packaged Mixes
chicken bouillon granules *(Tortellini Soup)*

Spices and seasonings
Salt
pepper
rosemary *(Turkey Cutlets)*

Condiments
Sherry *(Shrimp Newberg)*
balsamic vinegar *(Stuffed Chicken Breasts)*
Dijon mustard *(Turkey Cutlets)*
mustard *(Honeyed Ham Steak)*

Non-Food Items
Toothpicks *(Stuffed Chicken Breasts)*

Fall Grocery List #34 (does not include side dish suggestions)

Hawaiian Ham * Pesto Pork * Beef Stew * Chicken Casserole Ole' * Maryland Fish Fillets

Produce
1 medium onion *(Hawaiian Ham)*
1 green pepper *(Hawaiian Ham)*
12 Roma tomatoes *(Pesto Pork)*
4 potatoes *(Beef Stew)*
6 carrots *(Beef Stew)*
garlic *(Beef Stew)*
chives *(Maryland Fish Fillets)*

Meat, Poultry, & Fish
1 lb. lean cooked ham *(Hawaiian Ham)*
2-3 lb. pork roast *(Pesto Pork)*
1 ½ lbs lean stew meat *(Beef Stew)*
4 boneless chicken breast halves *(Chicken Casserole Ole')*
4 sole, flounder, or other skinless thin, white fish fillets *(Maryland Fish Fillets)*
skim milk *(Maryland Fish Fillets)*

Dairy
1 refrigerated package prepared pesto *(Pesto Pork)*
margarine or butter *(Maryland Fish Fillets)*
10 oz Monterey Jack cheese *(Chicken Casserole Ole')*
10 oz low fat cheddar cheese *(Chicken Casserole Ole')*
1 oz Gruyere cheese *(Maryland Fish Fillets)*
2 oz Monterey Jack cheese *(Maryland Fish Fillets)*

Pasta, Rice, & Legumes
16 oz rotini or spiral noodles *(Pesto Pork)*

Breads and Tortillas
12 8-inch flour tortillas *(Chicken Casserole Ole')*

Baking Aisle
raisins *(Hawaiian Ham)*
brown sugar *(Hawaiian Ham)*
cornstarch *(Hawaiian Ham, Beef Stew)*
1 can evaporated skim milk *(Chicken Casserole Ole')*
flour *(Maryland Fish Fillets)*

Canned
8 oz can pineapple chunks *(Hawaiian Ham)*
1 (28 oz) can tomatoes *(Beef Stew)*

Soups and Packaged Mixes
1 packet dry onion soup mix *(Beef Stew)*
beef bouillon granules *(Beef Stew)*
1 can (10 ½ oz.) Cream of mushroom soup *(Chicken Casserole Ole')*
1 can (10 ½ oz.) Cream of chicken soup *(Chicken Casserole Ole')*

Spices and seasonings
Salt
Pepper
dry mustard *(Hawaiian Ham)*

Condiments
vinegar *(Hawaiian Ham)*
Worcestershire sauce *(Hawaiian Ham)*

Asian
soy sauce *(Hawaiian Ham)*

Mexican
1 can (4 oz) diced green chilies *(Chicken Casserole Ole')*

Fall Grocery List #35 (does not include side dish suggestions)

*Pasta with Ham & Tomatoes * Foil Fish Bake * Steaks with Mushroom Sauce*
*Chicken & Brie Salad * Pesto Ravioli with Artichokes*

Produce
1 large onion *(Pasta with Ham & Tomatoes)*
1 small onion *(Foil Fish Bake)*
1 pint cherry or grape tomatoes *(Pasta with Ham & Tomatoes)*
fresh basil *(Pasta with Ham & Tomatoes, Pesto Ravioli with Artichokes)*
fresh parsley *(Foil Fish Bake)*
fresh dill sprigs *(Foil Fish Bake)*
fresh chives *(Foil Fish Bake)*
lemon juice *(Foil Fish Bake)*
8 oz sliced mushrooms *(Steaks with Mushroom Sauce)*
1 large head Romaine lettuce *(Chicken & Brie Salad)*

Meat, Poultry, & Fish
8 oz cooked lean ham *(Pasta with Ham & Tomatoes)*
4 fresh lake trout (about 8 oz each) or other whole white fish *(Foil Fish Bake)*
4 beef tenderloins *(Steaks with Mushroom Sauce)*
4 boneless chicken breast halves *(Chicken & Brie Salad)*

Dairy
Margarine or butter *(Foil Fish Bake)*
Small carton half & half *(Steaks with Mushroom Sauce)*
1 round of brie cheese (about 5 oz) *(Chicken & Brie Salad)*
1 (9oz) pkg. cheese ravioli *(Pesto Ravioli with Artichokes)*
1 container refrigerated pesto *(Pesto Ravioli with Artichokes)*

Pasta, Rice, & Legumes
16 oz gemelli or other medium pasta *(Pasta with Ham & Tomatoes)*

Baking Aisle
olive oil
sugar *(Chicken & Brie Salad)*
½ cup pecan halves *(Chicken & Brie Salad)*

Canned
1 can (15 oz) quartered artichoke hearts in water *(Pesto Ravioli with Artichokes)*

Soups and Packaged Mixes
beef bouillon granules *(Steaks with Mushroom Sauce)*

Spices and seasonings
Salt
Pepper
garlic powder *(Pasta with Ham & Tomatoes)*
crushed red pepper (optional) *(Pasta with Ham & Tomatoes)*

Condiments
light raspberry vinaigrette salad dressing *(Chicken & Brie Salad)*
small can sliced black olives *(Pesto Ravioli with Artichokes)*

Non-Food Items
Aluminum foil *(Pasta with Ham & Tomatoes)*

Fall Grocery List #36 (does not include side dish suggestions)

*BBQ Chicken Pizza * Linguine with Tuna Sauce * Beef and Snow Pea Stir-Fry*
*Chunky Tomato Soup * Gorgonzola Burgers*

Produce
1 small red onion *(BBQ Chicken Pizza)*
1 large onion *(Chunky Tomato Soup)*
1 small red onion *(Gorgonzola Burgers)*
Cilantro *(BBQ Chicken Pizza)*
5 large tomatoes *(Linguine with Tuna Sauce, Gorgonzola Burgers)*
parsley *(Linguine with Tuna Sauce)*
2 bunches green onions *(Linguine with Tuna Sauce, Beef and Snow Pea Stir-Fry)*
1 lemon *(Linguine with Tuna Sauce)*
6 oz pea pods *(Beef and Snow Pea Stir-Fry)*
2 red bell peppers *(Beef and Snow Pea Stir-Fry, Chunky Tomato Soup)*
6 celery stalks *(Chunky Tomato Soup)*
fresh basil *(Chunky Tomato Soup)*

Meat, Poultry, & Fish
2 boneless, skinless chicken breast halves *(BBQ Chicken Pizza)*
12 oz lean top round steak *(Beef and Snow Pea Stir-Fry)*
1 ¼ lb. lean ground beef *(Gorgonzola Burgers)*

Dairy
6 oz part-skim mozzarella cheese, shredded *(BBQ Chicken Pizza)*
4 oz crumbled gorgonzola cheese *(Gorgonzola Burgers)*
Store-bought pizza dough or Boboli bread *(BBQ Chicken Pizza)*
butter *(Chunky Tomato Soup)*
fat free half & half *(Chunky Tomato Soup)*

Pasta, Rice, & Legumes
16 oz linguine *(Linguine with Tuna Sauce)*
rice *(Beef and Snow Pea Stir-Fry)*

Breads and Tortillas
4 large, plain hamburger buns *(Gorgonzola Burgers)*

Baking Aisle
olive oil
cornstarch *(Beef and Snow Pea Stir-Fry)*
sugar *(Beef and Snow Pea Stir-Fry, Chunky Tomato Soup)*

Canned
12 oz canned tuna in water *(Linguine with Tuna Sauce)*
3 cans (14½ oz each) diced tomatoes *(Chunky Tomato Soup)*
sundried tomatoes, oil packed *(Gorgonzola Burgers)*

Spices and seasonings
Salt
Pepper
dried basil *(Linguine with Tuna Sauce)*
dried thyme *(Gorgonzola Burgers)*
garlic powder *(Gorgonzola Burgers)*

Condiments
BBQ sauce *(BBQ Chicken Pizza)*
dry sherry *(Beef and Snow Pea Stir-Fry)*
ketchup *(Chunky Tomato Soup)*

Asian
soy sauce *(Beef and Snow Pea Stir-Fry)*
1 can (8 oz) sliced Water chestnuts *(Beef and Snow Pea Stir-Fry)*

Fall Grocery List #37 (does not include side dish suggestions)

*Baked Ziti with Sausage * Chicken & Dumplings * Cod Chowder*
*Pot Roast w/Veggies * Vegetable Beef Tacos*

Produce
3 medium onions *(Baked Ziti with Sausage, Chicken & Dumplings, Vegetable Beef Tacos)*
garlic *(Baked Ziti with Sausage, Vegetable Beef Tacos)*
8 oz spinach *(Baked Ziti with Sausage)*
4 stalks celery *(Chicken & Dumplings)*
11 carrots *(Chicken & Dumplings, Pot Roast w/Veggies, Vegetable Beef Tacos)*
2 parsnips *(Pot Roast w/Veggies)*
5 med. red potatoes *(Pot Roast w/Veggies)*
4 oz mushrooms *(Vegetable Beef Tacos)*
1 large zucchini *(Vegetable Beef Tacos)*
3 Roma tomatoes *(Vegetable Beef Tacos)*
cilantro *(Vegetable Beef Tacos)*
Shredded lettuce *(Vegetable Beef Tacos)*

Meat, Poultry, & Fish
1 lb. hot Italian turkey sausage *(Baked Ziti with Sausage)*
1 large chicken *(Chicken & Dumplings)*
12 oz fresh cod *(Cod Chowder)*
turkey bacon *(Cod Chowder)*
3 lb boneless beef chuck roast *(Pot Roast w/Veggies)*
1 lb. lean ground beef *(Vegetable Beef Tacos)*

Dairy
8 oz part-skim mozzarella cheese *(Baked Ziti with Sausage)*
4 oz reduced fat sharp cheddar cheese *(Vegetable Beef Tacos)*
2 oz grated Parmesan cheese *(Baked Ziti with Sausage)*
1 container prepared pesto *(Baked Ziti with Sausage)*
½ pint skim milk *(Chicken & Dumplings)*

Pasta, Rice, & Legumes
12 oz penne pasta *(Baked Ziti with Sausage)*

Breads and Tortillas
8 tortillas (10 inch) *(Vegetable Beef Tacos)*

Baking Aisle
olive oil
flour *(Chicken & Dumplings)*
baking powder *(Chicken & Dumplings)*
cornstarch *(Chicken & Dumplings)*
1 can evaporated skim milk *(Cod Chowder)*

Frozen
1 package frozen hash browns *(Cod Chowder)*

Canned
1 (28 oz) can diced tomatoes *(Baked Ziti with Sausage)*

Soups and Packaged Mixes
chicken bouillon granules *(Chicken & Dumplings)*
1 can cream of shrimp (or potato) soup *(Cod Chowder)*
1 can cream of mushroom soup *(Pot Roast w/Veggies)*
1 pkg dry onion mushroom soup mix *(Pot Roast w/Veggies)*

Spices and seasonings
Salt
Pepper
dried parsley *(Chicken & Dumplings)*
dried dillweed *(Cod Chowder)*
dried rosemary *(Pot Roast w/Veggies)*
chili powder *(Vegetable Beef Tacos)*

Condiments
2 oz jar diced pimentos *(Cod Chowder)*
hot pepper sauce *(Vegetable Beef Tacos)*

Non-Food Items
red wine (optional) *(Pot Roast w/Veggies)*

Fall Grocery List #38 (does not include side dish suggestions)

*Oriental Chicken * Cuban Pork Sandwiches * Creamy Chicken & Broccoli Pasta * Vermont Ham & Cabbage * Hamburger Cornbread Bake*

Produce

4 carrots *(Oriental Chicken)*

1 red pepper *(Oriental Chicken)*

garlic *(Oriental Chicken, Cuban Pork Sandwiches)*

1 bunch green onions *(Oriental Chicken)*

1 small red onion *(Cuban Pork Sandwiches)*

2 yellow onions **(Creamy Chicken & Broccoli Pasta**, Hamburger Cornbread Bake)

4 cups broccoli florets **(Creamy Chicken & Broccoli Pasta)**

1 small head cabbage *(Vermont Ham & Cabbage)*

2 red apples *(Vermont Ham & Cabbage)*

Meat, Poultry, & Fish

2 boneless chicken breast halves *(Oriental Chicken)*

1½ cups cooked chicken breast (or buy 2 uncooked chicken breasts halves and cook them at home) *(Creamy Chicken & Broccoli Pasta)*

1 lb lean pork tenderloin *(Cuban Pork Sandwiches)*

1 fully cooked ham center slice, 1½ " thick *(Vermont Ham & Cabbage)*

1 lb lean ground beef *(Hamburger Cornbread Bake)*

Dairy

8 slices reduced fat Swiss cheese *(Cuban Pork Sandwiches)*

4 oz skim milk *(Creamy Chicken & Broccoli Pasta)*

3 oz. Reduced fat cream cheese *(Creamy Chicken & Broccoli Pasta)*

3 oz Grated Parmesan cheese *(Creamy Chicken & Broccoli Pasta)*

butter *(Vermont Ham & Cabbage)*

Pasta, Rice, & Legumes

16 oz. Spaghetti *(Creamy Chicken & Broccoli Pasta)*

Breads & Tortillas

sourdough bread *(Cuban Pork Sandwiches)*

Baking Aisle

honey or agave syrup *(Oriental Chicken)*

Sugar free pancake (or maple) syrup *(Vermont Ham & Cabbage)*

Small package corn bread mix *(Hamburger Cornbread Bake)*

Canned

1 (8oz) jar roasted red peppers *(sometimes found near the condiments) (Cuban Pork Sandwiches)*

1 (15 oz) can kidney beans *(Hamburger Cornbread Bake)*

1 (15oz) can diced tomatoes *(Hamburger Cornbread Bake)*

Soups and Packaged Mixes

1 can (10-3/4 oz.) reduced fat cream of chicken soup *(Creamy Chicken & Broccoli Pasta)*

Spices and seasonings

crushed red pepper *(Oriental Chicken)*

ground ginger *(Oriental Chicken)*

sesame seeds *(these are sometimes in the Asian food section) (Oriental Chicken)*

oregano *(Cuban Pork Sandwiches)*

ground cumin *(Cuban Pork Sandwiches)*

chili powder *(Hamburger Cornbread Bake)*

Condiments

sherry *(Oriental Chicken)*

cider vinegar *(Cuban Pork Sandwiches)*

Worcestershire sauce *(Hamburger Cornbread Bake)*

Asian

soy sauce *(Oriental Chicken)*

Chinese five-spice powder *(Oriental Chicken)*

peanut oil *(sometimes found in the baking aisle) (Oriental Chicken)*

Winter Grocery List #39 (does not include side dish suggestions)

*Chili Verde * Tilapia & Tomatoes * Roast Turkey Breast * Crispix Chicken*
Puffed Up Pizza

Produce
2 large onions *(Chili Verde, Puffed Up Pizza)*
garlic *(Chili Verde)*
cilantro *(Chili Verde)*
1 pint cherry or grape tomatoes *(Tilapia & Tomatoes)*
parsley *(Tilapia & Tomatoes)*
lemon juice *(Tilapia & Tomatoes)*
1 Red Apple *(Roast Turkey Breast)*
2 leeks *(Roast Turkey Breast)*
1 green pepper *(Puffed Up Pizza)*

Cereal
Crispix cereal *(Crispix Chicken)*

Meat, Poultry, & Fish
1 lb. lean pork *(Chili Verde)*
4 serving size portions tilapia fillets (or other thin white fish) *(Tilapia & Tomatoes)*
4 thinly sliced chicken (or turkey) cutlets (about 1 lb. Total) *(Crispix Chicken)*
1 bone-in Turkey breast *(Roast Turkey Breast)*
1 lb. lean ground beef *(Puffed Up Pizza)*

Dairy
3 oz reduced fat cheddar cheese (optional) *(Chili Verde)*
Small nonfat buttermilk *(Crispix Chicken)*
skim milk *(Puffed Up Pizza)*
eggs or liquid egg substitute *(Puffed Up Pizza)*
butter *(Roast Turkey Breast)*
4 oz Part-skim mozzarella cheese *(Puffed Up Pizza)*
1 oz Parmesan cheese *(Puffed Up Pizza)*

Baking Aisle
olive oil
flour *(Roast Turkey Breast, Puffed Up Pizza)*

Canned
1(16 oz) can kidney beans *(Chili Verde)*
1 (15 oz) can pinto beans *(Chili Verde)*
1 (15 oz) can chili beans with sauce *(Chili Verde)*
1 (15 oz) can stewed tomatoes *(Chili Verde)*
1 (15 oz) can tomato sauce *(Puffed Up Pizza)*

Condiments
4 oz pitted kalamata olives *(Tilapia & Tomatoes)*

Soups and Packaged Mixes
chicken bouillon granules *(Roast Turkey Breast)*
1 ½-oz. Pkg. Dry spaghetti-sauce mix *(Puffed Up Pizza)*

Spices and seasonings
ground cumin *(Chili Verde)*
Salt *(Tilapia & Tomatoes, Crispix Chicken)*
Pepper *(Tilapia & Tomatoes, Crispix Chicken)*
Rosemary *(Roast Turkey Breast)*

Mexican
16 oz green salsa *(Chili Verde)*

Winter Grocery List #40 (does not include side dish suggestions)

*Oriental Chicken with Stir-Fry Vegetables * Texas Stuffed Potatoes * Baked Pork Chops*
*Shepherd's Pie * Seafood Pasta*

Produce
2 large baking potatoes *(Texas Stuffed Potatoes)*
3 onions *(Texas Stuffed Potatoes, Shepherd's Pie, Seafood Pasta)*
garlic *(Texas Stuffed Potatoes, Seafood Pasta)*
1 zucchini *(Shepherd's Pie)*
4 oz sliced mushrooms *(Oriental Chicken)*
6 oz snow peas *(Oriental Chicken)*
2 cups bean sprouts *(Oriental Chicken)*
1 red pepper *(Shepherd's Pie)*
1 red or green pepper *(Oriental Chicken)*
2 stalks celery *(Oriental Chicken)*

Meat, Poultry, & Fish
2 boneless chicken breasts *(Oriental Chicken)*
8 oz ground turkey *(Texas Stuffed Potatoes)*
6 lean center-cut pork chops, 1/2" thick *(Baked Pork Chops)*
8 oz lean ground beef *(Shepherd's Pie)*
8 oz imitation crab *(Seafood Pasta)*
8oz shrimp *(Seafood Pasta)*

Dairy
6 oz reduced-fat Cheddar cheese *(Texas Stuffed Potatoes, Shepherd's Pie)*
eggs *(Baked Pork Chops, Shepherd's Pie)*
4 oz skim milk *(Shepherd's Pie)*
Parmesan cheese *(Shepherd's Pie)*

Pasta, Rice, & Legumes
16 oz thin spaghetti *(Seafood Pasta)*

Baking Aisle
Cornstarch *(Oriental Chicken, Seafood Pasta)*
1 can evaporated skim milk *(Baked Pork Chops)*
dry bread crumbs *(Baked Pork Chops)*
Olive oil

Cereal
cornflakes *(Baked Pork Chops)*

Canned
small can pineapple juice *(Oriental Chicken)*
8 oz can stewed tomatoes *(Texas Stuffed Potatoes)*
1 (14 oz) can Italian seasoned diced tomatoes *(Seafood Pasta)*

Soups and Packaged Mixes
Chicken bouillon granules *(Oriental Chicken, Seafood Pasta)*
instant mashed potato flakes *(Shepherd's Pie)*

Spices and seasonings
Salt
pepper
Ground ginger *(Oriental Chicken)*
Garlic powder *(Oriental Chicken, Baked Pork Chops, Shepherd's Pie)*
Chili powder *(Texas Stuffed Potatoes, Baked Pork Chops)*
Dried oregano *(Texas Stuffed Potatoes, Baked Pork Chops)*
Ground cumin *(Texas Stuffed Potatoes)*
Crushed red pepper *(Texas Stuffed Potatoes, Seafood Pasta*
cayenne pepper *(Baked Pork Chops)*
dry mustard *(Baked Pork Chops)*
Basil *(Shepherd's Pie, Seafood Pasta)*
paprika *(Baked Pork Chops)*
seafood spice *(Seafood Pasta)*
marjoram *(Seafood Pasta)*

Condiments
dry sherry *(Oriental Chicken)*

Asian
soy sauce *(Oriental Chicken)*

Winter Grocery List #41 (does not include side dish suggestions)

Chicken and Vegetable Medley * Stir-Fried Scallops & Vegetables * Beef with Potatoes & Greens
Ranch Chops & Rice * Cheesy Vegetable Soup

Produce

6 carrots *(Chicken and Vegetable Medley, Beef with Potatoes & Greens, Cheesy Vegetable Soup)*
2 red bell peppers *(Chicken and Vegetable Medley, Stir-Fried Scallops & Vegetables)*
1 med. yellow summer squash *(Chicken and Vegetable Medley)*
1 med. zucchini *(Chicken and Vegetable Medley)*
8 oz mushrooms *(Stir-Fried Scallops & Vegetables)*
6 oz snow pea pods *(Stir-Fried Scallops & Vegetables)*
8 small red potatoes *(Beef with Potatoes & Greens)*
1 Russet potato *(Cheesy Vegetable Soup)*
3 onions *(Beef with Potatoes & Greens, Cheesy Vegetable Soup)*
garlic *(Beef with Potatoes & Greens)*
1 bunch mustard greens, kale, or turnip greens *(Beef with Potatoes & Greens)*
2 stalks celery *(Cheesy Vegetable Soup)*

Meat, Poultry, & Fish

4 boneless chicken breast halves *(Chicken and Vegetable Medley)*
1 lb. Scallops *(Stir-Fried Scallops & Vegetables)*
turkey bacon *(Stir-Fried Scallops & Vegetables)*
1 lbs. top round steak *(Beef with Potatoes & Greens)*
4 boneless pork chops, 3/4" thick *(Ranch Chops & Rice)*

Dairy

4 oz skim milk *(Ranch Chops & Rice)*
4 oz. light Velveeta cheese *(Cheesy Vegetable Soup)*

Pasta, Rice, & Legumes

Rice *(Ranch Chops & Rice)*

Baking Aisle

cornstarch *(Stir-Fried Scallops & Vegetables)*

Frozen

10 oz. Frozen mixed vegetables *(Cheesy Vegetable Soup)*
10 oz. Frozen chopped broccoli *(Cheesy Vegetable Soup)*

Soups and Packaged Mixes

Chicken bouillon granules *(Chicken and Vegetable Medley, Cheesy Vegetable Soup)*
beef bouillon granules *(Beef with Potatoes & Greens)*
1 can cream of mushroom soup *(Ranch Chops & Rice)*
1 can cream of chicken soup *(Cheesy Vegetable Soup)*

Spices and seasonings

Thyme leaves *(Chicken and Vegetable Medley)*
Onion powder *(Chicken and Vegetable Medley)*
pepper
salt
paprika *(Beef with Potatoes & Greens, Ranch Chops & Rice)*
oregano *(Beef with Potatoes & Greens)*
chili powder *(Beef with Potatoes & Greens)*
garlic powder *(Beef with Potatoes & Greens)*
cayenne pepper *(Beef with Potatoes & Greens)*
dry mustard *(Beef with Potatoes & Greens)*

Condiments

1 pkg. (1 oz.) ranch salad dressing mix *(Ranch Chops & Rice)*

Asian

soy sauce *(Stir-Fried Scallops & Vegetables)*

Winter Grocery List #42 (does not include side dish suggestions)

*Pork Chops with Mushroom Gravy * Tuna Spaghetti * Deluxe Chicken Breasts*
*Pepper Steak * New Orleans Red Beans*

Produce

8 oz sliced mushrooms *(Pork Chops with Mushroom Gravy)*
3 onions *(Pork Chops with Mushroom Gravy, Pepper Steak, New Orleans Red Beans)*
garlic *(Pork Chops with Mushroom Gravy, Tuna Spaghetti, Pepper Steak, New Orleans Red Beans)*
2 large green peppers *(Pepper Steak, New Orleans Red Beans)*
1 large red pepper *(Pepper Steak)*
2 large stalks celery *(Pepper Steak)*

Meat, Poultry, & Fish

turkey bacon *(Pork Chops with Mushroom Gravy)*
6 boneless pork chops *(Pork Chops with Mushroom Gravy)*
4 boneless chicken breast halves *(Deluxe Chicken Breasts)*
1 lb. beef steak *(Pepper Steak)*

Dairy

butter *(Tuna Spaghetti, Deluxe Chicken Breasts)*
6 oz fat free half-and-half *(Tuna Spaghetti)*
2 oz Parmesan cheese *(Tuna Spaghetti, Deluxe Chicken Breasts)*
eggs *(Deluxe Chicken Breasts)*
8 oz skim milk *(Deluxe Chicken Breasts)*
3 oz reduced fat Cheddar cheese *(Deluxe Chicken Breasts)*

Pasta, Rice, & Legumes

1 pkg. (8 oz) Spaghetti *(Tuna Spaghetti)*
1 lb. dry red beans *(New Orleans Red Beans)*

Baking Aisle

cornstarch *(Pork Chops with Mushroom Gravy, Pepper Steak)*
flour *(Pork Chops with Mushroom Gravy, Deluxe Chicken Breasts)*
olive oil *(Pork Chops with Mushroom Gravy)*
dry bread crumbs *(Deluxe Chicken Breasts)*

Canned

1 can (9¼ oz) Tuna in water *(Tuna Spaghetti)*

Soups and Packaged Mixes

chicken bouillon granules *(Pork Chops with Mushroom Gravy, New Orleans Red Beans)*

Spices and seasonings

pepper
salt
basil *(Tuna Spaghetti)*
oregano *(Tuna Spaghetti)*
paprika *(Deluxe Chicken Breasts)*
bay leaves *(New Orleans Red Beans)*
parsley *(New Orleans Red Beans)*
dried thyme *(New Orleans Red Beans)*
celery seed (optional) *(New Orleans Red Beans)*

Condiments

pimiento-stuffed olives (optional) *(Tuna Spaghetti)*
Worcestershire sauce *(Deluxe Chicken Breasts)*

Asian

soy sauce *(Pepper Steak)*

Winter Grocery List #43 (does not include side dish suggestions)

*Ham Stuffed Potatoes * Pork & Broccoli Rotini * Chicken & Broccoli with Mushroom Sauce*
*Mom's Spaghetti * Grilled Salmon & Spinach*

Produce

2 large baking potatoes *(Ham Stuffed Potatoes)*
1 green pepper *(Ham Stuffed Potatoes)*
garlic *(Pork and Broccoli Rotini)*
2 cups broccoli florets *(Pork and Broccoli Rotini)*
4 carrots *(Pork and Broccoli Rotini)*
1 onion *(Pork and Broccoli Rotini)*
parsley *(Chicken and Broccoli with Mushroom Sauce)*
16 oz mushrooms *(Mom's Spaghetti, Grilled Salmon & Spinach)*
1 lemon *(Grilled Salmon & Spinach)*
10 oz spinach leaves *(Grilled Salmon & Spinach)*

Meat, Poultry, & Fish

1 ½ cups cubed fully cooked lean ham *(Ham Stuffed Potatoes)*
10 oz very lean pork *(Pork and Broccoli Rotini)*
1 lb. chicken breast *(Chicken and Broccoli with Mushroom Sauce)*
1 lb. Lean ground beef *(Mom's Spaghetti)*
4 salmon fillets (about 6 oz each) *(Grilled Salmon & Spinach)*

Dairy

8 oz non-fat cottage cheese *(Ham Stuffed Potatoes)*
2 oz part-skim mozzarella cheese *(Ham Stuffed Potatoes)*
Margarine or butter *(Chicken and Broccoli with Mushroom Sauce)*

Pasta, Rice, & Legumes

16 oz rotini, Twists, or Spiral Pasta *(Pork and Broccoli Rotini)*
16 oz spaghetti *(Mom's Spaghetti)*

Frozen

1 (10oz) pkg. frozen broccoli (florets or spears) *(Chicken and Broccoli with Mushroom Sauce)*

Baking Aisle

molasses *(Pork and Broccoli Rotini)*
dry bread crumbs *(Chicken and Broccoli with Mushroom Sauce)*
flour *(Chicken and Broccoli with Mushroom Sauce)*
olive oil *(Grilled Salmon & Spinach)*

Canned

1 (4oz) can mushrooms *(Chicken and Broccoli with Mushroom Sauce)*
1 (28 oz) can diced tomatoes *(Mom's Spaghetti)*
3 (8 oz) cans tomato sauce *(Mom's Spaghetti)*
1 (6 oz) can tomato paste *(Mom's Spaghetti)*

Soups and Packaged Mixes

chicken bouillon granules *(Chicken and Broccoli with Mushroom Sauce)*

Spices and seasonings

pepper
Salt
oregano *(Mom's Spaghetti)*
basil *(Mom's Spaghetti)*
onion powder *(Mom's Spaghetti)*
dried minced onion *(Mom's Spaghetti)*
garlic powder *(Mom's Spaghetti)*
garlic salt *(Mom's Spaghetti)*

Condiments

1 (2.25 oz) can sliced black olives *(Mom's Spaghetti)*

Asian

soy sauce *(Pork and Broccoli Rotini)*

Bin Foods

2 Tbsp dry roasted peanuts halves *(Pork and Broccoli Rotini)*

Winter Grocery List #44 (does not include side dish suggestions)

*Hearty Chili * Chicken & Sesame Noodles * Slow Cooked Pork Roast*
*Southwest Salad * Deviled Beef Rolls*

Produce

garlic *(Chicken & Sesame Noodles, Hearty Chili)*
green onions *(Chicken & Sesame Noodles)*
2 heads romaine lettuce *(Southwest Salad)*
2 onions *(Hearty Chili)*

Meat, Poultry, & Fish

4 chicken breast halves *(Chicken & Sesame Noodles)*
1 (3 lb) boneless pork loin roast *(Slow Cooked Pork Roast)*
4 beef cubed steaks *(Deviled Beef Rolls)*
1 lb. lean hamburger *(Hearty Chili)*
1 lbs. top round steak *(Hearty Chili)*

Dairy

4 oz reduced-fat Cheddar cheese *(Southwest Salad)*
Margarine or butter *(Deviled Beef Rolls)*

Pasta, Rice, & Legumes

1 lb thin spaghetti *(Chicken & Sesame Noodles)*

Baking Aisle

olive oil
brown sugar *(Chicken & Sesame Noodles)*
sugar *(Chicken & Sesame Noodles)*
flour *(Slow Cooked Pork Roast)*

Chip Aisle

baked tortilla chips *(Southwest Salad)*

Frozen

10 oz frozen corn *(Southwest Salad)*

Canned

2 cans (15oz) black beans *(Southwest Salad)*
1 (4oz) can mushrooms *(Deviled Beef Rolls)*
32 oz can diced tomatoes *(Hearty Chili)*
16 oz Tomato sauce *(Hearty Chili)*
2 (16oz each) Cans dark red kidney beans *(Hearty Chili)*

Soups and Packaged Mixes

chicken bouillon granules *(Slow Cooked Pork Roast)*
dry onion soup mix *(Deviled Beef Rolls)*

Spices and seasonings

Salt
Pepper
ground ginger *(Chicken & Sesame Noodles)*
sesame seed *(Chicken & Sesame Noodles)*
Chili powder *(Hearty Chili)*
basil *(Hearty Chili)*

Condiments

reduced fat ranch dressing *(Southwest Salad)*
horseradish mustard *(Deviled Beef Rolls)*

Asian

soy sauce *(Chicken & Sesame Noodles)*
teriyaki sauce *(Chicken & Sesame Noodles)*
sesame oil *(Chicken & Sesame Noodles)*

Mexican

12 oz salsa *(Southwest Salad)*

Non-Food Items

Toothpicks *(Deviled Beef Rolls)*

Winter Grocery List #45 (does not include side dish suggestions)

*Pecan Chicken * Creamy Bean Burritos * Fish & Potato Casserole ***
*Turkey Tetrazzini * Chipotle Pork Sandwiches*

Produce
green onions *(Pecan Chicken)*
1 green pepper *(Creamy Bean Burritos)*
8 oz sliced mushrooms *(Turkey Tetrazzini)*
1 onion *(Turkey Tetrazzini)*
garlic *(Turkey Tetrazzini)*
Small pkg. coleslaw mix *(Chipotle Pork Sandwiches)*

Meat, Poultry, & Fish
4 boneless skinless chicken breast halves *(Pecan Chicken)*
3 cups cooked turkey *(Turkey Tetrazzini)*
16 oz pork tenderloin *(Chipotle Pork Sandwiches)*

Dairy
Small fat free half-and-half *(Pecan Chicken)*
3 oz crumbled blue cheese *(Pecan Chicken)*
butter *(Pecan Chicken)*
8 oz reduced fat cheddar cheese *(Creamy Bean Burritos, Fish & Potato Casserole)*
4 oz reduced fat cream cheese *(Creamy Bean Burritos)*
egg substitute *(Fish & Potato Casserole)*
1 quart skim milk *(Fish & Potato Casserole)*
8 oz Parmesan cheese *(Turkey Tetrazzini)*
fat free sour cream *(Chipotle Pork Sandwiches)*

Breads and Tortillas
6 (10 inch) flour tortillas *(Creamy Bean Burritos)*
4 whole wheat hamburger buns *(Chipotle Pork Sandwiches)*

Baking Aisle
flour *(Pecan Chicken)*
brown sugar *(Pecan Chicken)*
3/4 cup pecans, finely chopped (may be cheaper in the bin section) *(Pecan Chicken)*
olive oil

Frozen
12 oz. frozen loose-packed hashed browns *(Fish & Potato Casserole)*
14 oz frozen fish sticks *(Fish & Potato Casserole)*

Pasta, Rice, & Legumes
instant brown rice *(Creamy Bean Burritos)*
16 oz spaghetti *(Turkey Tetrazzini)*

Canned
8 oz can diced tomatoes *(Creamy Bean Burritos)*
1 can (15 oz) Pinto beans *(Creamy Bean Burritos)*

Soups and Packaged Mixes
chicken bouillon granules *(Turkey Tetrazzini)*
3 cans mushroom soup *(Turkey Tetrazzini)*

Spices and seasonings
salt
pepper
rosemary, crushed *(Pecan Chicken)*
chili powder *(Creamy Bean Burritos)*
ground cumin *(Creamy Bean Burritos)*
ground coriander *(Creamy Bean Burritos)*
oregano *(Creamy Bean Burritos)*
minced dry onion *(Fish & Potato Casserole)*
seasoned salt *(Fish & Potato Casserole)*
dillweed *(Fish & Potato Casserole)*
Italian seasoning *(Turkey Tetrazzini)*

Condiments
BBQ sauce *(Chipotle Pork Sandwiches)*
fat free mayonnaise *(Chipotle Pork Sandwiches)*
Dijon mustard *(Chipotle Pork Sandwiches)*

Mexican
Salsa (optional) *(Creamy Bean Burritos)*
chipotle peppers in adobe sauce *(Chipotle Pork Sandwiches)*

Winter Grocery List #46 (does not include side dish suggestions)

*Creamy Chicken & Bacon Pasta * Meat Loaf Wellington * Chicken Stuffing Casserole*
*Cauliflower Soup * Mexi-Pork Skillet*

Produce
1 tomato *(Creamy Chicken & Bacon Pasta)*
2 small onions *(Creamy Chicken & Bacon Pasta, Cauliflower Soup)*
garlic *(Creamy Chicken & Bacon Pasta)*
1 red bell pepper *(Mexi-Pork Skillet)*
1 green pepper *(Mexi-Pork Skillet)*
2 celery stalks *(Cauliflower Soup)*
1 carrot *(Cauliflower Soup)*
parsley *(Cauliflower Soup, Meat Loaf Wellington)*
1 large head cauliflower (2 pounds) *(Cauliflower Soup)*

Meat, Poultry, & Fish
2 boneless chicken breast halves *(Creamy Chicken & Bacon Pasta)*
turkey bacon *(Creamy Chicken & Bacon Pasta)*
1 ½ lbs lean ground beef *(Meat Loaf Wellington)*
1 lb. Pork *(Mexi-Pork Skillet)*
4 cups cooked chicken (or Turkey) *(Chicken Stuffing Casserole)*

Frozen
10 oz frozen corn *(Chicken Stuffing Casserole)*

Dairy
1 quart fat free half & half *(Creamy Chicken & Bacon Pasta, Cauliflower Soup)*
skim milk *(Cauliflower Soup, Chicken Stuffing Casserole)*
2 oz reduced fat cheddar cheese *(Mexi-Pork Skillet)*
Butter *(Cauliflower Soup)*
4 oz part-skim mozzarella cheese *(Meat Loaf Wellington)*
1 tube (8 oz) refrigerated, reduced-fat crescent rolls *(Meat Loaf Wellington)*
eggs *(Meat Loaf Wellington)*

Pasta, Rice, & Legumes
16 oz spaghetti noodles *(Creamy Chicken & Bacon Pasta)*
instant brown rice *(Mexi-Pork Skillet)*

Baking Aisle
flour *(Creamy Chicken & Bacon Pasta, Cauliflower Soup)*
dry bread crumbs *(Meat Loaf Wellington)*

Canned
8 oz meatless spaghetti sauce *(Meat Loaf Wellington)*
2 cans (8oz) mushrooms *(Chicken Stuffing Casserole)*

Soups and Packaged Mixes
chicken bouillon granules *(Creamy Chicken & Bacon Pasta, Cauliflower Soup)*
1 envelope taco seasoning mix *(Mexi-Pork Skillet)*
2 packages (6 oz) chicken (or Turkey) stuffing mix *(Chicken Stuffing Casserole)*
2 cans cream of mushroom soup *(Chicken Stuffing Casserole)*

Spices and seasonings
salt
pepper
dill weed *(Cauliflower Soup)*
white pepper *(Cauliflower Soup)*

Condiments
1 can (2 ¼ oz) sliced black olives *(Creamy Chicken & Bacon Pasta)*
fat-free zesty Italian salad dressing *(Mexi-Pork Skillet)*

Non-Food Items
dry white wine (or chicken broth) *(Creamy Chicken & Bacon Pasta)*
Aluminum foil *(Meat Loaf Wellington)*

<u>Winter Grocery List #47</u> (does not include side dish suggestions)

*Now & Again Enchiladas * Lemon Rice & Chicken * Pistachio Fish Fillets **
*Penne Puttanesca * Marinated London Broil*

Produce
3 onions *(Now & Again Enchiladas, Penne Puttanesca)*
1 carrot (Lemon Rice & Chicken)
1 lemon (Lemon Rice & Chicken)
lemon juice *(Marinated London Broil)*
garlic (Lemon Rice & Chicken, Penne Puttanesca)
parsley *(Pistachio Fish Fillets)*

Meat, Poultry, & Fish
1 lb. Lean ground beef *(Now & Again Enchiladas)*
1 lb. ground Turkey *(Now & Again Enchiladas)*
2 boneless chicken breast halves (Lemon Rice & Chicken)
4 thin, mild white fish fillets (like orange roughy or cod) *(Pistachio Fish Fillets)*
1 London broil (round steak), 1-2 inches thick *(Marinated London Broil)*

Dairy
12 oz fat free cottage cheese *(Now & Again Enchiladas)*
12 oz free sour cream *(Now & Again Enchiladas)*
4 oz reduced fat cheddar cheese *(Now & Again Enchiladas)*
eggs *(Pistachio Fish Fillets)*
butter *(Pistachio Fish Fillets)*
Parmesan cheese (optional) *(Penne Puttanesca)*

Pasta, Rice, & Legumes
instant white rice (Lemon Rice & Chicken)
16 oz penne pasta *(Penne Puttanesca)*

Breads and Tortillas
12 (10 inch) tortillas *(Now & Again Enchiladas)*

Baking Aisle
½ cup shelled pistachios *(may be cheaper in the bin section)* *(Pistachio Fish Fillets)*
dry bread crumbs *(Pistachio Fish Fillets)*
olive oil

Canned
1 can (16 oz) tomato sauce *(Now & Again Enchiladas)*
1 can (28 oz) diced tomatoes *(Penne Puttanesca)*
anchovy paste *(find it by the tuna fish)* *(Penne Puttanesca)*

Soups and Packaged Mixes
chicken bouillon granules (Lemon Rice & Chicken)

Spices and seasonings
ground cumin *(Now & Again Enchiladas)*
ground coriander *(Now & Again Enchiladas)*
chili powder *(Now & Again Enchiladas)*
oregano *(Now & Again Enchiladas)*
garlic powder *(Now & Again Enchiladas, Marinated London Broil)*
thyme *(Now & Again Enchiladas)*
parsley (Lemon Rice & Chicken)
salt
pepper
ground ginger *(Marinated London Broil)*
red pepper flakes (optional) *(Penne Puttanesca)*

Condiments
1 (4oz) can sliced black olives (Lemon Rice & Chicken)
pitted kalamata olives *(Penne Puttanesca)*
capers *(Penne Puttanesca)*
fat free mayonnaise *(Marinated London Broil)*
mustard *(Marinated London Broil)*

Asian
soy sauce *(Marinated London Broil)*

Mexican
8 oz salsa *(Now & Again Enchiladas)*
1 can (7 oz) diced green chilies *(Now & Again Enchiladas)*

Non-Food Items
Disposable 9X13 inch baking dish (if needed) *(Now & Again Enchiladas)*
Aluminum foil *(Now & Again Enchiladas)*

Winter Grocery List #48 (does not include side dish suggestions)

*Vegetable Chili * Pizza Potatoes * Chicken Chipotle Tacos*
*Cranberry Ham * Pork Medallions in Mustard Sauce*

Produce
1 medium onion *(Vegetable Chili)*
1 carrot *(Vegetable Chili)*
2 green peppers *(Vegetable Chili, Pizza Potatoes)*
1 zucchini *(Vegetable Chili)*
8 oz fresh mushrooms, sliced *(Vegetable Chili)*
garlic *(Vegetable Chili, Pork Medallions)*
4 baking potatoes *(Pizza Potatoes)*
Shredded lettuce *(Chicken Chipotle Tacos)*

Meat, Poultry, & Fish
2 boneless chicken breast halves *(Chicken Chipotle Tacos)*
6 oz Turkey pepperoni *(Pizza Potatoes)*
4 boneless, fully cooked ham steaks *(Cranberry Ham)*
1 lb pork tenderloin *(Pork Medallions)*

Dairy
3 oz part skim mozzarella cheese *(Pizza Potatoes)*
6 oz Monterey Jack Cheese, shredded *(Chicken Chipotle Tacos)*

Breads and Tortillas
6 (8 inch) flour tortillas *(Chicken Chipotle Tacos)*

Baking Aisle
olive oil *(Vegetable Chili Pork Medallions)*
cornstarch *(Pork Medallions)*

Canned
1 (16 oz) can diced tomatoes *(Vegetable Chili)*
2 cans (16 oz each) kidney beans *(Vegetable Chili)*
1 (15oz) can pinto beans *(Chicken Chipotle Tacos)*
1 (16 oz) can tomato sauce *(Vegetable Chili)*
1 (26-28 oz) can spaghetti sauce, meatless *(Pizza Potatoes)*
1 can (15oz) jellied cranberry sauce *(Cranberry Ham)*
1 can (8 oz) crushed pineapple *(Cranberry Ham)*

Soups and Packaged Mixes
chicken bouillon granules *(Pork Medallions)*

Spices and seasonings
chili powder *(Vegetable Chili)*
oregano *(Vegetable Chili)*
ground cumin *(Vegetable Chili)*
paprika *(Vegetable Chili)*
crushed red pepper flakes (optional) *(Vegetable Chili)*
pepper
sea salt *(Vegetable Chili)*
salt
ground cloves *(Cranberry Ham)*
parsley *(Pork Medallions)*

Condiments
spicy brown mustard *(Pork Medallions)*

Mexican
1 (4 oz) can diced green chilies *(Vegetable Chili)*
Small can chipotle chilies in adobe sauce *(Chicken Chipotle Tacos)*
1 (16oz) jar salsa *(Chicken Chipotle Tacos)*

Winter Grocery List #49 (does not include side dish suggestions)

*Quick Mexi-Chicken & Rice * Minestrone Stew * Scallop Lo Mein*
*Pork & Potato Supper * Olive-Stuffed Chicken*

Produce
1 bunch green onions *(Quick Mexi-Chicken & Rice, Scallop Lo Mein)*
2 onions *(Minestrone Stew, Pork and Potato Supper)*
2 carrots *(Minestrone Stew)*
1 zucchini *(Minestrone Stew)*
1 lime *(Scallop Lo Mein)*
1 lb. asparagus *(Scallop Lo Mein)*
1 red bell peppers *(Scallop Lo Mein)*
garlic *(Scallop Lo Mein)*
parsley *(Pork and Potato Supper)*
3 potatoes *(Pork and Potato Supper)*

Meat, Poultry, & Fish
8 boneless chicken breast halves *(Quick Mexi-Chicken & Rice, Olive-Stuffed Chicken)*
3 oz turkey pepperoni *(Minestrone Stew)*
1 lb. sea scallops *(bay scallops are fine to substitute) (Scallop Lo Mein)*
4 Pork steaks (about 6 oz each) *(Pork and Potato Supper)*

Dairy
Parmesan cheese (optional) *(Minestrone Stew)*
4 oz reduced fat cream cheese *(Olive-Stuffed Chicken)*

Pasta, Rice, & Legumes
instant rice *(Quick Mexi-Chicken & Rice)*
elbow macaroni *(Minestrone Stew)*
6 oz vermicelli *(Scallop Lo Mein)*

Baking Aisle
olive oil
flour *(Pork and Potato Supper)*
seasoned bread crumbs *(Olive-Stuffed Chicken)*

Canned
42 oz canned diced tomatoes *(Minestrone Stew)*
2 cans (16 oz each) kidney beans *(Minestrone Stew)*

Soups and Packaged Mixes
chicken bouillon granules *(Quick Mexi-Chicken & Rice, Minestrone Stew, Pork and Potato Supper)*

Frozen
10 oz frozen spinach *(Minestrone Stew)*

Spices and seasonings
Salt
Pepper
garlic powder *(Quick Mexi-Chicken & Rice, Minestrone Stew)*
basil *(Minestrone Stew)*
oregano *(Minestrone Stew, Olive-Stuffed Chicken)*
Paprika *(Pork and Potato Supper)*

Condiments
Hot pepper sauce *(Scallop Lo Mein)*
1 (4 oz) can sliced black olives *(Olive-Stuffed Chicken)*

Asian
soy sauce *(Scallop Lo Mein)*
Sesame oil *(Scallop Lo Mein)*

Mexican
1 (16 oz) jar Salsa *(Quick Mexi-Chicken & Rice)*

Non-Food Items
Toothpicks *(Olive-Stuffed Chicken)*

Winter Grocery List #50 (does not include side dish suggestions)

*Feta Turkey Patties * Pork Chops & Apple Stuffing * Cuban Picadillo*
*Dijon Salmon * Cumin Chicken*

Produce
2 apples *(Pork Chops & Apple Stuffing)*
2 onions *(Pork Chops & Apple Stuffing, Cuban Picadillo)*
1 green pepper *(Cuban Picadillo)*

Meat, Poultry, & Fish
1 lb ground turkey (or chicken) *(Feta Turkey Patties)*
4 pork chops *(Pork Chops & Apple Stuffing)*
1 lb. lean ground beef *(Cuban Picadillo)*
4 boneless chicken breast halves *(Cumin Chicken)*
1 piece (6 oz) salmon **for each person** you want to serve *(Dijon Salmon)*

Dairy
4 oz crumbled reduced fat feta cheese *(Feta Turkey Patties)*

Pasta, Rice, & Legumes
rice *(Cuban Picadillo)*

Baking Aisle
raisins *(Cuban Picadillo)*

Canned
1 (8 oz) can tomato sauce *(Cuban Picadillo)*

Soups and Packaged Mixes
1 package pork stuffing mix *(Pork Chops & Apple Stuffing)*
chicken bouillon granules *(Cumin Chicken)*

Spices and seasonings
oregano *(Feta Turkey Patties, Cumin Chicken)*
salt *(Feta Turkey Patties)*
garlic powder *(Feta Turkey Patties, Dijon Salmon)*
ground cumin *(Cumin Chicken)*
garlic salt *(Cumin Chicken)*
black pepper

Condiments
apple cider vinegar *(Cuban Picadillo)*
pimiento stuffed green olives *(Cuban Picadillo)*
Dijon Mustard *(Dijon Salmon)*

Mexican
4 oz picante sauce *(Cumin Chicken)*

Winter Grocery List #51 (does not include side dish suggestions)

*Ravioli & Brown Butter * Mexican Lasagna * Crock Pot Chicken*
*Swiss Steak Strips * Lentil & Spinach Soup*

Produce
green onions *(Ravioli & Brown Butter)*
16-18 fresh sage leaves *(Ravioli & Brown Butter)*
optional - shredded lettuce *(Mexican Lasagna)*
optional- tomato *(Mexican Lasagna)*
3 medium onions *(Mexican Lasagna, Swiss Steak Strips, Lentil and Spinach Soup)*
Garlic *(Mexican Lasagna, Swiss Steak Strips, Lentil and Spinach Soup)*
9-12 oz spinach *(Lentil and Spinach Soup)*
green pepper *(Jambalaya)*

Pasta, Rice, & Legumes
1 box Rice-a-Roni chicken flavor rice *(Crockpot Chicken)*
pearl barley *(Lentil and Spinach Soup)*
dried lentils *(Lentil and Spinach Soup)*

Meat, Poultry, & Fish
1 lb. Lean ground beef *(Mexican Lasagna)*
6 boneless chicken breasts *(Crockpot Chicken, Lentil and Spinach Soup)*
1 ½ lbs. Round steak *(Swiss Steak Strips)*

Dairy
24 -28 oz fresh or frozen cheese ravioli *(Ravioli & Brown Butter)*
butter *(Ravioli & Brown Butter)*
6 oz Parmesan *(Ravioli & Brown Butter)*
optional - fat free sour cream *(Mexican Lasagna)*
6 oz reduced-fat Mexican blend cheese *(Mexican Lasagna)*

Breads and Tortillas
6 flour tortillas (10 inches) *(Mexican Lasagna)*

Baking Aisle
flour *(Swiss Steak Strips)*
olive oil

Canned
1 can (15 oz) black beans *(Mexican Lasagna)*
1 can (15 oz) garbanzo beans or chickpeas *(Lentil and Spinach Soup)*

Condiments
optional - sliced black olives *(Mexican Lasagna)*

Soups and Packaged Mixes
1 envelope taco seasoning *(Mexican Lasagna)*
2 cans Cream of Chicken Soup *(Crockpot Chicken)*
1 can Cream of Mushroom Soup *(Crockpot Chicken)*
beef bouillon granules *(Swiss Steak Strips)*
chicken bouillon granules *(Lentil and Spinach Soup)*

Spices and seasonings
sea salt *(Ravioli & Brown Butter)*
pepper *(Ravioli & Brown Butter, Mexican Lasagna, Swiss Steak Strips, Jambalaya)*
Paprika *(Swiss Steak Strips)*
Salt
Thyme *(Swiss Steak Strips)*
bay leaves *(Swiss Steak Strips)*

Mexican
32 oz salsa *(Mexican Lasagna, Lentil and Spinach Soup)*
1 can (16 oz) fat free refried beans *(Mexican Lasagna)*
1 can (10 oz) enchilada sauce *(Mexican Lasagna)*
1 can (4 oz) chopped green chilies *(Mexican Lasagna)*

<u>Winter Grocery List #52</u> (does not include side dish suggestions)

*Corn & Potato Chowder * Linguine with Gorgonzola Sauce * Glazed Chicken Breasts*
*Mini Meat Loaf Burgers * Seafood & Yellow Rice*

Produce

2 onions *(Corn and Potato Chowder, Seafood & Yellow Rice)*
2 large russet potatoes *(Corn and Potato Chowder)*
1 bunch fresh asparagus *(Linguine w/Gorgonzola Sauce)*
garlic *(Seafood & Yellow Rice)*

Meat, Poultry, & Fish

Turkey bacon *(Corn and Potato Chowder)*
4 boneless chicken breast halves *(Glazed Chicken Breasts)*
1 lb. lean ground beef *(Mini Meat Loaf Burgers)*
8 oz uncooked shrimp *(Seafood & Yellow Rice)*
8 oz bay scallops *(Seafood & Yellow Rice)*

Dairy

fat-free half & half *(Corn and Potato Chowder, Linguine w/Gorgonzola Sauce)*
4 oz Gorgonzola or other blue cheese *(Linguine w/Gorgonzola Sauce)*
16 oz reduced fat cheddar cheese *(Mini Meat Loaf Burgers, Chicken Stuffing Casserole)*

Pasta, Rice, & Legumes

12 ounces linguine *(Linguine w/Gorgonzola Sauce)*
rice *(Seafood & Yellow Rice)*

Baking Aisle

¼ cup chopped walnuts *(Linguine w/Gorgonzola Sauce)*
olive oil *(Seafood & Yellow Rice)*

Frozen

32 oz frozen corn *(Corn and Potato Chowder)*
10 oz frozen peas *(Seafood & Yellow Rice)*

Soups and Packaged Mixes

chicken bouillon granules *(Corn and Potato Chowder, Seafood & Yellow Rice)*
dry onion soup mix *(Glazed Chicken Breasts)*

Spices and seasonings

ground thyme *(Corn and Potato Chowder)*
cayenne pepper *(Corn and Potato Chowder)*
pepper *(Corn and Potato Chowder, Seafood & Yellow Rice)*
sea salt *(Corn and Potato Chowder)*
salt *(Linguine w/Gorgonzola Sauce, Seafood & Yellow Rice)*
garlic powder *(Mini Meat Loaf Burgers)*
turmeric *(Seafood & Yellow Rice)*

Condiments

fat free Catalina salad dressing *(Glazed Chicken Breasts)*
Simply Fruit apricot spread (or similar) *(Glazed Chicken Breasts)*
ketchup *(Mini Meat Loaf Burgers)*

Recipe Index